THE
Family Face
of
Schizophrenia

THE
Family Face
of
Schizophrenia

PRACTICAL COUNSEL
FROM AMERICA'S LEADING EXPERTS

Patricia Backlar

INTRODUCTION BY
NANCY C. ANDREASEN, M.D., PH.D.

A JEREMY P. TARCHER/PUTNAM BOOK
Published by G. P. Putnam's Sons
New York

A Jeremy P. Tarcher/Putnam Book
Published by G. P. Putnam's Sons
Publishers Since 1838
200 Madison Avenue
New York, NY 10016

Library of Congress Cataloging-in-Publication Data
Backlar, Patricia, date
    The family face of schizophrenia : practical counsel from
America's leading experts/by Patricia Backlar : introduction by
Nancy C. Andreasen.—1st American ed.
      p. cm.
  "A Jeremy P. Tarcher/Putnam book."
  Includes bibliographical references and index.
  ISBN 0-87477-748-8 (acid-free paper)
    1. Schizophrenics—Family relationships. 2. Schizophrenics—
Family relationships—Case studies. 3. Schizophrenics—United
States—Social conditions. I. Title.
RC514.B28 1994   93-18753
616.89'82—dc20   CIP

Commentary for "A Father's Story" by Bentson H. McFarland, M.D., Ph.D., copyright ©
1994 by Bentson H. McFarland; Commentary for "The Single Parent's Struggle" by Harriet
P. Lefley, Ph.D., copyright © 1994 by Harriet P. Lefley; Commentary for "Slipping
Through the Cracks" by Marsha Martin, D.S.W., copyright © 1994 by Marsha Martin;
Commentary for "Whereabouts Unknown" by Judith B. Krauss R.N., M.S.N. and Diane
M. Gourley, R.N., B.A., copyright © 1994 by Judith B. Krauss; Commentary for "Dial 911"
by Richard K. James, Ph.D., copyright © 1994 by Richard K. James; Commentary for "At
Risk" by Jeffrey L. Geller, M.D., M.P.H., copyright © 1994 by Jeffrey L. Geller;
Commentary for "Out of Control" by Jeffrey L. Rogers, J.D., copyright © 1994 by Jeffrey
L. Rogers.

Design by Irving Perkins Associates

Printed in the United States of America
1 2 3 4 5 6 7 8 9 10

This book is printed on acid-free paper.

For my mother
Jane van Gelder
nonpareil

Contents

Acknowledgments   9

Preface   11

Introduction   27
by Nancy C. Andreasen, M.D., Ph.D.

1. A Father's Story: Learning to Live with
Schizophrenia   43
Story by Patricia Backlar
Commentary by psychiatrist Bentson H. McFarland, M.D.,
Ph.D.

2. The Single Parent's Struggle: Schizophrenia and the
Adult Child   83
Story by Patricia Backlar
Commentary by psychologist Harriet P. Lefley, Ph.D.

3. Slipping Through the Cracks: Failure of the Mental
Health System   109
Story by Patricia Backlar
Commentary by social worker Marsha Martin, D.S.W.

4. Whereabouts Unknown: Searching for a Missing
Family Member   145
Story by Patricia Backlar
Commentary by nurses Judith B. Krauss, R.N., M.S.N.,
and Diane M. Gourley, R.N., B.A.

5. *Dial 911: Schizophrenia and the Police Response*   166
   Story by Patricia Backlar
   Commentary by psychologist Richard K. James, Ph.D.

6. *At Risk: Suicide and Schizophrenia*   201
   Story by Patricia Backlar
   Commentary by psychiatrist Jeffrey L. Geller, M.D.,
   M.P.H.

7. *Out of Control: Violence, the Law, and
   Schizophrenia*   224
   Story by Patricia Backlar
   Commentary by attorney Jeffrey L. Rogers, J.D.

   References and Notes   253

   Suggested Reading   259

   Resources   261

   Index   275

Acknowledgments

FIRST AND FOREMOST, I AM INDEBTED to the families who sought me out in order to tell their stories. Without these courageous women and men, this book could never have been written.

My cardinal debt lies with two persons: first, to my friend and mentor, Dr. Donald Moor, Chair of the Department of Philosophy, Portland State University, whose early interest and unflagging enthusiasm helped launch the project. I am grateful to him for his careful reading and criticism of the manuscript. Second, to Dr. Bentson McFarland, Director, Western Mental Health Research Center, Oregon Health Sciences University, without whose support and invaluable suggestions this particular enterprise could not have gone forward.

I am deeply indebted to Dr. Nancy Andreasen. She read the narratives in a single sitting during a flight from Iowa City to Portland, Oregon. When I picked her up at the airport, she told me that she had *already* started to write an introduction for this book. I am grateful to her for her spirited endorsement of this undertaking, and for the time and effort that she has so generously given.

Early on, before the book crystallized into its final form, several friends, Dr. David Cutler, Dr. David Helman, Dr. Daniel Labby, Margaret Neerhout, Bernard Rothman, Anita Taylor, read the narratives. I am appreciative of their criticism and approbation.

To Dr. Susan Tolle, Dr. Michael Garland, and Dr. Virginia Tilden, Director, Associate Director, and Assistant Director of the Center for Ethics in Health Care, Oregon Health Sciences University, respectively, I owe a substantial debt. They have sustained me with their confidence, patronage, and advocacy.

It is to Dr. Michael Reardon, Provost of Portland State University, that I am most grateful. Historically, Dr. Reardon has always given my various projects a free rein. Without his enduring support, this book could never have been brought to fruition.

I am especially indebted to my publisher, Jeremy Tarcher, who, from this project's infancy, has endorsed my efforts. After reading a few of the stories he urged me to complete the enterprise. By introducing me to Bernard Shir-Cliff, my literary agent, he ensured the book's realization. I owe to Bernard Shir-Cliff very singular thanks for his patient guidance, enduring kindness, and always impeccable advice. I have greatly benefited from the helpful direction given to me by my editor, Connie Zweig, and from her intelligent counsel. To Fred Sawyer, whose insightful copyediting greatly improved the work, I am exceedingly grateful. My special thanks to Lisa Chadwick and Allen Mikaelian, at Tarcher/Putnam, for their good-humored and steady support. I am indebted to Lorraine Duncan, manager of Portland State University's Faculty Resource Center, for her considerable and considerate assistance; and to Shahin Pourkhesali, whose computer expertise made my work much easier, I extend my deepest thanks.

In its final shape this book stands as a testament to its contributors: Nancy Andreasen, M.D., Ph.D.; Jeffrey L. Geller, M.D., M.P.H.; Diane M. Gourley, R.N., B.A.; Richard K. James, Ph.D.; Judith B. Krauss, R.N., M.S.N.; Harriet P. Lefley, Ph.D.; Marsha A. Martin, D.S.W.; Bentson H. McFarland, M.D., Ph.D.; and Jeffrey L. Rogers, J.D. I am grateful for their faith in and devotion to this project, for their eloquent and articulate insight, and for their dependable cooperation. That their contribution is indispensable is evident in the work.

It is to my own family that I am most indebted: To my mother, I lovingly dedicate this book in praise of her indomitable spirit. To my aunt, Mary Ann, who, from wartime London, used to send me books that stirred my sensibility. To my children, Jane Isbel, Michael, David, Roger, Fredric, Jennifer, and Nicholas, all of whom have enriched my life; each, in her and his own way, has contributed to this work, and I am grateful for their continued interest and encouragement. But the words "grateful, indebted, thankful" cannot express my greatest debt, which is to my cherished companion, my husband, Byron Backlar. Because he is a man of integrity, his careful reading of the manuscript (in its many and varied forms), his cautious criticisms, and his unstinting support have meant more to me than can be acknowledged.

Preface

[Schizophrenia] is the most solitary of afflictions to the people who experience it; but it is the most social of maladies to those who observe its effects.

—Michael MacDonald
Mystical Bedlam: Madness, Anxiety, and Healing in Seventeenth Century England

Public humiliation or private grief, which is worse? Was it the afternoon of her youngest son's high school graduation, when his older brother, Aaron, pranced around the auditorium, grimacing like a naughty monkey? And Jill, their mother, sat frozen in her seat, also grimacing. Or was it several months later, when she first saw Aaron in the hospital, after he had been diagnosed as having schizophrenia?

The year was 1981, the February evening, bleak and chill; Jill traveled directly from the airport to the hospital. As the bus jostled from stop to stop, she set her face against the grimy window and peered at the dismal city through the settling dusk. It was dark by the time she arrived at the hospital. Still shivering from the unaccustomed cold, she pulled her thin raincoat around her as she stood alone in the rising elevator.

Lethargically, a bored aide unlocked the door to the psychiatric ward. The fastened door was a surprise; she hadn't anticipated locked doors. Seated at the nurses' station, a dour woman told Jill she was too late for visiting hours. "It has been a very long journey," Jill said. "Aah," the woman acknowledged, and nodding her ponderous chin, she granted that they had expected a visitor for Aaron. Grudgingly, she gave permission for the mother to spend a few minutes with her son. Pointing down the dimly lit corridor, the attendant indicated Aaron's room.

On either side of the hall, open doors revealed small bare rooms with two or three beds. Women and men lay on the beds or slouched in chairs, many with their eyes closed, some staring aimlessly into space. No one appeared perturbed by the sound of muffled shrieks coming from behind a closed door.

Jill hesitated in an open doorway. Aaron lay curled up on a narrow hospital bed. His legs were drawn to his chest. His arms clasped his knees. The curve of his neck thrust his head forward into the circle of his body—a few wispy tendrils of hair emphasized the vulnerable nape. His open eyes appeared unseeing.

Two weeks previously, on a balmy California evening, Jill and her husband returned home after celebrating a friend's 50th birthday. A note was tucked under the telephone on Jill's night table. Her youngest daughter had scrawled a cryptic message: a Boston telephone number and a physician's name. Even though the doctor's name was unknown to her, Jill read the scribble with a deep sense of foreboding. She sat on the side of her bed, sliding off her shoes and absentmindedly rubbing her stockinged feet, back and forth, against the coarse carpet. Carefully, she pulled off her earrings; they were heavy and the clips squeezed her earlobes. The call could only be about Aaron.

Aaron, her third child and second son, was living in Boston. He was nineteen years old, a student, in his sophomore year at the university.

A psychiatry resident, polite but unbending, answered her call. "Your son," he said, "is a very sick young man. When he was admitted to the hospital this morning he was floridly psychotic, but we've given him some medicine and he's sleeping now." He paused, a silence hung awkwardly between them. "Nothing much will change over the weekend. On Monday, the attending physician will call and discuss the case with you." Jill made an undistinguishable sound, somewhere between a sob and a moan. "No," the young doctor said. "We prefer that you do not come right away. It may not be necessary. I expect we'll have him well in no time." She didn't really believe him, even then.

Years later Aaron told his mother that they had put him in restraints. They had left him alone, cold and afraid, strapped to a bed in an empty room. He had no recollection how long he had remained there. Unable to move, he remembered that he had soiled himself.

When Flaubert was asked who had been his model for Madame Bovary, he always maintained, "Madame Bovary, c'est moi!" And so too, I must acknowledge, Jill is *I*. And likewise, my *son* has schizophrenia.

Analogously, even though the stories in this book are authentic, each narrative is also my story. The family and personal details are unique, but the experiences are similar. I share, with the women and men in these accounts, their conflicting feelings of joy and hope, sadness and loss, anger and fear, and their intense absorption with the mentally ill person's well-being.

Initially, my son's illness consumed me much as it did him. There was little time for reflection. But in the intervening years his courage became my talisman, and my private distress matured into a public involvement.

My son's illness compelled me to find comfort for him; his disease forced me to recognize others like him. Only then was my personal pain eased— my own trouble becoming one among many. And thus this book had its genesis.

In 1989, as the project director of a symposium series on ethical issues in the public debate at Portland State University, I organized a program entitled "Who Cares? The Homeless Mentally Ill." The hall was packed. The downtown urban school attracted not only the more usual throng of students, professors, nurses, social workers, physicians, lawyers, and lay philosophers, but also a highly charged crowd of families who have mentally ill relatives and a number of mentally ill persons themselves. A few of the mentally ill people present were homeless. It was a miserably wet night and going home after the program to a warm supper and my comfortable bed, it was impossible not to think about the homeless mentally ill.

We've all seen them, but some we remember better than others. Firmly placed in my recollection is a middle-aged woman, whom I often saw standing at the corner of Wilshire Boulevard and 5th Street in Santa Monica, California. Week after week I could count on seeing her. A shocking pink bandanna bound her hair and scarlet lipstick was smeared clown-like around her mouth. "Shit, you mother fuckers," ballooned repeatedly from her crimson lips. She was in the habit of hurling her collected empty glass bottles from her Safeway shopping cart. Sharp splinters made a crazy paving on the road, and the dry hot sun glinted on the broken shards. Shoppers hurried past and averted their faces.

Also indelibly imprinted in my memory is a thin and fragile young man lying huddled on the damp concrete of a store doorway, shivering as he slept. There was a cold snap that autumn evening in downtown Seattle. We were on Pike Street, a stone's throw from the Sheraton. The young man might as well have been in a frigid desert, the Sheraton a mere mirage for him. As my husband bent over to place several dollar bills under the crook of his arm, the young man's head jerked up, his eyes wild and fearful. My own eyes welled up with tears: I envisioned my son.

Susan Sontag wrote in 1977, "Theories that diseases are caused by mental states and can be cured by willpower are always an index of how much is not understood about the physical terrain of a disease." She could have been writing specifically about schizophrenia. The etiology of this disease is still uncertain and because schizophrenia manifests through behavior, some people believe that the cure lies within the mental and emotional capacity of mentally ill persons themselves. When symptoms are evinced through behavior, and no physical pathology is discerned, it may appear that a person's will is weak and that the illness is her or his fault. Historically, for a diversity of reasons, the sufferers of various diseases (leprosy, TB, cancer, AIDS, to name a few) have borne the brunt of a culture's moral repugnance. Subliminally we may hear the leper's warning cry, "unclean, unclean," when we behold the homeless mentally ill.

Old and young, women and men, confused, suspicious, afraid, often angry, the homeless mentally ill are almost always alone. But somewhere, for many of them, there may be a person who cares. Inevitably these caring people are immediate family members. The compassionate parents of a person with schizophrenia are likely to be both heroes and victims. Attempting to help a mentally ill relative can be a Sisyphean charge. Albert Camus describes such a task: "The gods had condemned Sisyphus to ceaselessly rolling a rock to the top of a mountain, whence the stone would fall back of its own weight. They had thought with some reason that there is no more dreadful punishment than futile and hopeless labor."

But the metaphor does not hold: it is not a mythological stone which the families strain to bring to the top of the hill—it is a beloved child, whom they are striving to bring to safety. A *grown-up* child whose dependency binds and entwines the caretaker parent. Usually, the sympathetic parents may be aware that their adult child cannot properly care for herself or himself. They understand, only too well, that the disease has altered and inhibited their relative's ability to cope with the everyday business of life.

A few years past, in this city, a mother's worst nightmares came true. Ben, her fifty-year-old son, suffering from schizophrenia, was evicted to the streets from his downtown residence because of behavior due to his illness. His elderly mother, a widow, was unable to secure treatment for him, even though she signed papers initiating commitment proceedings. He died of peritonitis caused by a urinary infection. He had lived on the streets from early March until his death in May. His acute paranoia kept him from accepting any assistance.

Like Ben, many persons with schizophrenia suffer from paranoia. A feeling of being victimized by others is typically part of the paranoid schizophrenic experience. Sometimes this expectation becomes a self-fulfilling prophecy. How can they feel other than unwanted as they shuttle from family to hospital to supervised living arrangements to unsupervised living arrangements and—too often—to the streets? Mentally ill people are not mistaken: they *are* treated as pariahs.

However, mentally ill people are not the only ones who may be disenfranchised; their families also may feel like outsiders. More often than not, when a person is first recognized (not diagnosed, for it can be excruciatingly difficult to get that first official diagnosis) to have a mental illness, the well members of the family may rally round, making Herculean efforts to support and care for their ill family member. Too frequently, however, they find that their gallant exertions have come to naught. Like Ben's mother, they are unable to ameliorate the actual condition, and as the illness worsens there seems to be no concrete aid available. Helplessly, they may twist and turn through labyrinthine social services, watching their ill family member deteriorate. Confused, even disoriented, oftentimes the families feel that they have lost their way in what they had believed to be the familiar territory of their everyday lives.

In 1981, when my son was first diagnosed with schizophrenia, I too felt quite inept. Many years passed before I was able to begin to understand what I was dealing with. The disease itself was mystifying. And, with the cause unknown, myths were abundant. A common fiction assigned to mothers an extraordinary power: the mother was seen as being capable of causing her children to become ill with schizophrenia. For example, the following passage in a 1979 book by Colin Wilson is ascribed to psychologist Abraham Maslow: "Since my mother is the type that's called schizophrenogenic in the literature—she's the one who makes crazy people, crazy children—I was awfully curious to find out why I didn't go insane."

Maslow credits his deliverance from schizophrenia to a gentle uncle whose kindly ministrations saved him from his mother's smothering influences. Not surprisingly, even though there was already evidence that schizophrenia was a biological disease (meaning that mothers were not to be blamed), I sometimes felt as though I wore a scarlet letter "S" emblazoned upon my chest.

That "S" might stand for schizophrenogenic—mother of schizophrenics—but the "S" is as likely to impute personal shame. Shame is a powerful and destructive force. Subtly it can underlie the diverse and persistent dilemmas which abound for the families of people with mental illness. After all, it is not unusual for individuals to feel concerned about how they are regarded by their peers. A family group may respond similarly. If one of the family members behaves in a socially aberrant fashion, the group feels exposed and senses its vulnerability. They may perceive that they are being observed, scrutinized, and unofficially graded. How well the family is able to deal with these feelings about public examination may very well affect how they care for their mentally ill relation. A family's sensation of shame, with a naturally concomitant desire to avoid scandal, can significantly compromise the quality of care a mentally ill relative receives.

But without family assistance, the quality of life for a person with schizophrenia can be truly imperiled. Professor of education Agnes B. Hatfield, a founding member of the National Alliance for the Mentally Ill, has long been an advocate for close family involvement in the care of relatives with schizophrenia. There are four discrete but symbiotic spheres, she says, in which the family plays an essential role:

One: As the stories in this book illustrate, people with schizophrenia are usually unable to sustain a social network. A *supportive* family, therefore, is critical to the relative's well-being, inasmuch as they can provide and maintain a support system.

Two, and *three:* Unavoidably, a person with mental illness is dependent upon a variety of health care providers (psychiatrists, social workers, nurses). Because of confusions in our public policy and the nature of schizophrenia, these providers are not constant. An individual with schizophrenia may have an ever-changing and haphazard journey among various health care givers. It is crucial, therefore, that a family member be able both to *monitor* the services, and be a *resource* in order to supply adequately the ill person's history to appropriate providers.

Four, the family must be its relative's *advocate* in both everyday matters and the larger social and political sphere. Notoriously, schizophrenia robs a person of insight, and without judgment, people with mental illness can be unable to champion their cause—the cause itself being rendered quite opaque.

Theories are easily articulated: praxis, however, is not so simply obtained. Many parents would willingly, and naturally, follow Hatfield's exemplar. Probably, these families could not be other than supportive. They have the wit to act as an adequate resource, both monitoring the care provided, supplying appropriate history, and simultaneously functioning as an advocate in the public arena. But as the tales in this book demonstrate, the best intentions can be readily undermined.

Initially, I conceived this book as a collection of oral histories presenting stories of families whose lives have been altered by mental illness. The 1989 conference on the homeless mentally ill proved the catalyst to this idea. That evening made me determined to inquire into the family face of schizophrenia. After all, the people we see living on our streets who suffer from schizophrenia have (or once had) families just like the rest of us. I already knew my own situation. I knew that I loved and cared for my son; I also knew that caring for him was often arduous and complex. I wanted to tell, through families' voices, what it was like to live with, or care for, someone who has this puzzling disease.

A friend of mine had a brother who suffered from schizophrenia. He was run over and killed by an automobile when he was in his early thirties. I asked her if she would let me interview her. She was horrified. After that I approached no one directly. Seeking interviewees, I put a small paragraph about the projected book in the local Alliance for the Mentally Ill monthly newsletter. The rest was word-of-mouth. I interviewed everyone who telephoned and indicated an interest. Most of the conversations took place in my office. In all, some twenty-four individuals were interviewed. These included eighteen mothers, one father, a couple (mother and father together), one sibling (a sister), and two individuals (friends, not relatives) who were closely involved with a mentally ill person. The preponderance of the mentally ill individuals alluded to in the interviews were male; only three females were the subject of discussion.

As I listened to these people, it was transparent that no one among the interviewees had forsaken their mentally ill relative. It was also evident that often the family members felt as though they had been abandoned by the community in which they lived. Furthermore, four main threads, common to each family, were revealed: initial confusion, perpetual mourning, inescapable tumult, and conflict between the family and the community.

One, the initial confusion, is easily understandable. Usually, schizophrenia afflicts young people, becoming evident in late adolescence and the early twenties. The timing, therefore, often coincides with a natural breaking away from the family home, so that unusual behavior may be attributed to other causes. This can be a stressful time in ordinary circumstances. Misinterpretation of the early signals that indicate the onset of schizophrenia is not uncommon to the families and acquaintances of mentally ill persons. The narratives illustrate this familiar pattern. Lucille, in the chapter entitled "Dial 911," says: "What was happening in our home was so peculiar that we simply couldn't imagine that it could occur anywhere else. I think that in those early stages what was really paralyzing is that even though Tony's behavior was obviously not 'right,' it was not outrageously crazy. The total effect was that we always felt as though we were in some kind of muddle. All the time we were constantly questioning; we were always evaluating how Tony's behavior fit into what we called normal and what we called abnormal."

Two, as time goes on, the families experience a persistent feeling of perpetual mourning caused by the loss of a beloved child who remains strangely altered—an adult child—in their midst. It is as though nature has played some cruel prank. The family cannot help but love this stranger who reminds them of another. But, often, this stranger child is hard to love.

In a "Father's Story," Joe says: "What jarred us, what was so devastating was the loss—the loss of what we had had and what we now had in place of it. If I had to pick a person who could have succeeded in life it would have been Mark. He was gregarious, outgoing and what I want to describe as innovative. . . . We unashamedly enjoyed the promise that we saw in him. It was hard to lose that promise. . . . We keep hoping that maybe the promise will come back. But hope is a delicate thing and all the time we are hurting because we are not fooled. We have come to know that this is an irreparable loss."

Yet, even as Joe recognizes his loss, he stubbornly clings to the faith he has just denigrated when he says, "Times when I have thought, 'Damn it, Mark, even though you have a mental illness you cannot have lost all the values that you learned in your childhood—they have to be back there in that brain someplace.' "

There is not a mother or father, in any of these tales, who does not reminisce fondly about her or his child's past. What parents do not repeat to themselves—and to others—anecdotes about their children? When parents, however, have lost their adult child to mental illness, they face a formidable task: they must rewrite their dreams, but cannot relinquish their hope.

Three, more than anything else, these tales speak of tumult. These families are hurtled into a seemingly inescapable disorder. Dolores, in "At Risk," says, "Stanley gets overexcited when he's stressed. And yet, the way things are, when he gets sick he's thrown into more stress. They say that people who have mental illness do better with a peaceful life . . . they sure do get the opposite." One cannot help but sense that she is also talking about herself.

And Joni, in "The Single Parent's Struggle," echoes this. "I would have preferred that he had been locked up and medicated, so that he had a fighting chance. I would have preferred that he was OK. I would have preferred that I had a restful day."

Four, the central tension is conflict between the family, painfully aware of their ill relative's needs, and the community in which they live. In our culture we hold ingrained and asserted beliefs that "all men [and women] are endowed with certain unalienable rights . . . among these are life, *liberty* and the pursuit of happiness." We treasure our freedom and use it, unselfconsciously, in our everyday lives. We live in a society which gives high priority to personal choice in determining where, with whom, and how we live. As individuals we make intimate choices which inevitably affect every part of our being. By its nature, public policy reflects the community it serves: expectations and societal attitudes are expressed in our laws.

The family members come into direct confrontation with the law when they attempt to secure hospitalization and/or treatment for their ill relative. Our laws try to ensure that a person may not be coerced into accepting medical therapy. A patient's *understanding of* and *agreement to* any procedure must occur before initiation of treatment. But because of the nature of schizophrenia, this right to self-determination—the right legitimizing refusal of treatment—poses difficult and complex questions. At what point does a mentally ill person become unable to make coherent decisions? How can we be sure when chronically mentally ill individuals, taking their medications and living in the community, have attained the level of stability necessary to make decisions about their own health care? Are people who suffer from this disease, the measure of which is an inability to comprehend the consequences of their actions, ever able to give "informed consent" to treatment?

In many states, unless there is clear evidence that a mentally ill person is unable to care for herself or himself, or that she or he constitutes an immediate threat of danger to another, therapy may not be available. This standard, known as "harm to self or others," is usually read quite narrowly. No wonder Neal, in "Slipping Through the Cracks," says, "As I see it, the reasoning behind the laws which impede a diagnosis and commitment for mentally ill people is cockeyed."

And it is not the families alone who are undone by these laws. The mental health professionals—nurses, physicians, psychologists, social workers—also may be rendered impotent. The following paragraph, written by mental health care professionals and excerpted from a local Alliance for the Mentally Ill newsletter, speaks for itself: ". . . sometimes the only, and maybe most important, thing we can do is to offer you support and advice in dealing with situations in which we cannot directly intervene due to legal constraints. Sometimes, we are as powerless as you, given legal constraints, to make your family member accept the treatment that we both know is needed."

Coincidently, as I was preparing the oral histories recorded in this book, I was invited to join, as a senior scholar, the Center for Ethics in Health Care, at Oregon Health Sciences University. The Center had just been formed by a diverse group of health care professionals dedicated to the concept of working together as equals. Each discipline's contribution is seen to be of equal value. Health care is, in fact, a collaborative reality.

The Center's fundamental principle of cooperative enterprise came to play a significant part in the composition of this book. It became evident to me that the families' stories, which I had been collecting, needed additional perspectives. The narratives, confined by the families' views, delineate only a partial picture. We cannot extricate ourselves from the framework in which we live. Plainly there can be multiple people involved with a single individual who has schizophrenia: judges, lawyers, nurses, police, psychiatrists, psychologists, social workers, and so forth.

These people are not simply a backdrop to a family's drama. If the family members are to perform the vital role which Agnes Hatfield outlines for them, the helping professionals need to interact with the parents and to view them as the *indispensable* resource which they can be. For the most part, the families are eager (sometimes desperate) to establish an open dialogue with the providers.

But it is not necessarily clear how these connections can be made. For instance, because initial impressions can color succeeding relationships, families are especially vulnerable to the circumstances in which their ill relative first receives treatment. As Harriet Lefley wrote in 1987: "For most families . . . the first encounter with officially sanctioned helpers occurs in the context of the psychiatrist's office, a clinic, a hospital, or a crisis emergency room. This may be the family's first experience with mental health professionals—the experts who presumably will know how to heal their relative. The nature and quality of this encounter, occurring during a period of profound anguish and stress, may greatly affect the family's subsequent capability to comprehend and cope with their relative's mental illness."

When my own son first became ill, I remember that I received a lot of advice (some of it dreadful, some, in retrospect, excellent), but because I was without experience it took me a long time to sift through what worked and what didn't. Of course, my son did not remain "still," so to speak, while I attempted to secure adequate care for him. Consequently, as the oral histories in this book confirm, on-the-job-learning was the rule. But most of us, myself included, are impatient when needlessly we must start things from scratch. Without information, families are hindered from becoming full associates with the various service providers, which they must be—especially at a time of scarce resources—if their relatives with schizophrenia are to receive the attention that they require. Therefore, it appeared valuable to gather together, in one book, the knowledge and perspectives of the diverse helping professionals.

Thus, the narratives have become the spine of the book and form the foundation for a multiprofessional project that provides practical information to help families recognize and understand schizophrenia as an illness, prepare them for what lies ahead, and advise them on where to turn for help. Each story, serving as a springboard, is followed by a commentary written from the viewpoint of a specific discipline. These essays emphasize cooperation between family and service providers; they also underwrite the necessity for interprofessional teamwork. "Professional fences need to come down," emphasizes psychologist Richard James, in his essay about the police and mental health providers. In order to achieve a synergism, collaboration and candid communication between all the players are required.

The commentators represent the following disciplines: law, nursing, police, psychiatry, psychology, and social work; in addition, their geographic distribution is national, many regions of this vast country are included—Connecticut, Florida, Iowa, Massachusetts, New York, Oregon, Tennessee. The essayists furnish realistic data about current care available for those who suffer from schizophrenia, providing guidance and enabling families to find their way through the thicket of confusions which confront them. Furthermore, some national material is supplied, along with suggestions for improving the social services.

Schizophrenia is the most important of the major mental illnesses, writes Dr. Nancy Andreasen in her introduction. She says, "Although the classical Greeks and the medieval Arabs viewed mental illnesses as true illnesses and treated their victims with compassion, throughout much of the history of western society attitudes have been more negative and judgmental." Bringing the account up to date, Dr. Andreasen explains the social and medical background that lies behind our current opinions about mental illness. She gives a clinical description of schizophrenia, defining it "as legitimately physical as cancer or heart disease." Dr. Andreasen stresses the importance of advocacy, education, and research as ways to improve the grim difficulties which most persons with schizophrenia face. And although most individuals cannot do research, she urges them to support it. Research, she emphasizes, will "provide the long-term hope for mental illness."

Psychiatrist Bentson McFarland has written the commentary which follows "A Father's Story." Depicting the variety of health care professionals trained to provide aid for persons with schizophrenia, Dr. McFarland describes their education and explains the assistance which they can furnish. His guide details the medications available for schizophrenia, delineating what each drug can do and specifying its side effects. He sorts out the confusing mixture of public and private services which are financed by an astonishingly complicated set of payment systems, and reveals how financing determines the type of service available. He further clarifies the monetary picture, enumerating costs of drugs, hospitalization, insurance (including both medicaid and medicare), and counsels on how to access federal and state financial assistance.

"A study of burden of care for families of young persons with schizophrenia found that single mothers were especially vulnerable to stress," writes psychologist Harriet Lefley in her commentary to the tale "The Single Parent's Struggle." She chronicles common ordeals and shows how they affect both the family and, more specifically, the single parent. Dr. Lefley emphasizes the importance of communication. When health care providers fail to inform and educate, they exacerbate patient and family difficulties. "In Western culture," Lefley writes, "which places great stock in personal control and solutions for every problem, guilt seems to be a ubiquitous response to illness in a child." In addition to pinpointing various sources of guilt feelings, Dr. Lefley reports, "Family members are caught in the double-bind of feeling remiss if they do not follow professional advice, and feeling remiss if following that advice produces an unsatisfactory outcome." She explains how guilt can interfere with an objective assessment of professional wisdom. In her account of grieving and loss, Dr. Lefley observes that mourning is experienced not only by parents but also by the young adults who suffer from schizophrenia. She proffers hope, however, when she notes that the ill individual's "positive personal qualities and premorbid talents may still be intact and ready to be released under favorable circumstances."

Social worker Marsha Martin writes about the mentally ill homeless population in her commentary which follows the story, "Slipping Through the Cracks." Dr. Martin reports that *one-third* of homeless men and women have a severe mental illness such as schizophrenia. This is primarily due to two causes: one, a mental health system which does not have enough resources to provide care to all people who are in need, and two, a mentally ill person's legal right to refuse treatment even when treatment is available and clearly in her or his best interest. Consequently, says Martin, many individuals do not receive treatment, fall through the cracks, and join the ranks of the homeless. Martin chronicles how the symptoms of the disease—delusions and paranoia—can make a person with schizophrenia exchange a warm and comfortable home for the anonymity of street life. She shows how behaviors considered maladaptive to indoor living can become a means of protection for living outdoors, and explains why it is so difficult to get some people with schizophrenia to give up their homeless lifestyle. Nevertheless, Martin assures families that even though finding a missing family member can be very difficult, it is not an impossible task. She provides a list of suggestions for families searching for their mentally ill relative. However, she notes that the return of a previously homeless family member will challenge even the most talented and sophisticated families. She urges families to work with agencies which provide specialized services for homeless individuals and families. Families who cope best with their ill relative, Martin says, are characterized by being more relaxed, less intrusive, better able to listen, have a lack of fear and a positive attitude. Dr. Martin warns that unless returned ill relatives receive mental health treatment "they will be right back where they were before they left."

The story "Whereabouts Unknown" is a postscript to the preceeding narrative, "Slipping Through the Cracks." The commentary, authored by Judith Krauss and Diane Gourley, presents a psychiatric nursing perspective. Professor Krauss and nurse clinician Gourley write, "When the helping professions allow a person to suffer the ravages of schizophrenia for fear of being accused of coercion or violation of confidentiality, it is a sign that the system is getting in the way of the common goals of health professionals and families." They target five areas which demand attention and rectification: early diagnosis and education, inclusive treatment planning, the needs of siblings, the need for family respite, and system reform. While analyzing these issues, the authors scrutinize many important concerns: how treating a psychiatric diagnosis as a secret simply reinforces the stigma associated with it; the significance of finding a way to create centralized clinical, administrative, and fiscal authority for care if patients and families are to survive our decentralized system; and, significantly, how laws dealing with the mentally ill are outmoded and need to be reexamined to see if they still serve the people they were intended to protect. The psychiatric nurse can play an important role in the life of both people with chronic schizophrenia and their families: "Psychiatric nurses are a good source of information about disorder and treatment, expected main effects and side effects of medication, symptom management (from both a patient and a family perspective), and how to navigate the system."

Most of us have read lurid newspaper accounts about inept and disastrous police handling of the mentally ill. Dr. Richard James puts his finger on a cause when he describes such a scene: "After a tremendously violent struggle to control a psychotic adolescent, [the police officer] turned to the hysterical mother and said, "Sorry, lady, but we just aren't *trained* for this." In his essay, which follows the story "Dial 911," psychologist James reconstructs the fears and difficulties police face when dealing with a crisis situation, and also gives concrete evidence that by training police to deal with the mentally ill, the mental health system can form an extremely strong alliance and rapid response system. Graphically, Professor James outlines the successful Crisis Intervention Team *training* program that they have in Memphis, Tennessee. He lauds the Alliance for the Mentally Ill and their member families for bringing this about, and provides heartwarming evidence of effective advocacy in action. He writes, "Can such a program be adopted in your community? The answer is 'Yes!' if someone like you is willing to start the ball rolling."

In the essay which follows the narrative "At Risk," psychiatrist Jeffrey Geller writes, "For generations people appear to have been fascinated by how society provides care and treatment to those with the chronic mental illness we now call schizophrenia." Suicide, Dr. Geller says, also piques our interest. However, he notes that suicide by individuals with schizophrenia appears to be simply less newsworthy. Tragically, Dr. Geller concludes, "Suicide is the main cause of increased mortality among individuals with schizophrenia." Geller surveys the alterations in patterns of care for persons with schizophrenia, and asks whether there are better methods now (as opposed to two or three generations ago) for governing the potential for suicide in individuals with schizophrenia. He answers his rhetorical question negatively by exploring the risk factors shared by the general population and persons with schizophrenia: "Persons with schizophrenia have a mortality rate that is twice that of the general population." He spells out specific risk factors for suicide in this population. Importantly, Geller provides treatment considerations in lessening the risk of suicide in persons with schizophrenia.

"Out of Control," the final narrative in the book (and the only story recounted by a friend, not a relative), precedes attorney Jeffrey Rogers' commentary. Studies indicate, Rogers writes, that most people with schizophrenia are not violent. However, he notes that the small fraction of people with schizophrenia who are dangerous to others have a disproportional influence on public opinion. He examines the psychiatrist's legal duty to protect third parties, and explains both civil and criminal commitment. Rogers reports on the composition and duties of a Psychiatric Security Review Board, illuminating its usefulness. Because rules of law so often play a significant part in the life of a person with schizophrenia, he intersperses sensible advice to families throughout his account of the legal territory. But as Rogers points out, "the answer to the scourge of schizophrenia will come from medical research, not from the law."

Everywhere we turn we see how our public mental health system has failed us, whether we look to our homes, to our hospitals, to our jails, or to our streets. The stories in this book underscore this fact. These tales of madness describe not only schizophrenia but also how our society treats people who suffer from this biological disease. In America, people with schizophrenia find themselves in double jeopardy: on the one hand, they suffer from a chronic disease which in its acute forms can terrorize them, and on the other hand, they are punished by a society which, for complex reasons, often witholds aid to those who most desperately need assistance.

Like moths flitting about an incandescent light bulb, mentally ill people, their families, and the helping professionals hover around the bright glow of high expectations: hoping for an explanation of and restorative treatment for schizophrenia. What can we do? How can we help? To whom can we turn? When will our hopes be realized? Our daily lives inform us, and I trust this book demonstrates, that we must rely on the cooperative relationships among people with common goals to guide and order how resources—whatever they may be—are utilized.

Introduction

By Nancy C. Andreasen, M.D., Ph.D.

Dr. Andreasen is the Andrew H. Woods Professor of Psychiatry in the Department of Psychiatry of the College of Medicine, the University of Iowa. She is the Director of the Mental Health Clinical Research Center, which is one of four major research centers dedicated to the study of schizophrenia in the U.S. Dr. Andreasen has received many awards and prizes. She was recently elected to the Institute of Medicine of the National Academy of Science and was named Editor of the American Journal of Psychiatry. *She has served as president of the Psychiatric Research Society and the American Psychopathological Association. She has received the American Psychiatric Association Prize for Research, the highest award given by that organization, as well as the 1992 Stanley R. Dean Award from the American College of Psychiatrists, the major international prize in schizophrenia research. She is currently the recipient of a Career Scientist Award and a MERIT Award from the National Institute of Mental Health. Her current work emphasizes the use of several major neuroimaging techniques, including magnetic resonance, single photon emission computed tomography, and positron emission tomography. Assisted by contributions from computer science and cognitive neuroscience, she uses these techniques to study the living human mind and brain in health and disease. She has written more than 200 scientific articles and seven books, including* The Broken Brain: The Biological Revolution in Psychiatry *(1984), written to explain the neurobiology of mental illness to lay readers. Before Dr. Andreasen went into medicine she was an English professor at the University of Iowa.*

This book portrays the impact that a terrible illness, schizophrenia, has had on six people who suffer from it and on their families and friends. Its story is told with chilling candor. The stories are true and truly terrifying. In case after case, decent people who should be the guardians of social welfare—lawyers, doctors, policemen, judges, nurses, social workers, psychologists—have turned their gaze away from patients and families who are experiencing nearly unbearable pain, fear, torment, and life-threatening danger. These patients and families have been ignored or abandoned by the medical and legal structure of society that should comfort and protect them. The experiences portrayed could easily be stories by Kafka. Nothing is fair. Nothing makes sense. Good people suffer. Indifferent or callous people control the reins of power. *But these stories are true.*

How did this Kafkaesque world come to exist within our enlightened and progressive society? This, unfortunately, is the world of mental illness. As this book vividly portrays, the attitudes and regulations of much of society toward the mentally ill are perhaps crazier than the patients themselves. Doctors often go to extraordinary lengths to maintain life in patients with cancer, renal disease, or other "physical illnesses" (even when the quality of life is extremely poor and the long-term outcome is certain death). Yet doctors may be prevented from prescribing simple effective medications for patients doomed to decades of pain and even "living death" if the patients suffer from a "mental" illness such as schizophrenia. Judges ignore such clear evidence of danger as a man holding a knife to his mother's throat, since he isn't doing it before their eyes in the courtroom, and rule that there is no evidence of dangerousness and no need for treatment. A patient who has run wild during a psychotic break will receive medical care for the cuts on his feet, but none for the torments in his mind that drove him to run amok. Disease of the body is palpable and understandable. Disease of the mind is not.

For much of human history, attitudes toward mental illness have been ambivalent and ambiguous. Although the classical Greeks and the medieval Arabs viewed mental illnesses as true illnesses and treated their victims with compassion, throughout much of the history of western society attitudes have been more negative and judgmental. Typically, the mentally ill were isolated from the remainder of society—locked up (often even in chains) in jails or poorhouses. Depending on the point of view being expressed, either the mad were spared having to deal with the rational and sane, or the rational and sane were spared the sight of madness. This situation was remedied during the nineteenth century by the development of movements all over the world to free the mentally ill from the prisons where they were typically housed to create asylums where the mentally ill received treatment. But now, in the 1990s, a new constellation of social forces has emerged and led to "deinstitutionalization," which sometimes has the quality of a nightmare. The mentally ill have been freed from their chains for a second time, but this freedom has released them into a technologically complex, economically stringent and socially indifferent world.

No one likes to see the homeless mentally ill wandering the streets. We naturally react negatively toward their strange behavior and their apparent lack of purposefulness and initiative. The sense of helplessness and inconvenience we experience at the sight of their suffering leads us to feel anger and to find someone to blame. The most logical targets of blame are the mentally ill themselves, the families who have failed to care for them properly, or the doctors who have failed to treat them properly. Much of the time this imminently sensible and comforting set of conclusions puts the blame in the wrong place. How did such a misunderstanding come to pass?

WHY DID SUCH ATTITUDES ARISE?

Many sources can be identified for the situation in which we currently find ourselves. Perhaps the most fundamental is the so-called mind/body problem. Most of us assume that our minds are somehow separate from our bodies and that they have a different kind of reality. In order to make sense of our world as we perceive it, we assume that something that we call the "mind" governs the "body." We subjectively experience ourselves deciding to eat chicken instead of steak, to watch television instead of reading a book, or to take a half hour nap instead of going to the gym to exercise. We assume that there is an "executive" somewhere inside us that makes these decisions. As we become increasingly sophisticated about how our bodies work, we realize that this "executive function" resides in our brains. Nevertheless, most of us tend to think in a rather linear way and to assume that one thing has to cause another in a chain of events. The mind is conceived of as something that causes the brain to act, which in turn has a subsequent impact on what the rest of the body does. A body is like a machine, while the mind is the capacity to turn the machine on and off—often thought of as "the ghost in the machine." A dualistic way of thinking about the world as containing "mind vs. matter" permeates human thinking from very early times, usually with the assumption that mind is somehow "higher" than matter.

This sense that there is a "mind/body dichotomy," leading to a dualistic and hierarchical way of thinking about the mind and body, has important implications for the way people think about mental illness. The first major implication is that aberrations in thinking must somehow be under personal control. If the mind is the executive that runs the body, then when it performs badly, the mind itself must be at fault. The mind, after all, is running the machine. Mental illness is just a case of the mind running the machine badly. Each person's mind is perceived as that person's particular identity or property. Since mind and "personhood" are intertwined, if the mind is doing a bad job of governing thinking and behavior, then the person to whom the mind belongs must be a bad human being. This is, of course, an oversimplification.

A second implication of "mind/body dichotomy" is that a person who displays symptoms of mental illness must be considered personally responsible for all aberrations in thinking or behavior that he displays. We all have the sense that we make choices and that the decision is made by our minds. If a person behaves in a way that is strange or socially inappropriate, the source of this behavior is his mind, and he must be choosing to behave in that way. Obviously, his mind is free to choose differently. If it chooses to do things that society regards as unacceptable or bad, those bad choices are freely made, and each person must be considered morally responsible for his bad choices. From here it is an easy step to see people who have mental illness and behave in an aberrant way as innately bad people. This is, of course, a conceptual error.

A third implication of the "mind/body dichotomy" is that any so-called mental disease is less real because it is not apparently "physical." We can all sympathize with the pain of a broken leg, a heart attack, or the ravages of cancer. Mental pain is often, however, considered to be less real. We constantly hear statements such as "it's all in your mind" or "it's just psychological." That "mental suffering is the worst kind" is another truism we also hear, however. In fact, distinctions between mental and physical suffering are arbitrary, the subjective experience of suffering is individualized, and comparisons between people who are suffering from various illnesses are probably inappropriate. As the stories in this book will attest, however, mental suffering is certainly real and can be extremely painful.

A final implication of the "mind/body dichotomy" is that mental illnesses may in fact be spiritual problems. In some languages, such as German, the same word is used to refer to "mind" and to "spirit" (i.e., "geist"). As recently as 200 years ago, the mentally ill were considered to be "bewitched" and were handed over to the church for treatment, which was likely to consist of being tortured or burned at the stake. While we tend to pride ourselves for living in more enlightened times, remnants of this attitude persist in many people's minds. The concepts of mind and spirit are mixed together, and the assumption is made that people who suffer from mental illness (or their parents) must have done something wrong for which they are being punished. Although further retribution through torture or fire is no longer recommended, the alternate possibility of restitution through prayer and spiritual support is often seen as sufficient "medicine" to "cure" a spiritual disease. People are urged to exert more mental and moral control, to have more self-discipline, or to adopt a more positive attitude. This is a very unfair way to treat people who are suffering from a tragic and painful illness that they cannot in fact control. To ask them to "shape up" is like asking a person with a broken leg to run a marathon.

All these various ideas and attitudes feed into the problem of stigmatization toward mental illness. Because mental illnesses are seen as different, separate from physical illness, perhaps less painful, and perhaps less real, their victims are not usually given equal status with those suffering from other illnesses in the health care system or by society. Instead, they are at best second-class citizens and at worst seen as "locos" or "crocks" who are worthless or a waste of time. The worst expression of such attitudes occurred when the Nazis herded the mentally ill off to the gas chambers along with the mentally retarded, the Gypsies, and the Jews.

Our vocabulary is replete with words that refer to mental illness that are pejorative in nature. Hospitals are "looney bins" or "institutions." Psychiatrists are "head shrinkers." When problems of modern society are described in a critical way, they are often referred to as "schizophrenic." Admitting to a past history of psychiatric treatment may be grounds for being refused admission to medical school or the military, life or health insurance, or even a reasonable opportunity for employment. People who have experienced mental illness are inevitably ashamed to admit they have it or have had it, and most families are reluctant to admit the existence of a mentally ill relative. Pressure is great to "keep mental illness in the closet." Largely because they have a poor understanding of the nature of mental illness, most ordinary people react to it with fear, embarrassment, or rejection.

Issues of health care delivery and social politics have interacted with the problems of stigmatization and the mind/body dichotomy to make the plight of the mentally ill especially poor at the present time. Until the 1970s and 1980s, the majority of people with very serious mental illnesses such as schizophrenia remained in hospitals. This kept mental illness out of the public eye, no doubt reducing the opportunity to understand it better. During the 1960s it was estimated that every other hospital bed was occupied by a person suffering from a serious mental illness.

A variety of factors led to the movement known as "deinstitutionalization." Medications became available that were effective in reducing some of the symptoms of serious mental illnesses, making it more likely that people could function outside a protected hospital setting. A renewed interest in the importance of civil rights focused on the rights of the mentally ill, in addition to the rights of blacks and women. In this context, hospitals were often viewed as "institutions" where the environment was excessively controlled. The coupling of effective medications with an emphasis on the importance of civil liberties led many to argue that the mentally ill would benefit from discharge into the community, where they would be able to live in a more normal and natural environment. An ideal health care system was proposed, in which community mental health centers would be dotted around the country and would provide health care services for the mentally ill in their local community environment.

Thus, in the 1980s, the majority of hospitalized patients were steadily discharged and the hospitals that housed them were closed. This new policy was based largely on humanitarian arguments. Several things went wrong in the process, however. In most areas the expected community services did not materialize. Patients were not provided with adequate housing, adequate income or sheltered employment opportunities, or adequate medical services. In fact, many patients were much worse off. Many of the state hospitals were in fact small communities in themselves, where patients lived together as a family and were given a chance to be productively employed by the hospital farm, kitchen, or laundry. While such work was seen as potentially demeaning in the environment of the 1970s, the retrospectoscope of the 1990s makes it look considerably better than wandering the streets without any employment at all and without adequate food and housing. Most of us would agree that wheeling a shopping cart containing one's life possessions down the street is not superior to working in a garden or canning the vegetables it produces, while living in a sheltered environment with warm food, clean sheets, and clothing.

Economic issues entered the picture as well, and they may be the driving force for the mess we are currently in. In addition to suggesting that community services would be more humane and efficacious, some advocates of this approach also suggested that they would be cheaper. The deinstitutionalization movement coincided with the emphasis on substituting outpatient care for inpatient hospital care in health services as a whole, with the goal of placing a cap on skyrocketing medical costs. As physicians and patients are beginning to discover, rapid discharge from the hospital after childbirth, cataract surgery, or spine surgery can turn into a nightmare for a person who lives alone and who has no available surrogate nurse to assist with the functions that were previously managed in the hospital—a human detail that health economists seem to have ignored or forgotten. In the case of the mentally ill, it seems that no one remembered to factor in the cost of providing adequate housing, food services, transportation to centralized medical services, or organized daily activities that the seriously mentally ill need in order to maintain structure and stimulation in their lives.

The problem with escalating health care costs has gotten worse rather than better, in spite of the diminished services that are being provided for the mentally ill. Yet serious mental illness remains a favored target for additional cuts in health care services. "Rationing benefits" is a popular term these days. In this rationing process, most private insurance companies cover only one or two months per year for hospital care for mental illness, although they do not have corresponding caps for other types of illness, many of which can be far more costly. Huge sums are spent liberally (even if progressively less cheerfully) for very costly surgical procedures, such as transplantations, that require subsequent long-term care. Many state governments, the traditional refuge for the care of chronic illnesses, have been driven into insolvency by the burdens placed on them through federal cutbacks. Once the state institutions have been closed and the patients have been moved to the community, they have conveniently ceased to be a state responsibility. And so it goes. The mentally ill are often unable to speak articulately for themselves. Family members have been intimidated by shame and blame, or simply worn out by the worries and responsibilities of caring for a seriously ill loved one.

What is the answer to these various problems? Easy solutions are not in sight. But as a beginning it must be stated explicitly, clearly, and repeatedly that mental illnesses *must* be raised to equal status with other forms of illness in the public consciousness and in the minds of those who are responsible for allocating health care resources. It is essential to recognize that major mental illnesses—schizophrenia, Alzheimer's disease, and manic depressive disease—are important and legitimate illnesses that should be accorded an equal investment in resources for health care and in research concerning their treatment and causes.

The old arguments, based on the mind/body dichotomy and stigmatization, will no longer work in the 1990s. During the past 20 years, a new discipline—neuroscience—has emerged and has substantially advanced our understanding concerning the mechanisms that govern brain function from the abstract level of the mind to the finely detailed level of the molecule. Although a great deal remains to be learned, neuroscientists have begun to discover how nerve cells develop and grow in the brain and form complex circuits that regulate and modulate behavior, how chemical messengers are generated to communicate in these circuits, how genes control functions of growth and development, and how information is assembled and stored as memories at the molecular level.

In the context of all this neuroscience research, it has been repeatedly demonstrated that mental illnesses are diseases of our most human organ, the brain. Again, a great deal remains to be done, but masses of information have been assembled that suggest many different kinds of brain abnormalities in serious mental illnesses—abnormalities in nerve cell structure, in the genetic programs that regulate the growth and development of neural circuits and cells, in brain chemistry and metabolism, and in the storing and processing of information. The molecular structure of the nerve receptors that receive and send messages in the brain have been cloned for many types of chemical messengers, raising the hope that new medications can be designed to specifically target these receptors so that more effective treatments will be available.

After centuries of fear and ignorance, we are finally beginning to understand the most important organ in our bodies, the brain, and the diseases that afflict it, the major mental illnesses. As brain diseases, mental illnesses are as legitimately physical as cancer or heart disease. As legitimate physical illnesses, the various mental illnesses must be given equal treatment by health care providers. People who suffer from these illnesses must be seen as genuinely ill, accorded the sick role, and provided with comprehensive and humane treatment.

In recognition of the importance of neuroscience and brain disease, Congress has designated the 1990s as the "The Decade of the Brain." Recognition is growing that major mental illnesses are perhaps the most important and human illnesses that people experience, since they afflict an organ in the body that is uniquely developed in human beings. The very recognition of the importance of the brain/mind/spirit, which has produced such fear and stigmatization of mental illness in the past, should be used to move it to its appropriate status as perhaps the most significant disease that human beings experience.

WHAT IS SCHIZOPHRENIA?

Schizophrenia is the particular mental illness which afflicts the six patients described in this book. It is the most important of the major mental illnesses. Most people have serious misconceptions about the nature of this illness. Because the name "schizo-phrenia" literally means "split mind" in Greek, this illness is often confused with multiple personality or "split personality." This disease was given its name, however, by a Swiss psychiatrist, Eugene Bleuler, in order to convey the concept that in schizophrenia the mind has somehow become shattered, fragmented, or destroyed.

The earlier name for schizophrenia, dementia praecox, may convey its fundamental nature better to the modern reader. Emil Kraepelin called this illness dementia praecox because it typically produces serious disabilities in thinking and feeling, much as occurs in Alzheimer's disease. Dementia praecox literally means "a dementia that occurs in young people." Kraepelin chose this name in order to distinguish it from the other common form of serious mental deterioration that he often saw in his patients, which differed primarily because its onset was later in life. By studying the brains of elderly patients with this other dementia, Kraepelin's colleague, Alzheimer, was able to define a characteristic abnormality in nerve cells that became a defining feature at the laboratory level. Consequently, this dementia of the elderly is now known as Alzheimer's disease.

Alzheimer and other scientists working in laboratories in Kraepelin's department early in the 20th century also did exhaustive studies of brain changes in dementia praecox, but were never able to find a single specific defining characteristic that was consistently present, like the exploded and dying nerve cells seen in Alzheimer's disease. Because some young people who developed this condition had a milder form that did not lead to a severe dementia-like deterioration (in spite of a significant decline in functioning), Bleuler suggested the name "schizophrenia" to replace "dementia praecox," and it slowly caught on.

While the older name for schizophrenia may have implied a more devastating outcome than occurs in some patients, it does convey well the essentially tragic nature of schizophrenia, as the disease manifests itself in many who suffer from it. Schizophrenia strikes young people, many of whom had been functioning at a normal or high level. At times it strikes precipitously, and at others more insidiously. But both victims and their families typically note a change in personality, behavior, and thinking. These changes tend to progress inexorably, and sometimes they are so profound that parents feel as if they have "lost" their child.

The young person with schizophrenia also may recognize that he is losing mental and emotional capacities, and this recognition drives many to suicide (which occurs in about 15 percent of patients with schizophrenia). Just as a husband, wife, or child of a person with Alzheimer's disease experiences sorrow and despair over the decline of someone whom they love, so too do the parents of a schizophrenic child. The sense of loss in schizophrenia is probably more painful, however, because the young person is stolen away while in the full bloom of youth. Further, the young person with schizophrenia typically lives on for another 40 or 50 or even 60 years, while death usually rescues Alzheimer's patients from their affliction within five to 10 years.

We have no effective medical treatments that arrest the decline in either Alzheimer's disease or schizophrenia at present. Both are chronic illnesses that persist throughout the remainder of the victim's lifetime. The tragedy of schizophrenia is greater, however, because the pain of watching the slow steady decline of a young person, who will remain ill for a lifetime, is worse than having one's personality and mental capacity snatched away after one has already completed a full life. Further, the pain of watching one's own child suffer is also probably the greatest that human beings can experience.

A large body of research literature has demonstrated that schizophrenia is very much a physical illness. Although brain scientists carefully studied postmortem tissue from patients who suffered from schizophrenia during the first several decades of this century, the availability of newer technologies was necessary in order to demonstrate the importance of brain mechanisms in schizophrenia. Computerized tomography (CT), the oldest of the modern neuroimaging techniques, was invented in the early 70s and applied to the study of schizophrenia for the first time in 1976. Since then, more than 50 studies have demonstrated that patients with schizophrenia may have abnormalities in brain structure that can be seen visibly with the naked eye on CT scans. Only a subset of patients with schizophrenia have these visible abnormalities, but they are frequent enough to indicate that schizophrenia must be understood as an illness that affects nerve structure.

The most common structural abnormality is an increase in the size of the ventricles, fluid-filled cavities inside the brain, as well as a corresponding increase in fluid on the surface of the brain. The presence of these abnormalities suggests that nerve tissue either has been lost or has failed to grow normally; the bulk of the current evidence suggests that the abnormality may be neurodevelopmental (i.e., a failure in normal growth processes), because these structural brain abnormalities have been observed in patients at the time when they first develop the symptoms of schizophrenia, indicating that the disease process in the brain antedates the onset of symptoms.

Several investigators also have used neuroimaging to study identical twins, one of whom has developed schizophrenia. In these studies, the ill twin can nearly always be distinguished from the well twin on the basis of the appearance of the brain when visualized with either CT scanning or magnetic resonance imaging (MRI). The study of identical twins, one of whom has schizophrenia, is an especially elegant research design, since it also permits investigators to examine the role of both genetic and environmental factors in producing an illness such as schizophrenia. Since identical twins have exactly the same genetic material (DNA), the traits they share in common are likely to be genetically based, while the ways that they differ must have some kind of nongenetic (i.e., environmental) component. Since both twins have schizophrenia approximately 40 percent of the time, we learn that schizophrenia has an important genetic component; since 60 percent of identical twins do not share schizophrenia, however, we also learn that genetics alone cannot explain the cause of schizophrenia.

The neuroimaging studies add to this information by demonstrating that the brains of patients with schizophrenia are different from those who do not have it. These visible differences in brain structure suggest that schizophrenia must have an important environmental cause. Various factors that could serve as environmental causes include viral infections, toxins, and birth injuries.

WHAT ARE THE SYMPTOMS?

Psychiatrists conventionally divide the characteristic symptoms into two groups: positive and negative. The "positive" symptoms represent exaggerations or distortions in functions that are normally present. Perhaps the most common positive symptoms are disorders in perception; hearing voices of various kinds (auditory hallucinations) is especially common. The voices often say critical or nasty things to the patient or may give him commands to do things. Delusions are another common type of positive symptom. They involve misinterpreting various cues from the environment and developing a belief system that is often quite complex, clearly wrong in the eyes of others, but firmly believed by the patient. Typical delusions include the belief that one is being spied on, persecuted, tormented, or harmed. Such experiences as delusions or auditory hallucinations are usually unpleasant and even terrifying to the person who experiences them. These symptoms are also sometimes referred to as "psychotic" symptoms because they represent distortions of reality.

The other large group of symptoms experienced by patients with schizophrenia are called "negative symptoms." They represent a decline in functions that are normally present. While the positive symptoms are more striking, and often call attention to the patient early in the course of the illness, the negative symptoms tend to be more important and severe over the long-term, since they seriously impair the person's capacity to function in a daily living environment. Negative symptoms include loss of interest, loss of initiative, loss of emotional attachments, loss of the ability to think fluently and abstractly, and loss of drive. Negative symptoms may appear early and be the first harbingers of schizophrenia. Parents may notice that a child who was formerly a "go-getter" has become apathetic, asocial, and withdrawn. It is often difficult for a parent to decide whether the youngster is simply going through a "typical adolescent experience" or whether something is really wrong. Negative symptoms are especially common after the illness has developed into its full florid state.

Medications currently available to treat schizophrenia are reasonably effective in diminishing delusions and hallucinations, but at present they have less effect on the negative symptoms. Consequently, a young person may be admitted to a hospital and treated, with good remission of psychotic symptoms. When he tries to return to daily life, however, he is no longer able to achieve at his previous level in school or in a work setting. The negative symptoms are especially frustrating because one has the sense that they should be responsive to encouragement, support, and various forms of psychological motivation. The schizophrenic's difficulty in sticking with a job or schoolwork is sometimes seen as simple laziness or stubbornness, and his lack of "get up and go" can be quite annoying. With time, however, most parents realize that their child is unable to complete tasks because he has lost some central drive mechanism that is normally present in most of us. He truly can't help his lack of interest, motivation, and energy.

The long-term outcome of schizophrenia can be quite variable. Approximately two-thirds of patients with this illness are relatively handicapped, in that they are unable to work or to have a successful and normal independent living arrangement. The majority are in and out of the hospital during the first five to ten years of their illness, and they tend to steadily "drift downward." This mixture of positive and negative symptoms, which characterizes most people who have schizophrenia, produces an illness that is very handicapping. The various positive symptoms make the person fearful and sometimes angry and unpredictable. Patients may become upset and agitated because of the things that their voices tell them or the various delusional thoughts that they have developed. After the illness has been present for several years, the negative symptoms prevent most people from being able to hold a job or to have a normal social life. When the symptoms are especially severe, the person's ability to care for himself at even simple levels deteriorates; he cannot plan meals, do grocery shopping, or maintain normal hygiene. For these reasons, patients with schizophrenia sometimes require care in halfway houses, sheltered environments, or long-term hospitals. Some patients with schizophrenia do have a relatively good outcome, however. These patients are able to work at some level, and some at a relatively high level.

Since the deinstitutionalization movement, the majority of patients with schizophrenia have been discharged to the community. Unfortunately, in some cases neither the community nor the patient has been prepared to accept one another. People with schizophrenia have joined the ranks of the homeless. The majority live in marginal housing on marginal income, receiving the bulk of their medical care from the relatively ungenerous auspices of Medicaid.

WHAT CAN BE DONE?

After you read the stories that follow, which describe six people who have suffered from schizophrenia and who have been cruelly mistreated by society as a consequence, you will no doubt feel frustrated and angry. Frustration and anger are negative emotions, however, and they do little good. They must be counterbalanced by a constructive drive to change an ugly situation and to improve it. How can this be done? How can a single individual help? The battle must be fought on three fronts: advocacy, education, and research.

Advocacy refers to the importance of making strong public statements on behalf of the mentally ill. People who have been patients must be willing to admit it and to describe their good and bad experiences with illness and with the health care system. Many people with serious mental illness have been successfully treated and are living very normal lives, particularly those with mood disorders such as manic depressive illness. A reluctance to place one's previous suffering on display is understandable, but speaking out can be helpful to other sufferers. Many public figures, such as Dick Cavett, William Styron, and Patty Duke have been very helpful through their portrayals of their own struggles with mood disorder and their eventual recovery. Family members of patients must advocate as well. This is especially important for illnesses such as schizophrenia, whose victims often cannot speak clearly on their own behalf. As long as patients and families remain in the closet, the public will never be aware of the hundreds of thousands of people who suffer from mental illness.

Advocacy can be facilitated through participation in group advocacy efforts. While people have organized in groups for years to fight polio, birth defects, diabetes, cancer, and other ailments, the advocacy groups for mental illnesses are relatively young. The National Alliance for the Mentally Ill (NAMI), the oldest of the advocacy groups, celebrated its tenth birthday in 1990. This particular organization is complemented by another, the National Depressive and Manic Depressive Association (NDMDA). NAMI targets all serious mental illnesses, but has many members who are parents of young people with schizophrenia, while NDMDA has a strong input from patients who suffer from mood disorders. Joining an advocacy group provides an important source of support for patients and family members, and it also provides a framework from which large scale advocacy efforts can be mounted. One need not be either a patient or the relative of a patient to join an advocacy group, however. Many loyal supporters are simply people who have developed an understanding of the importance of mental illness and a resultant desire to work on its behalf.

Education is another important vehicle for implementing change. People interested in mental illness must first educate themselves, and subsequently they must work to educate others. Most of the advocacy groups can provide a list of useful reading materials. Fortunately, during the last decade many high-quality books have been written for the average layperson. An educated patient or family member is better equipped to assess the appropriateness of treatment and to identify new developments in diagnostic evaluation as they occur. Public education is as important, however, as self-education.

While good books have become increasingly available, an ongoing need for other kinds of educational materials also exists, particularly those that appeal to broad audiences, such as films or videotapes. The film *Rain Man* informed people about one serious mental illness, autism. One hopes the film industry will learn something from its public success. The average person cannot produce a *Rain Man,* of course, but should not discount the importance of quiet individual education. At a minimum, people who make callous or inappropriate remarks about mental illness should be gently informed about the insensitivity of their behavior, at least if there is any hope that they are likely to listen.

Research is the last vehicle for implementing change. Again, the average individual cannot do research, but he or she can support it. The various advocacy groups have taken a strong stand on behalf of increasing public funding for research, and they actively lobby Congress on its behalf. Congressmen take letters from their constituents very seriously, and no single individual should discount the importance of just writing a letter in support of research in mental illness to a person in power.

Research is without question the long-term hope for mental illness. Exciting new technologies are available in neuroscience, molecular biology, and neuroimaging. These techniques have given scientists a new type of telescope and microscope to see far and finely into the brain. Much has been learned already, and much more will be learned in the future. The study of mental illness is at a threshold much like that in the rest of medicine prior to the development of penicillin. That single discovery wiped out a host of infectious diseases that had been the scourge of mankind for centuries. While identifying the causes of mental illness and ultimately preventing it will almost certainly not be as simple as the discovery of penicillin, powerful techniques for discovery are already at hand, and it is virtually certain that people's lives will be improved through research during the next several decades.

1.

A Father's Story:

Learning to Live with Schizophrenia

"I AM TIRED OF TELLING TALES of woe. I think we should talk less and do more. We need to change the way we care for our large group of citizens who are mentally disabled. Yet I know darn well that talk is necessary too. People need to talk—they need to get it out—to get rid of the grief that they carry."

Joe Talbot is a bear of a man. His voice is deep and gruff and raspy. Joe is retired and proud of being a self-made man. "My father died when I was thirteen and I put myself through school. I've always made my own way. I didn't depend on anybody. It is my belief that if you work hard enough, everything else being equal, you can accomplish your goal." Brimming with this kind of energy, Joe has brought his pragmatic skills to the aid of the local and National Alliance for the Mentally Ill organizations.

More than a committeeman, more than a chairperson with an agenda for social alteration, Joseph Talbot has taken his youngest son's mental illness—this personal and family wound—as a catalyst for change within himself.

A fiercely independent man who twenty years ago would have happily and proudly proclaimed himself a male chauvinist and deemed that nursing the sick is women's work, Joe has devoted himself to daily toil in the care of his ill son. Joe Talbot's story is a love story.

His private sorrow funds his exertions—his ceaseless travail—on the part of all those who are mentally ill. His fecund imagination perpetually provokes and irritates in order to produce results, to produce a "real return" as he might describe it. Fancy oratory is not to his liking and he finds it inappropriate to the job at hand. He is a plain man who wants to furnish broadbased meat-and-potato services for mentally ill people, but he also wants to supply the tools which will provide them with a modicum of self-respect. Joe's own work experience has proven to be a heuristic activity by which he has come to understand fully the significance of self-respect.

"I have become very cynical," Joe said, "with many things that are going on right now in the mental health system. As I see it, we are creating another group of people who will want to live on welfare. We have in place some kinds of provision—albeit grossly inadequate—for housing mentally ill people. And now we have some organizations that provide some socialization activities. We have much more available in this line than we used to. Don't get me wrong, though, I'm not saying that even these attempts are satisfactory. But—and this is a big but—in the area of vocational rehabilitation we have very little going on."

Joe made a little jab in the air with his fist. "There is no emphasis on job training. As far as I am concerned, we have lost sight of a goal that we shouldn't have lost sight of: a return of mentally ill people to society and meaningful work. What I think we are doing is creating a society of people who congregate together and become content to live in poverty.

"I am sure that at least a good percentage of the people who have a mental disorder, with proper medication and proper medication management, can exist not only in society but also contribute to society. I bet if we set this as a goal we would be very surprised to find that we had a real good outcome.

"Look, there has to be a happy medium, a balance between the consumer organizations, the socialization programs, and vocational rehabilitation. They are all important, but right now it appears to me that the emphasis is more on the problems of becoming eligible for social security supplements, welfare, and finding a place to live. I am not denying that these are the nuts and bolts without which mentally ill people cannot survive. But vocational rehabilitation has been relegated to the background—way in the background.

"What we have in the area of vocational rehab, especially in our state"—again Joe made little jabs in the air with his fist clenched—"is demeaning. Occasionally, I volunteer at a mental health center, and the workshop that this particular center supervises contracts with private industry. The young people wire components for computers. Sometimes there is too much work for the mentally ill people to handle, so then the unit goes to the employment office and they hire workers for minimum wage. They pay the mentally ill person for piecework, which is less money than minimum wage, so right away that disabled person is made to feel, yet again, that they are not up to snuff.

"What I'm saying is that that type of workshop is not what I'm looking for. I'm looking for training programs that prepare people for meaningful and rewarding work. I know it can be done.

"A lot of mentally ill people have abilities that are not being tapped. Some of these individuals have developed a very high level of skill before they became ill and there is no reason to waste any of this high-level functioning."

Joe paused, took a deep breath, and then, speaking slowly and carefully he said, "OK, OK, I'll get off the soap box. I want to tell the story about our child, our youngest son, Mark. Maybe that will help to affix a perspective onto the larger picture.

"Mark's illness started eleven years ago, when he was a junior in high school. It came on very suddenly. He had gone on a student tour to Europe and when he returned home we, his mother Ginny and I, recognized an extreme change in him. Mark left here one very nice young man. He came back an absolute hellion."

Shaking his head, Joe remembered: "When he came back from Europe we pretty much lost control of him. He became involved with drugs. His senior year of high school was a nightmare for us; both his mother and I felt sick about his behavior. Initially we thought that the problem was primarily drugs, we never imagined it to be anything else. We were just certain that Mark had become a bad boy.

"Mark had always been a polite and responsible kid. He was a nice-looking—big fellow—straight-arrow young man. He had never given us any trouble with our family rules. He'd always been compliant about that kind of stuff. Don't get me wrong, he was no sissy. But after that Europe trip"—Joe shook his head—"well, most of the time we didn't even know where he was. When he did drop in—and it was just that: dropping in—he was a shocker. He was dirty, slovenly. His hair, which is a sandy color, looked black, it was so grimy and greasy, his language was unrepeatable, and he was always explosive. He was raging like a madman. You'd have thought we would have picked up on that. And school, that was a laugh, he never went there. He thumbed his nose at all the things we held in respect.

"Ginny and I tried everything. We tried withholding money, we kept laying down stricter and stricter rules, curfews were imposed, we were yelling, we were screaming, we even offered bribes. Nothing, nothing worked. Eventually we realized that this was beyond a family issue; if this was to be resolved, we would have to go outside the family.

"We went to see the school counselor, and she suggested we take Mark to a psychologist. The psychologist did quite an extensive testing of Mark and then called us in for his evaluation. He was blunt: 'Your son has a mental illness.' So it wasn't just the drugs.

"We were shocked—stunned—to find out that Mark was mentally ill and that the drugs were simply magnifying the underlying problem. Mental illness was completely foreign to us. We felt helpless. Many were the times we came to wish that Mark had simply been a delinquent kid. The psychologist sent Mark to a psychiatrist and within a few weeks our son had his first hospitalization."

One morning, not long after Joe and Ginny learned that their son was mentally ill, Mark—without any warning—erupted into a rage and struck his mother over an incident that normally would have appeared slight and trivial. Ginny, attempting to keep some order in her house, had asked her son to make his bed. Speaking quietly and more from habit than any expectation of some result, she told Mark that she would prefer him to do some of his chores before he ate his breakfast. Mark, giving no indication of what he was about to do, turned suddenly and swung out, striking his mother with so much force that she lost her balance and fell backward. The back of her head hit the floor with a sickening thwack. Groggily, she pulled herself upright and very gingerly seated herself on Mark's bed. Mark ran out of his room and shut himself in the bathroom.

Slowly and carefully, Ginny managed to walk downstairs to the kitchen. Joe was drinking his second cup of coffee and listening to the morning news on the radio. Using her peacemaking skills, Ginny quietly explained to Joe what had occurred without arousing him to anger. She was able to persuade her husband that, first, she was only slightly bruised, that she was going to be fine, and second, now that they knew that Mark was ill it would not be beneficial in any way to punish him. Even so, they were unnerved and scared by this impulsive and irrational behavior. They immediately phoned the psychiatrist. The doctor, who had seen Mark only a few times, quickly moved to hospitalize him and increased his course of medication.

Joe remembered that even though the psychiatrist had been prompt to help, and he was grateful for that, he and Ginny had been very uncomfortable in their relationship with this doctor. "This fellow told us that the whole family should be treated. So my wife Ginny, our older son Fred, and I started to see this doctor on a regular basis. We had always seen ourselves as a regular middle-class family—a close family—but the psychiatrist seemed to have the idea that we were the cause of Mark's problems. The term dysfunctional wasn't so popular back then, but I guess that is how he might have described us.

"We didn't get along too well with that psychiatrist," Joe recalled. "The so-called family treatment turned out to be more destructive than constructive. We had a very sick boy whom we had to attend to, and pointing fingers at us—the only ones willing and capable of caring for him—was not only outrageous but also stupid. We needed positive help, not negative criticism. Believe me, the work of looking after a mentally ill person is difficult enough without having extra hazards thrown in your direction."

After this first hospitalization Mark returned to live with his family, but very soon, disregarding Ginny and Joe's entreaties to the contrary, he stopped taking the prescribed medicine and quickly became quite ill again.

"Mark was the type of boy who could not stand to be in one place when he started one of his what we called episodes. He might get in his car in the middle of the night and head for Phoenix, for instance." Joe spoke in a resigned voice. "In fact, one time that is just where Mark headed. On the way there he was picked up for reckless driving in northern California and put in jail. He didn't have enough money to pay the fine, so he took the time in jail to pay his debt.

"We didn't hear a thing from him until he was released from jail, and then he phoned us—collect of course. I remember him sounding a little sheepish. 'Dad, I'm stuck down here in a place called Yreka. Can you help me out?' I called a motel, gave them my credit card number, booked a room for him, and asked them to advance him some money so at least he could eat until I got there. I flew down, and Mark and I drove back together.

"All the way home Mark told me he didn't think that he should be living as well as he was living. He was embarrassed that I had come down to rescue him. He felt shamefully aware that he and I had stayed in a nice motel and we had eaten well. 'I don't think I'm entitled to all that,' he said to me. He seemed so genuinely distressed that he was unable to restrain himself from doing wrong things.

"I had begun to educate myself about this schizophrenia. Slowly, I was beginning to understand that Mark couldn't help himself. That it wasn't Mark's intention to be bad. When this began to dawn on me I didn't know which was worse: Mark as a bad boy or Mark as a young guy who had no ability to control his own behavior."

When father and son returned from California, Joe put Mark in a motel near the family home. The Talbots thought that Mark might find it more peaceful if he wasn't living at home. They also knew it might be more peaceful for them. Joe and Ginny began to explore the different routes and options that might be open to them as they attempted to find ways of coping with their son's illness.

"I had been reading various articles," Joe said, "and had seen some messages on television which told me something about the kind of care that might best benefit someone with schizophrenia. I understood that without medication the mentally ill folks would go nowhere—wouldn't be able to function at all. After our unpleasant and discomforting experience with the psychiatrist, I figured that a family doctor could administer medication just as well as a psychiatrist. Ginny and I took Mark to our general practitioner and after he did all kinds of tests he told us, 'No, you really need to have Mark see a psychiatrist. They specialize in looking after these kinds of diseases.'

"Well, we followed his advice and did just that," Joe said. "But we were pretty careful not to go back to the doctor who had made us feel that we were the cause of Mark's disease." Because Mark was still pretty shaky and very negative about taking medicine, the family and the new psychiatrist decided that he should be hospitalized in order for him to simmer down. But Mark was quite resistant to another hospitalization.

"Since he had been behind locked doors before," Joe remembered, "Mark had no intention of going into another hospital, so we called our minister—whom Mark was real fond of—and he talked him into entering the hospital voluntarily. That was an enormous relief because I had already heard many disaster stories where families couldn't persuade their kids into a voluntary hospitalization. The commitment laws are written in such a way that you have to show, and often have to persuade a judge, that the mentally ill person intends to harm others or himself—well, more times than not this is impossible to deal with. Lawyers and judges are meddling with medical judgments. Clearly this is an inappropriate way to deal with this disease. You have only to look around our streets to see the results of these policies."

Mark remained in the hospital for a number of months until he was stabilized. "Then we decided," Joe said, "that maybe it would be best for him to live in a group home. The hospital staff told us that it might be easier for Mark and for us if Mark didn't live at our house. We had already come to this conclusion, but they felt that he needed to have some kind of full-time supervision. And we were more than willing to go along with that. Hah." Joe grinned mirthlessly. "We were still naive enough to believe that something appropriate—and affordable—could be found.

"The social worker at the hospital gave us very little help or assistance as we looked around for decent housing for our son. We did all the legwork ourselves. We went to the mental health center in our county and got names and addresses of group homes.

"When we started looking at these places, Mark didn't like any of them. Neither did I, for that matter. For the most part, the homes were filthy, smelly, disgusting, and degrading. They looked to me like the snake pits that deinstitutionalization was supposed to eliminate. I was shocked. If my son had not become mentally ill I would never have known that we—in our country—could tolerate such places.

"We finally settled on an organization in the west suburbs which was started by a group of families. They had secured apartments and houses, which they ran in a kind of loose fashion. Two patients would be put together to share a room or an apartment.

"That didn't work out either. It had looked OK to us in the beginning, but it turned out that the supervision wasn't very good. These mentally ill folk were a pushover for anyone selling drugs, so drugs were real prevalent there and no one was willing to do anything about it—maybe it was impossible."

Joe sighed. "I've gotten tired. I can't get as excited and wrought up about these things as I used to. You can fight on only so many fronts. And my first priority was to get Mark out of that place.

"One doesn't know whether to say fortunately or unfortunately, but we were able to get Mark out of there quite easily. He had this convenient access to drugs, so it didn't take long for him to become quite psychotic. He was like a loose cannon—no impulse control—he trashed his apartment and became very belligerent. He smashed a couple of windows, he threw his garbage outside his front door and"—Joe's face colored—"he stopped flushing his toilet. There were feces all over the bathroom floor.

"As bad as this sounds, we actually became afraid that he might do much worse than mess up his apartment. We were afraid that he might harm someone. He was that psychotic that we easily got him committed to the state mental hospital—for six months. There was a court hearing and there was no problem in getting a judgment for a commitment. The judge was quick to see that Mark was very sick.

"It's funny when you think about it. Things are so topsy-turvy that you're glad when your child gets out of control because only then can you get him the suitable attention and care."

Joe paused and cleared his throat. "After that I finally realized that if anyone was going to help Mark it had to be us. I knew that nobody else was going to do it, so we brought him home.

"When we made this decision we interviewed yet another psychiatrist—this was the third psychiatrist we had seen. This doctor told us he would see Mark once a month and that that would be adequate for monitoring his medication.

"I doubted that it would be enough but—I'm ashamed to say—I was still very green about this whole business. I felt awkward about questioning a doctor's authority. I had to get burnt quite a few times before I realized that just because people were doctors it didn't mean they were automatically going to be satisfactory.

"It also took a long time for me to understand that this was a disease that the medical community didn't really have a handle on. I knew that I was in the dark about mental illness, but I began to realize that even though I didn't know anything about chemistry and biology, I wasn't so far behind many of the guys who were presenting themselves as authorities."

A few months after Ginny and Joe brought Mark back home to live with them, they got a call from the mental health center workshop where Mark was spending his days. Mark had gone over to the emergency room of a small hospital which was near the workshop because he was becoming very frightened and anxious. He was literally trembling with an uncontrollable fear that something or someone was going to harm him. But there was no psychiatric unit at this local hospital where he had gone for help, so the caseworker at the workshop alerted Joe to his son's plight. Joe jumped in his car and raced over to rescue Mark.

Mark's current psychiatrist had just reduced his medication even though Joe had strongly advised against it. Deeply distressed by what he believed to be bad management of his son's case, Joe had already planned to switch Mark's treatment to another doctor.

Because of his volunteer work, Joe had come to know some prominent psychiatrists in the state. Now he turned to these physicians for assistance. Joe had already started the process of following through on one of the referrals that they had given to him. He had telephoned a young psychiatrist, and they had set up an appointment just before this current emergency had transpired.

Mark was distraught. He was begging for help. For once he was desperate to be admitted into the safe care of a hospital. Joe scooped up his son. But where to go?

The psychiatrist who had been seeing Mark didn't, or wouldn't, answer their calls. The new doctor, with whom they had an appointment the following week, wouldn't hospitalize Mark. She said, "He's not yet my patient." She was emphatic. "Mark is still in another doctor's care." But the Talbots were unable to contact Mark's psychiatrist.

"This was a Friday afternoon. It's almost impossible to get admitted to a psychiatric ward on a Friday afternoon. I call it the weekend syndrome. They all take off and leave a minimum staff. So I was sure we were lost. Of course," Joe said, "I could have taken him to an emergency room, but I was afraid that even that might not work. Mark was in turbulent straits, he needed help, and I didn't want to chance our being turned away. I knew how easily that could happen.

"The head of the Community Training Services at the Medical School was a psychiatrist whom I had met when I was doing voluntary work at the various local mental health organizations. I called him, and I guess I must have sounded pretty excited. 'I'm desperate,' I told him. 'I need to get my boy into a hospital *now*. And not only that, I need to find a psychiatrist who will work with us cooperatively from now on in.' Well, this good and decent man did both of these things. Right away he arranged for Mark to be hospitalized immediately, and subsequently he found the fine young doctor who has been helping us with Mark for the past few years."

Joe jammed his fist into his open hand. "I know how lucky I have been to get good help for my son. When I say lucky, I don't mean that good fortune fell out of the sky. What I do mean is that there are many unfortunate folks who don't have the wherewithal or the time to be able to organize adequate care for their mentally ill kids.

"Not only did it take me a number of years to understand what Ginny and I needed to do, so we could be a proper support system for Mark, but also it took a while—and a lot of mistakes—for us to know who to turn to if we were to fulfill Mark's needs. None of that could have occurred if I hadn't had time and funds. When I think how difficult and painful it has been for us, I can't help imagining what it must be like for all those families who have to struggle to get by just for themselves.

"Mark lives at home now." Joe gave a pinched smile. "He manages pretty well. No, he *barely* manages. I guess disorderliness is just one of those things that goes with this disease. In other words, he's not as neat or as clean as he should be."

Joe paused. "He's completely self-centered. For instance, in our home we have a daylight basement and that's where we have our family room. Mark prefers to sleep down there rather than in his own bedroom. We don't like it, because after a couple of years he has completely destroyed this room. Oh, I don't mean that he's torn things up or thrown things around. It's that he is so inconsiderate. He's taken away a room that we used to enjoy, and even if he vacated it tomorrow he's used it in ways that would take time and money to repair.

"First of all, the couch is gone. It's finished. It sags, the springs are done for, even if it was re-covered it would be useless. It was never meant to be slept on night after night. It was meant as an extra bed for the occasional out-of-town guest.

"And he smokes. That's a very dirty habit. Ginny, Fred, my older son, and I don't smoke. We hate the smell." Joe looked down and made a small futile gesture with his hands. "This all sounds so petty." He almost moaned.

"Maybe the worst part is the noise. Mark has an auditorium-style speaker, which he hooked up to the television, to the stereo, and to his electric guitar. The noise from down there, from that room, is something else. There is no place in the house to escape from the incessant blare coming from that basement room."

Twisting in his chair as though he could not find a comfortable fit, Joe continued. "He is very independent. Mark does not like us to correct him. We have made many attempts to find a way to deal with this problem. It is very difficult to live with someone who refuses to cooperate, especially if that person has a disease like schizophrenia. Any kind of criticism, even the mildest direction or recommendation, can cause the kind of repercussions that the caretakers—*we*—are going to great pains to avoid.

"Look, here we have our son Mark, whom we are trying to protect from what appears to him to be a hostile world. And for him it *is* a hostile world, because any kind of criticism feels—to him—like a vicious attack. It's as though he lacks a layer of skin, as though he has no cover or armor which the rest of us take for granted. Usually none of us think much about the fact that we manage to live our lives without collapsing every time someone says or does something unpleasant to us.

"But my son is like some poor pathetic creature whose immune system has gone berserk. He lacks that special something that he needs and is essential to him if he is going to be able to get along in the world. I often say to Ginny that trying to take care of Mark without upsetting him is comparable to trying to walk on eggs without breaking them.

"When you are responsible and care for someone whom you cannot direct or criticize, you become helpless. Ginny and I are Mark's prisoners. We are in jail. This disease is not Mark's illness alone. We have also been captured by it."

The Talbot family have made an innovative effort at partly solving their dilemma. Every second week they accompany Mark when he goes to see his psychiatrist. They are so acutely responsive to their son's sensitivity to criticism that now, instead of confronting Mark, they relay their concerns about his behavior to the physician.

"We spend the first five to ten minutes telling Mark's doctor about our current troubles with Mark. Big problems, little problems—whatever is going on—we tell them all to Mark's psychiatrist. Then we leave and sit out the rest of the appointment in the waiting room. We get out of being the bad guys. We let the doc handle it in any way he sees fit.

"Ginny and I feel comfortable in chatting with this psychiatrist. For the first time we feel we have some positive relief from the strain. And that's because we can see that this young fellow helps Mark as well as us. It's nice to be able to ease up a little.

"Mark's personality before he was ill was quite different. He was loving, friendly, considerate, caring—all of those qualities that he doesn't now have." Stretching his legs, Joe remembered, "We had never known anyone who was mentally ill. We knew nothing about the disease. It was very difficult for us to accept that Mark had schizophrenia. Even though we were ignorant about the disease, we were not unaware of the stigma attached to mental illness.

"Oh, yes." Joe stopped talking and leaned back in his chair. "Oh, yes, we felt the shame. We were embarrassed. We didn't want to talk about it. We didn't want to let anyone know about our trouble. But we did, and what a surprise—we had a support system that wouldn't quit. None of our friends turned away from us. They rallied around us and gave us the kind of backing that enabled us to go on.

"What jarred us, however, what was so devastating was the loss—the loss of what we had had and what we now had in place of it. If I had to pick a person who could have succeeded in life, it would have been Mark. He was gregarious, outgoing, and what I want to describe as innovative. Mark was a handsome, loving, and intelligent boy, and we unashamedly enjoyed the promise that we saw in him. It was hard to lose that promise.

"Aah," Joe sighed. "We keep *hoping* that maybe the promise will come back. But hope is a delicate thing, and all the time we are hurting because we are not fooled. We have come to know that this is an irreparable loss.

"Perhaps what would chill us most was when he would run."

Woven into the patchwork made up of Mark's many hospitalizations and diverse living arrangements was what his father called a run. On one of these runs, Mark took off for New York City. He was twenty-three and had been sick for about six years. He bought himself a plane ticket and flew to the big city. He had no money with him. He had no plans. Often schizophrenia robs people of prudence. Consequences have no meaning for Mark. Without medicine and careful supervision, he lives a life propelled by impulse.

The New York incident had a good outcome. Mark was lucky. It was early fall, and the evenings were only beginning to get nippy. After a few weeks on the street, eating at soup kitchens and scrounging around for places to sleep, Mark walked into a police station. He was looking for a warmer place to sleep; he was just beginning to feel a little chilled. He walked into the right place. His psychotic condition was blatantly evident. The police had no doubt that Mark Talbot was very ill.

Fortunately for Mark (and Ginny and Joe), the New York police did not turn him back out on the street. They placed him in a mental hospital. Mark was treated there, the Talbots were notified, and Joe flew to New York. And so again a patient and loving Joe Talbot brought his son home.

Whenever Mark was on a run, whenever Joe and Ginny did not know his whereabouts, when they didn't know if he was in New York, Florida, Arizona, or dead in a ditch, their anxiety for their son's well-being placed them in a crucible. They were unable to function. They couldn't eat without thinking about the possibility of his being hungry. They couldn't sleep without terrible anguished fears about where he was sleeping. Was he starving? Was he sheltered? They could think of nothing but their poor mad son wandering about strange city streets, unable to care for himself.

The excruciating torture of not knowing, not knowing where or how he was, was ceaseless. To keep their son at home and safe—to save themselves—the Talbots are willing to live very inconvenient lives. The unbearable pain of not knowing negates the charm of a comfortable life. For Ginny and Joe, burdens and benefits easily tilt the scales in favor of knowing and discomfort.

"We do much better knowing that he is at home, knowing that he is safe, knowing that he has a place to sleep, knowing that he's been fed. Now we rest easy. We are assured he is being cared for. Ginny and I would rather put up with the problems of living with Mark than the much worse problem we had when we didn't know where the hell he was. When we didn't know if he was alive or dead."

Joe cleared his throat and spoke quietly. "I have observed in many families when a child dies, or becomes ill with an incurable disease like cancer, the disease afflicts not only the child but the family as well. Tragically, not only do they lose the child, but the parents may lose each other. The mother and father appear unable to face each other and often a divorce is the result.

"In our predicament that did not happen. We became closer. When one of us would lose our cool, the other could be counted on to maintain strength. I can't even number the times my Ginny has done this for me. I only hope I've proved to be a support to her too. Whenever I flew off the handle, Ginny would be there for me. I could always rely on her for a stable and measured response.

"And there have been—this is no whitewash—real angry moments." Emphatically, Joe repeated himself. "Real angry moments, times when I have thought, 'Damn it, Mark, even though you have a mental illness you can't have lost all the values you learned in your childhood—they have to be back there in that brain someplace.' "

Joe praises his wife. He feels that women are better at dealing with the hostility and anger that people with schizophrenia may present.

He believes that women, being gentler, are not so quick to react with outrage; that intuitively women understand that schizophrenia causes people to behave in ways that they cannot control; that women naturally are more easily compassionate. Joe, on the other hand, sees himself as being easily roused to anger. A quick retaliation to any offense, he says, is part of his instinctive nature. "The first reaction of the male—at least in the animal kingdom—is to fight back."

But for all that Joe Talbot is an "old-fashioned" man with "old-fashioned" views of gender. He is unashamed of his tender heart. "With this disease there is no fighting. You may not fight. You just have to take it and take it calmly. And remember to keep your voice down. It is imperative that you ignore the schizophrenic person's angry eruptions. His rage will evaporate as quickly as it started. Punishment doesn't work with this disease. Now that I have lived with a person with schizophrenia, it makes me very upset when I see mental health workers try to correct their clients' adverse behavior by punishment, because I know it doesn't work.

"I'm taking a long time to say it." Joe looked down at his hands. "I think the thing that has happened with us, we—my wife and I—are probably closer at this point in our life than we ever have been. Really, all of us are closer, the older boy Fred, the younger boy when he can be, and Ginny and I."

Commentary

BY BENTSON H. MCFARLAND, M.D., PH.D.

Dr. McFarland is a graduate of Yale University and the University of Washington School of Medicine. He completed his psychiatric residency at Oregon Health Sciences University and trained in geriatric psychiatry at Maudsley Hospital in London. Dr. McFarland is associate professor of Psychiatry, Public Health and Preventive Medicine at Oregon Health Sciences University, and an investigator at the Kaiser Permanente Center for Health Research. His research includes studying the effectiveness and safety of medications and the organization and financing of mental health services for persons with severe mental disorders. Dr. McFarland is President of the Oregon Psychiatric Association.

Joe Talbot, the father in the preceding story, believes that "if you work hard enough, everything else being equal, you can accomplish your goal." But Joe knows only too well that everything else isn't equal for persons with schizophrenia. The origins of the conditions are mysterious. Persons with schizophrenia suffer stigma and discrimination. There is treatment but no cure, and resources for treatment are often limited. There is a large and sometimes confusing variety of helping professionals who get involved in providing services.

This chapter introduces the professionals and programs aimed at helping persons with schizophrenia, summarizes the types of treatment available, and discusses how to pay for care. The chapter is designed to be a concise guide to the resources available for persons struggling with this condition.

PROVIDERS

Who Are the Professionals and What Do They Do?

There are several types of professionals trained to provide services for persons with schizophrenia (see Table 1).

Psychiatrists are physicians who specialize in the prevention, diagnosis, and treatment of mental or emotional disorders. Psychiatrists have four years of college, four years of medical school, and three or more years of residency training. Many psychiatrists are *psychopharmacologists,* who have a particular interest in brain chemistry and its modification by medications. Psychopharmacologists often have had special training in the field and may conduct research as well as treat patients. All psychiatrists can prescribe medications and have special knowledge about drugs that affect the brain. In many states psychiatric *nurse practitioners,* who usually have four years of nursing school and two years of graduate study, also can prescribe medications for treatment of schizophrenia. Clinical *psychologists* have four years of college and usually four or more years of graduate study. Psychologists specialize in evaluation, testing, and behavioral treatment of mental conditions. Clinical *social workers* have two years of graduate work following four years of college and have considerable expertise in working with social service agencies and families. *Counselors* typically have four years of college training and often two years of graduate work. Physicians (including psychiatrists) and nurses (including nurse practitioners) are licensed by state agencies. Nearly all states also license psychologists and social workers, and many states also regulate counselors.

This array of mental health professionals can offer a variety of services to persons with schizophrenia. While medications can be useful in reducing symptoms like hallucinations or delusions, taking pills alone cannot find a person food, shelter, or a job. Psychosocial rehabilitation, including the vocational training Joe described, is an important component of treatment for schizophrenia. Joe points out that many persons with schizophre-

TABLE 1.
Helping Professionals

TITLE	COLLEGE	GRADUATE SCHOOL	INTERNSHIP	RESIDENCY	LICENSED
Counselors/case managers	Usually	Two years (usually)	No	No	Some states
Nurses	Yes	Two years (often)	No	No	Yes
Clinical social workers	Yes	Two years	No	No	Yes
Clinical psychologists	Yes	Four years	One year	One year (often)	Yes
Psychiatrists	Yes	Four years (medical school)	One year	Three years	Yes

nia can learn or relearn the skills needed to become productive members of society.

For a typical person with schizophrenia, the illness begins in the late teens or early twenties and causes considerable disruption for the next ten to twenty years. However, by the time the person is in his or her forties, it is not unusual to see a lessening of symptoms and a resumption of social activities, including work. Mental health professionals can be helpful in assisting the person's reintegration into society.

Finding a compatible provider is not necessarily easy. For example, in the preceding story we saw that Mark's first psychiatrist recommended "family treatment" when medication seemed more appropriate. Family members are often "accused" by the schizophrenic person of interfering with an alternative lifestyle. By its very nature, schizophrenia leads to disruption in the family. The disruption, in turn, may well worsen the symptoms experienced by the mentally ill person. The family may tell the provider one version of events and the patient may give a completely different story. Not surprisingly, it can be difficult for a health care provider to satisfy the needs of all the family members.

Persons with schizophrenia and their family members also may differ in their beliefs about the value of drug treatment. Drugs used to treat schizophrenia may be unpopular with users owing to side effects, lack of complete cure, and stigma. As in "A Father's Story," it is not uncommon for someone like Mark to stop taking the prescribed medicine. On the other hand, drugs are less unpopular with family members because they often see that the medications are effective—even though they are not perfect. Joe and Ginny's entreaties to Mark to take his medicine are typical between patients and families. Other problems in finding a care provider include the tendency of persons with schizophrenia to drift from the private health care sector to the public as the costs of illness overwhelm available health insurance.

Reluctant Providers

As Joe discovered, there is often a reluctance among mental health professionals, including psychiatrists, to work with persons who have schizophrenia. One of the chief reasons for this situation is financial. Mark is typical in that he has difficulty sustaining employment—and consequently in obtaining health insurance. Mark is different from many others in that his family is able to provide for his health care. Too often, persons with schizophrenia have no income and no way of paying doctor or hospital bills. Unfortunately, but perhaps not surprisingly, mental health professionals, physicians, and hospitals develop a belief that they will not be paid for providing care. Consequently, health care providers often hope "someone else" will be willing to treat the patient. This "someone else" may be a local community mental health program.

Community Mental Health Programs

Community mental health programs may be operated by state or local government or by private (usually nonprofit) agencies or some combination thereof. As noted in the introduction, at the beginning of the deinstitutionalization movement, policymakers hoped that community programs would provide services that state mental hospitals were formerly expected to offer. While some states have done a good job serving people with schizophrenia in the community, other localities have nonexistent or nonfunctional programs. We would expect that a community mental health program will at least be able to assist the consumer in obtaining food stamps, welfare, and access to low-income housing. The program should provide a crisis line as a source of information during emergencies. Medications and their monitoring are also typical community mental health services. More advanced programs offer alcohol and drug treatment, rehabilitation (including job placement and training), as well as a spectrum of housing ranging from strictly supervised "respite" facilities to semi-independent apartments. Interestingly, leadership and advocacy like that provided by Joe in his community are often as important as funding in the development of services for people with schizophrenia.

Community mental health program services are listed in Table 2. The public mental health system in most states includes state mental hospital services and community mental health programs. Public mental health programs, of course, must compete with education, criminal justice, transportation, etc., in the contest for state and local dollars. Some states are more generous than others, and some states are better organized than others. Programs in some states will include all the services in Table 2, while other states will offer only a few. Community mental health programs are often listed in the blue pages of the telephone book under "Mental Health."

TABLE 2.
Community Mental Health Program Services
for Persons with Schizophrenia

Minimal:

1. Mental health care: Diagnosis, treatment planning, medication management, rehabiltation
2. Crisis service: 24-hour availability of staff
3. Case management: Linking the client with the needed services and advocating for service provision
4. Assistance with basic needs: Helping the client obtain food, shelter, and clothing
5. Protecting client rights and dealing with client grievances
6. Involvement of families, landlords, and other persons who interact with the client

Highly desirable:

7. Backup support and respite for families, landlords, and others who deal with the client
8. Housing appropriate to the client's needs
9. Psychosocial services: Vocational training, supported employment
10. Outreach services to inform potential clients of services

Hospitals

Even with the best housing, rehabilitation, and medication, persons with schizophrenia are at risk of deterioration in their condition. As in Mark's case, drug or alcohol abuse often leads to a return of psychotic symptoms like hallucinations or delusions. Discontinuing medications is another reason for relapse. Stresses such as poverty, homelessness, malnutrition, being raped, robbed, or assaulted can bring back hallucinations or delusions that were once under control. While many flare-ups of schizophrenia can be handled in the community, sometimes closer supervision is necessary. Reasons for hospital admission are chiefly danger to self or others. Danger to self can and often does include inability to feed or clothe oneself due to psychosis.

Several types of facilities provide psychiatric services (see Table 3). General hospitals may have a psychiatric ward. Some private hospitals specialize in psychiatric treatments. Most states have at least one state mental hospital. In recent years, "non-hospital" facilities have been developed. Many but not all veterans' hospitals also provide psychiatric services, which may be reserved for those veterans whose "service-connected" mental health problems developed while they were in the military.

All these institutions attempt to guarantee the patient's and the public's safety, while addressing problems such as drug intoxication, malnutrition, and noncompliance with medications. Because of the concern for safety, patients may initially be housed in locked wards or a locked room. All health care providers have a responsibility to protect patients from themselves and to protect others from violent patients. As we saw with Mark, it is not unusual for a person with schizophrenia to spend at least some time in an environment with restrictions on personal liberty.

The state mental hospital was formerly the chief source of care for persons with schizophrenia. Several factors contributed to the decline of these institutions. Some scholars feel that the development of nursing homes, and ways to pay for nursing home care by way of the Federal Medicaid program, was the chief stimulus for the decrease in size of state mental hospitals. Many researchers have questioned the therapeutic value of large "warehouse" state facilities. In any event, nowadays it is not unusual for state hospitals to be restricted to involuntary patients only.

TABLE 3.
Types of Hospitals

General Hospitals
include medical and surgical as well as psychiatric services
private or public
usually nonprofit

Psychiatric Hospitals
only psychiatric services
often private
often for profit

State Mental Hospitals
only psychiatric services
often restricted to involuntary patients

Veterans Hospitals
can be general hospitals or strictly psychiatric
only some veterans hospitals have psychiatric services

This situation leads to the common complaint of persons with schizophrenia: "If you want to be admitted, you can't come in; if you don't want to be admitted, you'll be dragged in by the police." State hospitals typically have ten patients for each staff member, while other types of hospitals will have only one patient for each staff member. On the other hand, lengths of stay in state hospitals can be rather long—weeks or months as opposed to days.

Many states limit state hospital admissions to involuntary patients— those brought in by the police or committed by a judge. These individuals are typically dangerous to themselves or to others and may not be interested in hospitalization. The irony of this situation for persons with schizophrenia is that people who seek admission will be denied, but those who refuse will be forced to enter the state hospital. Owing to limited staffing, state hospitals should not be expected to provide much more than safety, shelter, food, sobriety, and medications. It is not uncommon for persons seeking admission to be turned away from an overcrowded state hospital. For example, lack of housing, in and of itself, is generally not grounds for admission to a state hospital even when the homeless person is mentally ill. Danger to self or others is usually the key to admission.

Private psychiatric hospitals are often run by profitmaking companies. Therefore, to be admitted a potential patient needs adequate funding. One is well advised to check one's insurance beforehand; mental health might not be covered at all. In most cases, prior authorization from a "managed care" entity will be required before a patient can be admitted to a private psychiatric hospital. The managed care entity also will ensure that the length of stay in a private psychiatric hospital will most likely be only a few days.

Although general hospitals are often nonprofit or public facilities, they too must avoid bankruptcy. The patient with schizophrenia may well experience a very short length of stay in the general hospital. Some general hospitals have psychiatric facilities and some do not. A telephone call beforehand can avoid a frustrating trip to an inappropriate hospital. Also, the hospital, particularly a public facility, might be full.

A frequent frustration for family members is that hospitalization is not available on demand. Family members of persons with any chronic illness often need a break ("respite") and would like to see the individual admitted to hospital. Joe's difficulties in arranging admission for his son are not unusual. As Joe discovered, the providers who can facilitate hospitalization may be difficult to contact on a weekend.

Involuntary Treatment

Danger to self or others is usually the reason for psychiatric hospitalization. Persons with schizophrenia often request hospitalization when their condition makes them unable to care for themselves or places them at risk of harming someone, including themselves. However, sometimes the person may not appreciate the seriousness of the situation, and one must consider the possibility of involuntary treatment.

Family members who are concerned that their mentally ill relative might be dangerous to self or others can initiate involuntary treatment in any of several ways. In many states the process can be started by contacting a local community mental health program. The agency may send a staff member to evaluate the situation and to interview the person who is believed to be mentally ill and dangerous. Sometimes the agency may request that the mentally ill person come to a clinic or hospital for an interview. Usually the evaluation is summarized in a report to a judge who then decides whether to commit the person for involuntary treatment. Family members testifying at such a hearing are well advised to be prepared to provide specific examples of the person's dangerous behavior.

Involuntary treatment, of course, is very different from the usual encounter between a health care consumer and a service provider. Under ordinary circumstances it is assumed that the patient voluntarily decides whether to accept the recommended treatment. Indeed, the consumer has a well-established right to refuse treatment. Ordinarily, the health care consumer gives "consent" to treatment.

Since the consumer of involuntary treatment does not give consent for services, the process raises numerous concerns about possible violations of civil rights. Consumers sometimes say they are afraid to talk freely with mental health professionals for fear they will be held for involuntary treatment. On the other hand, family members often echo Joe's statement that involuntary treatment means lawyers and judges are meddling with medical judgments. Surveys of mental health consumers indicate that a slight majority feel involuntary treatment is worthwhile in emergencies.

Involuntary treatment is clearly acceptable in a life-threatening emergency. The person who is imminently dangerous to self or others needs to be treated—voluntarily or involuntarily. Also, health care providers have a duty to warn identified persons who are specifically threatened by a client. This duty stems from a well-known legal case called the *Tarasoff* ruling.

Transporting a dangerous, mentally ill person to a clinic can itself be dangerous. Joe's "disaster stories" about arranging an emergency evaluation for a person with schizophrenia are only too common. In an emergency the police can transport a dangerous mentally ill person to a hospital for evaluation and possible treatment. Usually the person can be detained involuntarily in the hospital pending an evaluation. In most states, a court hearing is required before a person can be detained involuntarily more than a few days.

Once admitted to the hospital, the duration of the "emergency" then becomes an open question. Long-term (i.e., months or years) involuntary treatment has several disadvantages, including the cost to patient, family, and society. For the involuntary patient, one cost is "institutionalization," in which the person loses the ability to attend to his or her own basic needs. Also, there is little or no scientific evidence of benefit for long-term hospitalization versus short-term hospitalization or community treatment. In fact, the biggest problem facing state hospitals is finding placements for patients, because even a state hospital is better than the streets.

These practical considerations, plus concerns for civil liberties, have resulted in several checks and balances surrounding involuntary treatment. This area of the law is referred to as "civil commitment." The word "civil" indicates that the person in question is not a criminal, and the word "commitment" refers to involuntary treatment. Although the civil commitment laws vary from state to state, there is typically a time limit, usually a few days, for the "emergency" phase of involuntary treatment. Often a community mental health professional will "investigate" the situation to determine if the person should be released or if the case should be presented to a judge. If the case is brought before a judge, the patient can be released or committed for a longer period of time. In some states, the judge can commit the person to an outpatient treatment program. An interesting feature of civil commitment is that, in the absence of an "emergency", the committed person retains the right to refuse medication.

DIAGNOSIS AND TREATMENT

Whether voluntary or involuntary, treatment of schizophrenia is complicated but rewarding. Although the condition cannot be cured, medications can reduce many of the symptoms. Rehabilitation is possible and, in fact, likely. The flagrant symptoms experienced by a young adult like

Mark tend to decline with age. By age 30 or 40 a person with schizophrenia is often able to take advantage of training programs designed to help him or her resume life in society.

As with many young persons who develop schizophrenia, Mark underwent major changes in his thinking, behavior, and ways of relating to others. Mark exhibited many of the difficulties persons with schizophrenia often experience, including confused thinking, impulsive behavior, and an inability to provide for his basic needs. Mark's uncontrollable fear that someone would harm him is very common in persons with schizophrenia. As Joe discovered, even though abuse of alcohol or drugs like cocaine can worsen these problems, the cause lies deep within the brain itself. In a few cases, these symptoms of psychosis can be caused by medical conditions, for instance epilepsy. Before making the diagnosis of schizophrenia, it is important to rule out other possible causes by taking a careful medical history, performing a physical examination, checking blood counts and blood chemistries, and in some cases doing a brain scan or X ray.

Diagnosis of Schizophrenia

Schizophrenia is known as a "diagnosis of exclusion." Inconveniently, there is at the moment no blood test, brain scan, or X ray that will establish conclusively that the person does have schizophrenia. Rather, the health care provider needs to exclude other possible causes of the person's condition. For example, use of illegal drugs such as cocaine or amphetamines can often cause many of the symptoms of schizophrenia, such as hallucinations or delusions. Because these symptoms sometimes can be caused by medical problems such as disorders of the thyroid gland, epilepsy, or brain tumors, the person should have a physical examination, blood tests, and urine tests. In rare cases it may be worthwhile to have a brain scan.

The most important information used in making the diagnosis of schizophrenia is the person's history. It can be very helpful to know what the problem is now, when the problem began, whether it has been better some times and worse at other times, whether it has been getting worse lately, and whether any treatments have improved the situation. Other useful information includes whether or not alcohol and drugs are involved and whether or not anyone else in the family has ever had a similar problem.

Since there is no definitive laboratory test for the condition, persons with schizophrenia often acquire different "labels" from health care providers. For example, it can be difficult to tell whether alcohol or drug use is causing a person to have hallucinations or delusions, or whether the drug use is simply worsening an underlying problem. At times it also can be difficult to distinguish between two types of mental illness: schizophrenia and bipolar (manic depressive) disorder. The situation is rather like trying to decide whether a person has migraine headaches or tension headaches. In any event, the history is usually the most important guide to the diagnosis.

Medications

Once the diagnosis is made, medications (Table 4) can be helpful for persons with schizophrenia. Since the 1950s antipsychotic drugs like chlorpromazine (Thorazine) or haloperidol (Haldol) have been used in the treatment of schizophrenia. These drugs can reduce the "positive" symptoms of the disease that were described in the introduction. For about 70 percent of patients medications can reduce auditory hallucinations (voices the schizophrenic person hears that no one else can hear). These drugs can also decrease the schizophrenic person's delusional thinking, often reducing his or her belief that he or she is being spied upon or followed or poisoned. In the majority of cases, the medicines can help the person to think more clearly.

Typically, the person with schizophrenia is bombarded by internal messages that have no connection to the real world. These "internal stimuli" may take the form of mocking voices or a belief that others are controlling the individual's thoughts. Persons with schizophrenia often experience unusual bodily sensations ("My bones have turned to mush") or believe the impossible ("Martians have implanted radio receivers in my teeth"). Not surprisingly, it sometimes can be difficult to provide routine medical or dental care for persons with schizophrenia. Does the complaint of "radios in my teeth" mean a worsening of the schizophrenia or development of tooth decay?

Many scientists believe that these psychotic symptoms are caused by an excess of a brain chemical called dopamine. The antipsychotic drugs moderate the effects of dopamine and reduce the "positive" symptoms of schizophrenia. When the hallucinations and delusions are reduced, the schizophrenic person often finds that thinking is easier and more logical. The medications may reduce the patient's agitation; hence their alternative name of "major tranquilizers."

The antipsychotic medications are certainly not perfect. One problem

TABLE 4.
Medications for Schizophrenia

GENERIC NAME	TRADE NAME	TYPICAL ADULT DOSE
Low potency:		
Chlorpromazine	Thorazine	30–800 mg per day
Promazine	Sparine	40–1200
Triflupromazine	Vesprin	60–150
Thioridazine	Mellaril	150–800
Mesoridazine	Serentil	30–400
Acetophenazine	Tindal	60–120
Prochlorperazine	Compazine	15–150
Chlorprothixene	Taractan	75–600
Molindone	Moban	15–225
Loxapine	Loxitane	20–250
High potency:		
Perphenazine	Trilafon	12–64
Fluphenazine	Prolixin	0.5–40
Trifluoperazine	Stelazine	2–40
Thiothixene	Navane	8–30
Pimozide	Orap	1–10
Haloperidol	Haldol	1–15
Clozapine	Clozaril	300–900
Lithium	many names	900–1800
Side effect medications:		
Benztropine	Cogentin	0.5–6
Biperiden	Akineton	2–8
Diphenhydramine	Benadryl	10–200
Procyclidine	Kemadrin	7.5–20
Trihexyphenidyl	Artane	1–15
Amantadine	Symmetrel	100–200

is that the drugs address the positive symptoms of schizophrenia but generally do rather little for the negative ones. Persons with schizophrenia often have difficulty taking the initiative, showing emotional attachment, and developing an interest in the normal activities of life. Unfortunately, most of the antipsychotic drugs do not specifically correct these symptoms.

Another problem is that the drugs do not produce their main effects

immediately. It may take several weeks for a person taking an antipsychotic drug to develop full benefits in terms of reducing hallucinations or
delusions, but the side effects can arise much sooner.

Side effects of the antipsychotic drugs can range from troublesome to
devastating. It is helpful to divide the drugs into two classes: the "low-
potency" drugs such as chlorpromazine (Thorazine) or thioridazine (Mellaril), and the "high-potency" drugs, such as haloperidol (Haldol),
fluphenazine (Prolixin), or thiothixene (Navane). Potency refers to the fact
that 100 milligrams of a drug like chlorpromazine is equivalent to one
milligram of a drug like haloperidol.

The low-potency drugs like chlorpromazine may put people to sleep,
lower blood pressure, and cause dry mouth or constipation. The high-
potency drugs tend to affect people's movements, so that they may walk
stiffly, shake, drool, or develop muscle contractions. Many of these side
effects can be relieved by taking additional medicines such as benztropine
(Cogentin).

The person taking an antipsychotic drug may feel a need to move his
or her legs, walk about, or rock in a chair. This problem may be due to
a puzzling side effect called "akathisia" or motor restlessness. It can be
difficult to determine whether or not a patient like Mark, who frequently
paces about (or even runs away), is experiencing agitation due to schizophrenia or akathisia due to the medication. Side-effect medication like
propranolol (Inderal) or benztropine may be helpful in dealing with akathisia.

All these short-term side effects are reversible; that is, they go away
when the drug is stopped. Some patients may experience the side effects
frequently, and others will not notice any at all. Generally speaking, the
more medicine one takes during a day, the more likely one is to develop
the side effects. On the other hand, many patients adjust to the medicines
since the side effects tend to diminish after the first few weeks or months.

These short-term side effects are one reason why antipsychotic drugs
are not particularly popular. As in Mark's case, the patient may feel that
the side effects are worse than the benefits from the medication, while
family members not surprisingly might have a different view. Some people
notice the side effects first and stop the drugs before receiving their main
benefits. Consequently, there is a tendency for the drugs to be stopped
before they have been given a chance to be effective. Also, if the response
to the drugs is not complete, e.g., hallucinations are reduced but delusions
persist, there is a tendency to increase the dose. Unfortunately, high doses

of the antipsychotic medications often produce side effects but only infrequently yield increased benefits.

The worst long-term side effect is known as tardive dyskinesia. This potentially irreversible condition is characterized by abnormal involuntary movements, usually of the tongue or lips but sometimes of the arms or legs. It can develop from using any antipsychotic drug (with the exception discussed below) for a few months, but more usually requires several years of use. Some persons can use antipsychotic drugs for decades and never develop abnormal movements. Others seem to be at higher risk—especially persons over age 65 and women. Careful monitoring of patients taking antipsychotic drugs is important to prevent development of tardive dyskinesia. The condition may temporarily worsen when the antipsychotic drug dose is reduced, but frequently improves over a period of several months when less medicine is used.

Until recently it was fair to say that the main effects of antipsychotic drugs were similar, as were many of the side effects. Of course, some people are greatly helped by the medications, and others do not receive much benefit. Some do better with one drug and not so well with another. Some people dislike taking pills every day and prefer to receive an injection once or twice monthly. Sometimes people find the sedating effects of drugs like chlorpromazine helpful for sleep. All the oral antipsychotic drugs remain in the body for about 24 hours, so they can be taken once daily, usually at bedtime. Medications for side effects, if they are needed, are often taken twice daily.

Clozapine was recently introduced into the United States. It has been shown to help persons who have not responded to conventional antipsychotic drugs. Interestingly, clozapine does not cause side effects like stiffness or restlessness. Although it has been used for decades in Europe, there is no evidence that it causes tardive dyskinesia. Indeed, it is not uncommon for older patients with severe tardive dyskinesia to show considerable improvement when they stop their usual medicines and take clozapine instead.

Unfortunately, clozapine has its own side effects. It often causes sleepiness, low blood pressure, drooling, and weight gain. However, these may disappear after the first month or two of use. More worrisome side effects include seizures in about 5 percent of patients and reduced white blood cell counts. Because the reduced white blood cell counts may leave patients vulnerable to infection, users of clozapine need to be carefully monitored and to have their blood tested weekly.

On the other hand, clozapine seems to improve the "negative" symptoms of schizophrenia. Individuals with this illness may have limited reasoning and diminished communication skills. Some patients taking clozapine report a return of these seemingly lost capabilities. Many have described this experience as an "awakening" from psychosis and a return to society. This awakening sometimes may be seen more readily by family members than by the patients themselves.

As is commonly found in treating persons with chronic conditions, a few users of clozapine have had "miraculous" responses, some have had no response at all, and more than a few have shown substantial improvement but certainly are not cured. Persons taking clozapine may find that their hallucinations and delusions are gone, but they are still uncomfortable talking with people. Many report that they need to learn or relearn social skills, such as how to make friends, go shopping, and manage money.

A feature of clozapine that has generated much controversy is its cost. Unlike the older antipsychotic drugs, which typically cost only a few cents per day, clozapine can cost ten to fifteen dollars per day. This price includes the blood testing. Paying for the drug and for mental health services generally presents substantial problems.

Besides the antipsychotic drugs, other medications can be used in the treatment of schizophrenia. For example, lithium is a natural substance that, like gold or lead, comes out of the ground and can affect human health. Although used chiefly by persons with bipolar (manic depressive) disorder, lithium can be helpful for some persons with schizophrenia. Persons taking lithium must have their blood monitored to determine if the level of medication is appropriate. Lithium can have several side effects, including tremors, diarrhea, excess urination, and weight gain. However, many do not experience any of these problems. Lithium can affect many body systems, especially the thyroid gland, and can harm the fetus in a pregnant woman. Again, it is important that persons taking lithium work closely with a health care provider who has experience with this drug.

Adherence to treatment is a problem for many people taking medications, not just those with schizophrenia. In the father's story, we saw that Mark is very negative about taking his pills. In addition to the side effects, other problems with medications include having to remember to take the pills, their cost, and their stigma. People, especially younger people, generally dislike being thought ill by others.

Taking pills every day is a reminder of illness, something that most people would rather avoid thinking about. This problem is particularly apparent with medications like antipsychotic drugs, which patients should take even when feeling healthy. Battles between family members and persons with schizophrenia about taking the medications are not uncommon. Many psychosocial treatment programs include educational activities aimed at helping people understand the value and necessity of their medications.

Psychosocial Treatment

Mental health professionals generally believe that medications are but one part in a complete program of treatment for persons with schizophrenia. The other aspects include case management and rehabilitation.

Case management refers to the provision of services necessary for the client to survive in the community. Persons with schizophrenia, especially in the early years of the condition, often need assistance finding shelter, obtaining food, keeping appointments, and taking medication. Case management programs provide counselors who work with them to ensure that these basic needs are met. Some community mental health programs provide "assertive" case management, which emphasizes outreach to clients by a team of providers available seven days per week, twenty-four hours per day. Unfortunately, in many parts of the country it can be difficult to locate a program that provides case management. Also, case managers may change jobs or programs may shrink when funding is lost. It is important for family members to keep in contact with both the schizophrenic person and the case manager.

Rehabilitation addresses the handicaps associated with schizophrenia. For example, a person with schizophrenia may have hallucinations, which may lead to an impaired ability to concentrate. The inability to concentrate in turn can lead to difficulty maintaining employment. A rehabilitation program would deal with this situation by placing the client in a supported work environment. The program would assure the employer that the job would be performed by either the client or a program staff member. Then the client would be trained to perform those job tasks that were within his or her capabilities. Program staff would continue to support the client as needed following the training period. Rehabilitation techniques have been devised for a number of the handicaps associated with schizophrenia, including grooming, managing medications, and avoiding alcohol or drug abuse. Rehabilitation programs may be provided in the context of a "clubhouse" that clients ("members") operate.

As Joe Talbot points out, work is an important part of any rehabilitation program, especially one aimed at persons with schizophrenia. State agencies use federal and state funds to operate vocational rehabilitation services. Unfortunately, these "voc-rehab" programs typically have few openings but many applicants. Persons with schizophrenia must, in effect, compete with other disabled persons for entrance into voc-rehab. This area is one of many in which "everything else being equal" does not apply to persons with schizophrenia. The individual with schizophrenia often finds it difficult to be accepted into voc-rehab and, once accepted, may not obtain the assistance needed to complete the program. Consequently, persons with schizophrenia often spend much of their adulthood unemployed and in poverty.

COSTS

One of the features distinguishing schizophrenia from other long-term conditions is the contorted and inadequate financial system surrounding treatment for mental disorders. The ideal of community care for persons with schizophrenia certainly has not been attained. What we have instead is a confusing mixture of public and private services financed by an astonishingly complicated set of payment systems. The person with schizophrenia may have drugs prescribed by a private psychiatrist; receive counseling at a publicly funded community mental health center; reside in a supervised apartment subsidized by local, state, and federal funds; spend a couple of days per year in a local, general hospital during a crisis; and be committed for several months to a state mental hospital after a relapse. For other chronic conditions (e.g., diabetes), care is often provided by a comprehensive program that offers a variety of coordinated services. In contrast, the person with schizophrenia (or, more likely, the family) is expected to fashion a care system from a variety of unconnected programs.

Personal Finances

Since competitive employment is often challenging for persons with schizophrenia, financial support can be difficult. In many states persons with schizophrenia may be eligible for General Assistance (welfare) by virtue of disability and/or poverty. Typically one must be certified unable to work by a physician or clinical psychologist. Not surprisingly, there is usually a substantial amount of paperwork to be completed before funds are provided. Community mental health program staff should be able to assist their clients in obtaining the state benefits to which they are entitled. The amount of benefits varies from state to state and from month to month depending on the state's budget.

Often one can apply simultaneously for welfare and food stamps. However, in some areas two applications at two different agencies are required. The role of the case manager is to ensure that these benefits are provided. The case manager can be particularly helpful in dealing with the bureaucratic problems (lost checks, denied eligibility, etc.) that inevitably arise.

The federal Social Security Administration provides financial assistance programs that are often used by persons with schizophrenia. Supplemental Security Income (SSI) is intended for persons who are determined to be disabled (i.e., unable to work) due to illness, including schizophrenia. Although the program is funded by the federal government, disability determination is typically performed by state agencies. The process of attaining SSI is complicated and frustrating for all applicants, let alone those with schizophrenia. The application process typically takes one or two years. Commonly the applicant with schizophrenia is rejected initially but becomes successful on appeal. Again, community mental health programs should be able to help persons with schizophrenia to obtain SSI. Social Security Disability Income (SSDI) is a federal program similar to SSI but generally aimed at persons who have had some paid employment prior to becoming disabled. The Social Security programs are confusing and constantly changing. Family members are well advised to keep in touch with the local Social Security Administration office in order to learn about new developments in these programs.

Becoming certified as disabled by schizophrenia is no simple task. The applicant must start by obtaining a diagnosis from a physician or a clinical psychologist. However, the diagnosis itself is not sufficient. Next, one must show that the disorder has left the individual impaired in some way. For example, hallucinations may prevent the person from concentrating enough to follow instructions. The evaluators appreciate examples of situations in which the applicant attempted to work but could not do so because of symptoms. In other words, the process is one of showing that symptoms lead to impaired function, which in turn renders the applicant unable to work. The process of application and evaluation is confusing for anyone and especially so for persons with schizophrenia.

The application process is similar for SSDI except that the dates at which disability developed become important. Records of psychiatric hospitalizations can be helpful in obtaining SSDI. It is possible for a parent or spouse who is nearing age 62 to apply for SSDI on behalf of their disabled relative.

Enrollment in SSDI is desirable for several reasons, including the availability of Medicare. In addition, under the rules of SSDI, it is legally permissible to set up a trust fund for the benefit of the family member. The local Social Security Administration office can provide more information on SSDI.

Re-evaluation may be required after the person has had SSI or SSDI for a couple of years to make sure he or she remains unable to work. Of course, there are many administrative problems with SSI and SSDI, including checks deposited in the wrong bank or sent to the wrong address and inappropriate terminations from the program. Again, case managers should be helpful in keeping the funds flowing.

Although relatively modest, the monthly check from SSI can be either a blessing or a curse for the person with schizophrenia. Many persons with this condition have difficulty managing money and, as in Mark's case, may spend the funds on drugs or alcohol rather than food or shelter. At least during the early years of schizophrenia, it can be helpful to have a person or an agency designated as the payee for the SSI check. This payee dispenses the money in small amounts to the client, while ensuring that food and housing are obtained. Being a payee can be challenging, since the client may at times become demanding. For example, the client may wish to obtain all of the monthly check at once in order to buy drugs or alcohol. Conversely, the payee may feel that the client should be given only a portion of the check each week. On the other hand, payees can often develop close relationships with clients and provide wanted social interaction.

Given this precarious financial situation, the person with schizophrenia may often have trouble buying food. Indeed, nutrition for the schizophrenic individual can become a major problem. Delusions about food being poisoned are not rare. Some people lack the concentration to buy and prepare food. The person with schizophrenia may dine from a dumpster. Food stamps can be helpful, and missions or soup kitchens are often lifesaving. Shoplifting food (or more often cigarettes) is unfortunately all too common for schizophrenic individuals and can result in confrontations with the police.

As Joe Talbot points out in the preceding chapter, persons certified as disabled may well feel that they have been devalued. Also, certification for SSI often carries the implicit and explicit message that the beneficiary should not seek gainful employment. Despite its drawbacks, SSI does provide income. The amount varies from time to time and from place to place for reasons few outside the Social Security Administration can understand. Typically, the person receiving SSI will get about $500 per month. Ironically, in some states persons on SSI are too wealthy to qualify for state assistance programs such as Medicaid.

Financing Health Care

Unfortunately, financing determines the type of services available for persons with schizophrenia rather than the other way around. Medicaid is the joint federal-state program that pays health care providers to serve clients enrolled in this system. While there are 50 or more different Medicaid programs, one in each state and territory, in most cases persons become eligible by virtue of poverty. Not surprisingly, many but certainly not all persons with schizophrenia are poor enough to qualify for Medicaid. Once enrolled in Medicaid, clients become eligible to have their medical bills paid to the extent that their state's program will do so. Many states have strict limits on the amount of outpatient mental health treatment that can be reimbursed under Medicaid. Similarly, many states restrict the number of general hospital psychiatric days they will reimburse during a given year. Some states cover the costs of drugs like clozapine under their Medicaid programs, but others do not. In general, Medicaid will not pay for state mental hospital services, which are financed almost entirely by state funds. Medicaid reimbursement rates are typically low and may not cover the costs to the physician, mental health professional, or hospital providing the service. Not surprisingly, then, providers may be reluctant to offer services to Medicaid clients.

Medicaid, at least, offers the possibility of paying something. Unfortunately, many persons with schizophrenia are not even enrolled in Medicaid. There can be several reasons for this strange situation. States typically require applicants to complete reams of paperwork to enroll in Medicaid and maintain that enrollment. People with schizophrenia are often unable to organize their thoughts sufficiently to answer the many questions on the application forms. Sometimes schizophrenia leaves its victims so suspicious that they refuse to accept assistance, including Medicaid. State require- ments that clients return to welfare offices for recertification every six months or so (known as churning) effectively eliminate some people with schizophrenia. Also, states may have separate systems and applications for food stamps and low-income housing, again providing more stumbling blocks for the psychotic individual to overcome.

Interestingly, sometimes people with schizophrenia can be too wealthy to qualify for Medicaid. Persons like Mark who live with their families may have "too many" financial assets to be enrolled in a Medicaid program. These rules, of course, vary from state to state. Similarly, many states offer a variety of welfare programs often known as General Assistance. Again, the poverty that frequently accompanies schizophrenia is the chief qualification. In many states, enrollment in General Assistance (welfare) guarantees Medicaid eligibility. Community mental health programs often are motivated to help persons with schizophrenia attain General Assist- ance and/or Medicaid because the agency's funding may thereby be in- creased. Similarly, local hospitals (but not state mental hospitals) generally have an interest in helping patients enroll in Medicaid. The local hospital's motivation derives from the fact that the patient's bill might be paid, at least in part, if he or she is enrolled in Medicaid. On the other hand, there is no financial incentive for state hospitals to enroll their patients in Medicaid because federal law effectively prevents Medicaid funds from flowing to these hospitals.

Enrollment in SSDI typically includes eligibility for Medicare, which will pay for some mental health services. Medicare's regulations are rap- idly changing. At present Medicare will pay for a total of 180 days (per lifetime) of psychiatric hospitalization in facilities other than state mental hospitals. Medicare also provides some limited outpatient mental health benefits. Some mental health professionals are reluctant to serve Medicare patients due to the low levels of outpatient reimbursement.

In some rare cases a person with schizophrenia may be eligible for both Medicaid and Medicare. However, if one must choose, in most states Medicare is at the moment the preferred coverage because it at least pays for general hospital services. Also, changes underway in Medicare may increase the amount of reimbursement for outpatient mental health ser- vices.

Medicaid, of course, varies markedly from state to state. However, it is safe to say that having Medicaid coverage is much better than having no health insurance at all.

Hospitalization of all types is expensive, and psychiatric hospitalization is no exception. General or private psychiatric hospital charges at the moment can run from $500 to $1,000 daily. A state hospital may cost $100 to $300 daily. And a "nonhospital" alternative facility could cost anywhere from $50 to $200 daily. There are several reasons for the different charges. The majority of hospital costs go for nursing staff salaries, with room and board, record keeping, laboratory testing, etc., accounting for smaller shares of the bills. While room and board costs will be much the same at various types of facilities, the ratio of staff to patients can be quite different. Typically, a general hospital will have five to ten times as many nurses per patient as does a state hospital or a nonhospital alternative facility. Another confusing feature of hospital accounting is that physicians typically bill separately for their services at general hospitals and private psychiatric hospitals but not at state hospitals. A common feature is that no facility can operate at a deficit. Someone must pay the bills.

Paying for hospitalization can be an overwhelming problem for people with schizophrenia. As noted, Medicaid is typically quite frugal about paying for inpatient or outpatient mental health services. Medicare is more generous—until the lifetime 180-day limit expires. Private health insurance may entirely omit coverage for mental health problems. The insurance industry conveniently takes advantage of the public ignorance about mental illness that Joe described. Since schizophrenia affects only one percent of adults, few know anyone with schizophrenia. Naturally enough, most people have no problem with a health insurance policy that offers no benefits for this disorder.

On the other hand, there are a number of initiatives aimed at eliminating some of this discrimination against providing care for people with schizophrenia. Some states have legally defined schizophrenia as a physical brain disease like meningitis or epilepsy that must by law be covered by health insurance in the same way that physical conditions are. Other states have mandated mental health benefits that are typically a certain amount of money for hospitalization during a year, e.g., $10,000 per person for all mental health hospitalization during a year. In almost all areas of the country mental health services are coming to be provided by managed-care systems that attempt to control costs by regulating use of services. Often, physicians must get prior approval from a managed-care organization before patients can be hospitalized. Length of stay in the hospital is carefully monitored, and discharge may come sooner than providers, consumers, or family members think necessary. At the national level, development of a health care system for all Americans may lead to some improvements or may result in worse discrimination against persons with schizophrenia and other mental illnesses. The new Americans with Disabilities Act may be useful in reducing the stigma suffered by those with mental disorders like schizophrenia.

Housing

Housing is another challenging area for persons with schizophrenia. Joe's difficulties in finding shelter for his son can be traced to several sources. At the beginning of the deinstitutionalization movement during the 1960s, persons discharged from state hospitals often moved into single-room occupancy (SRO) hotels in central city areas. While by no means ideal, these SRO hotels did at least provide affordable shelter. Unfortunately, urban renewal and gentrification led to a decline in this type of housing stock. Low-income persons, including those with schizophrenia, find it difficult to compete for housing in the current marketplace.

Alternatives to SRO hotels have been developed over the years including nursing homes, "sheltered care" (the group homes described by Joe as snakepits), and other, more innovative forms of supervised or semi-independent housing. The challenge lies in finding a form of housing that supports the desire of mentally ill persons for independence but minimizes the less desirable aspects of unsupervised living, such as the drug abuse that led to Mark's return to the hospital.

Sheltered care facilities ("group homes") range in quality from outstanding to disastrous, but typically involve a few to a few dozen clients living in a house or apartment building under live-in supervision. Clients may all be persons with mental disorders like schizophrenia or there may be a mix of people including persons with developmental disabilities, head injuries, or Alzheimer's disease. Often the client must arrange for the provider to receive the resident's SSI check. The provider in turn dispenses small amounts of pocket money to the client while using the bulk of the SSI check to finance room and board. Some facilities, especially those known as "adult foster homes," dispense medications, while other homes leave the clients to manage their own pills.

Not surprisingly, group living appeals to some persons with schizophrenia, but most prefer to live independently. Persons with schizophrenia are sometimes eligible for low-cost, federally subsidized housing known variously as HUD (Housing and Urban Development) or "Section Eight" housing. Although originally designed for the elderly, many of these federally subsidized housing projects now find that their occupants include younger persons with schizophrenia, who sometimes enliven the facility.

Safety and Crime

Persons with schizophrenia occupy two ends of the violence spectrum. Because of their difficulties in thinking clearly, schizophrenic individuals are much more frequently victims than victimizers. Running away (as Joe terms it, going on a run) is not uncommon in persons with schizophrenia. While this activity may be related to the medication side effect akathisia, it occurs commonly enough in individuals who decline to take medications. In any event, the schizophrenic person on the streets of a strange city is easy prey, and may be beaten, raped, or robbed.

Looking at the perpetrator side of the violence spectrum, persons with schizophrenia are rarely mass murderers. On the other hand, they do seem to be overrepresented in the ranks of prominent-person assassins— for example, John Hinckley, who wounded President Reagan. Violence to family members is not rare.

Consequently, the question frequently arises whether the schizophrenic individual should or should not live with family. The father in the preceding story reviewed the risks and benefits. On the one hand, the family knows where the schizophrenic person is. On the other hand, the family's lifestyle may be altered substantially. Different families have different perspectives. It is clear, however, that families provide the bulk of support for many schizophrenic persons.

HOW TO IMPROVE CARE AND SERVICES

We all need food, shelter, companionship, and a reason to get up in the morning. The person with schizophrenia can have difficulties in all these areas. Unfortunately, our current treatment system may only compound these problems. We spend considerable energy deciding who is disabled, but we spend less energy helping those in need. We have many systems but little effective service.

We should recognize that schizophrenia is a long-lasting problem that does improve, in some cases, a little each year. Once we have determined that a person has schizophrenia, he or she should automatically be entitled to food, housing, treatment, and rehabilitation with little or no paperwork required.

Housing, and especially appropriate housing, is sorely lacking. Persons with schizophrenia by and large are less interested in living in an institution and more interested in living independently in the community. We need to devise ways to support them in independent or semi-independent housing. This goal involves multiple tasks, including providing affordable housing, minimizing alcohol and drug use, and arranging for close supervision during crises.

Our treatment system is geared toward recovering from catastrophe but not toward its prevention. The schizophrenic person who wants to volunteer for a few days of respite will find it difficult to obtain that service. Conversely, the flagrantly psychotic person who has become dangerous and refuses treatment will be transported involuntarily to a hospital. We need to redeploy our resources away from high-cost crises and toward lower-cost prevention.

We place many mutually incompatible demands on our treatment system, and then we are surprised to find that it fails in several areas. On the one hand, we would like our mental health system to rehabilitate disabled persons who volunteer for and, indeed, participate in planning a treatment program. On the other hand, we expect our system to protect society from potentially dangerous individuals. These functions are, of course, very different and not easily accomplished within one service delivery system. We may need to accept a small degree of risk from those few potentially dangerous persons with mental illness, while gaining enhanced services for the large numbers of people with schizophrenia who need constant support to function in the community.

We have difficulty translating well-established research findings into everyday practice. Assertive case management and psychosocial rehabilitation clubhouses are well studied, highly regarded programs that are rarely available. Lack of funding is part of the explanation, but lack of leadership may be a larger part. Our system is fragmented and our financial incentives perverse. Persons with schizophrenia would benefit from having access to a unified mental health system with stable funding. Managers of such a system would benefit from having clear outcome measures that could be used to judge their performance. The many skills and capabilities of mental health consumers need to be incorporated into our mental health programs. The basic needs of food, shelter, companionship, and meaningful activity could become goals for both consumers and providers.

How do we get from where we are to where we want to be? Advocacy is the most important mental health development in the last two decades. It is essential that schizophrenia be taken out of the closet and brought before the public. The Americans with Disabilities Act may well be a useful tool to increase understanding of and services for persons with schizophrenia. The national debate on health care reform provides a forum for reducing the stigma associated with schizophrenia and for abolishing the discrimination against those affected by mental disorders. Family members always will be the key to advocacy and service improvement.

2.

The Single Parent's Struggle:

Schizophrenia and the Adult Child

"SOMETIMES I SAY THAT I AM not ashamed of this happening—of my son being mentally ill—that I am not embarrassed by it, but I have found in the past that this is not really true. At one time or another I have had feelings of shame and anger. I like to think that I don't have a problem with it, but when I'm really honest I have to admit that there is always a little residual embarrassment, a kind of tightness that makes me feel that I must both explain and hold myself back."

Joni Lindsey is a single parent. She is a small, pretty, fair-haired woman. In earlier times, she might have been called pert. Tiny-boned and energetic, she presents a picture of an alert, bright, and spunky person. And yet it is quickly apparent that Joni is also fragile and vulnerable, which makes her unselfconscious feistiness all the more poignant.

Twenty-one years old, Joni's son Stuart has paranoid schizophrenia. With crew-cut sandy hair and deep blue eyes, he is a good-looking young man who still has the appearance of a youthful, all-American college preppy. He is the middle child, with an older brother and a younger sister. And according to his mother, Stuart is, or was until he became ill, the brightest of her three offspring.

Stuart was a mathematics major at the state university. His mother remembers that at the beginning of his sophomore year there was an undeniable onset of mental illness. Joni describes it as "when the real tense part began." She admits, however, that it actually probably started when he was a senior in high school. But she didn't recognize it then, and neither did anybody else.

An outstanding athlete and student, Stuart played varsity baseball and varsity soccer. He also was in accelerated academic programs in English, science, and math. Gradually, however, during his senior year at high school he seemed to become sluggish and was unable to last out and play a full game in either of his sports. At the same time he was unable to keep up his schoolwork.

Stuart not only appeared to lose his ability to concentrate, he also acted as though he were intimidated by his friends. This was really puzzling because Stuart was an easygoing fellow who had had very relaxed, long-term relationships with his buddies. He had been the kind of child who loved to play and was always in a good humor. He was the sunny kid on the block: "Good at everything but no sweat," Joni said. "All the neighborhood kids wanted to play with Stu."

Although it became evident that, in his senior year, Stuart was becoming incapable of coping with even minor matters, Joni simply dismissed this behavior as his apprehension about going away to college. She says now that she must have just very conveniently ignored everything.

Daphne, Stuart's sister, did notice that his behavior was odd and bizarre. But Joni said that she didn't want to listen to her daughter. She distinctly remembers that she put down Daphne's observations to sibling rivalry. In hindsight she thinks that she knew something was awry, but she stubbornly ignored her own concerns. She felt compelled to stand firm against the possibility that anything might be wrong with her handsome and gifted son.

Joni is nagged by a feeling of wrongdoing. Did she make her son's subsequent schizophrenia worse by inattention to the early signals? Slowly she has come to understand that the outcome—Stuart's chronic mental illness—is unaltered by her earlier neglect. Even so, she continues to find it difficult to set aside this worry.

Somehow Stuart managed to get through his first year at college without attracting much attention to himself. He was no longer an outstanding student or much of an athlete, but he was able to keep out of harm's way. Ironically, when he came home for the winter and spring breaks, Joni attributed his quietness and reticence to a welcome maturation.

At the end of his first university year, Stuart took a summer job selling books and magazines in Alabama and Georgia. This was itinerant work.

The job required that he go from door to door making a rote sales pitch. The company that he worked for would drop him off in the morning and pick him up in the evening—if he named his pickup point.

Joni said she found out later that he spent most of his nights out in the woods sleeping under trees, eating scraps, and begging for bread in stores. She said, with a wry smile, that "he came back a very slender person." He ended up owing the company a lot of money. He had sold their products and never collected any money; confused, Stuart had given the books away.

Stuart went back to school and started his sophomore year, but after six weeks he came home. His mother was not surprised to see him. By now she had admitted to herself that something had to be wrong. He appeared disoriented and incapable of completing even simple tasks. He hadn't been sleeping, his days and nights were turned around, and his hygiene habits were deplorable. Joni recalled her shocked realization that her son smelled bad.

She telephoned an old and trusted friend who worked in a doctor's office and asked her if she could recommend a psychiatrist for Stuart. Meg told her to call a Dr. Martin Sweeney in northwest Portland. The doctor prescribed Mellaril for Stuart, which apparently helped him sleep but certainly did not alter his behavior, which continued to grow stranger and stranger.

Joni was told by Dr. Sweeney that her son had an emotional disorder, but he never actually said what it was. She remembers that "he never gave it a name." He was also quite emphatic that he would be able to help Stuart. Unfortunately, the treatment was unsuccessful and Stuart grew worse.

At the time Joni felt bewildered. Now she believes that this psychiatrist helped prolong the ordeal before the inevitable hospital stay. She felt very frustrated about this then, and still feels very angry. As a working widow, she felt that the family had been victimized by those additional six months. She paid a lot of money for her son's treatment and it wasn't, as she put it, "the right thing."

By the end of December, Stuart's behavior was becoming more distinctly bizarre and he was "getting heavily into religion." Joni thought this was very odd because as a family they had never put much emphasis on religion.

"It appeared," Joni said, "as though he felt that everything was to be resolved by religion. He was reading the Bible all the time, and staring—for hours at a time—at a picture of Jesus Christ." He was also posturing in weird ways: standing or sitting, for long, long periods of time, sometimes even five hours, in strange and sometimes contorted positions. Joni recalled, "He would stay absolutely still, as though he was frozen. It was scary."

On Christmas day she told him to get washed up for dinner. Stuart went into the bathroom. He took off all his clothes and slathered his mother's moisturizing lotion all over his face, his hair, and his body. Joni and her family had invited guests for Christmas dinner, including some young children. A four-year-old girl walked into the bathroom just as Stuart was walking out. When she saw this naked, greasy apparition she screamed with terror.

Joni ran to the bathroom. She calmed and hushed the child and took her back to her parents in the living room. She told Daphne and her older son, Bob, to serve dinner while she settled Stuart.

Running back to her disoriented son, she spoke soothingly to him. And just as she had when he was a small child, she placed him in the bathtub and washed him off. She dressed him in his pajamas, gave him two Mellaril, and put him to bed. He went to sleep.

The next morning Joni told him, "Stuart, it is time that you go to the hospital." Her voice trembled as she remembered this. She took him to a hospital that was near their apartment. He went very willingly. Stuart was admitted, and he stayed in the hospital for two months.

Joni visited him every day. She met with the social worker who was assigned to her son's case. The social worker and the hospital staff were making plans for Stuart's living arrangements and follow-up treatment in preparation for his hospital discharge. Her voice falling to a whisper, Joni said she was a "total wreck."

The staff evinced a certain antagonism toward her. They felt that Joni was not—in her words—"buying into the program." She knew that Stuart needed help and needed assistance to set up an appropriate living situation. She was agreeable to all of this, but she was still telling herself that this was a "temporary deal"—that Stuart was going to be just fine. Joni was tenacious and she didn't want to give up so easily. She was clinging to the idea that her son was going to come out of this all right.

Kate Arthur was a social worker on Stuart's ward whom Joni would never forget. One day, late in Stuart's stay at the hospital, Kate asked Joni to come into her office for a quick chat. Kate came right to the point. "Look, Joni," she said. "I know that the hardest thing for any mother to face is that her child is not living up to her dreams. You have carefully nurtured certain expectations for your son. Now it's time, Joni, that you face the life that is *possible* for Stuart. Stop fooling yourself with fantasies. It's harmful for your son."

Initially Joni felt affronted. She perceived this as an accusation and it hurt her feelings terribly. She felt painfully and publicly exposed, as though unknown to her she had been evaluated and suddenly she was being told that she had not passed a test. She was being told it was common knowledge that she had stumbled as a mother, and her son's illness marked her as a failure.

But Joni Lindsey is a resilient woman. "I have come to be very grateful to Kate. This woman's remark made me realize that I had to learn to deal with what was best for Stuart. I had to accept this present son. He was not to be the Stuart that I had fancied him to become."

Stuart was released from the hospital, but the only place the hospital staff could find for him to live was in a very undesirable group home. The Hathaway Guest Home was a fetid, filthy, slovenly place. In the nooks and crannies there was a thick greasy grime that had layered with time. The entire residence smelled of stale food, recooked soups, and garbage left sitting around too long.

It was simply a place where the sick, young and old, women and men, were warehoused, nothing more. They were given their medicine and fed. Most of the men roomed in the basement area. Usually there were eight to ten men in a room. The bunks were lined up against the wall. The rooms stank of old urine and unwashed bodies.

Joni was horrified. Even so, she took Stuart to the group home and left him there. She had been told that if she took him to her home, he would revert to being a child and would never learn to get along in society. The hospital staff made it clear to her that Stuart would be better off living away from her. They told her that this was the only route if she wanted him to become independent. Joni Lindsey wanted so much to "do the right thing."

"After I knew more about schizophrenia I found myself questioning this," Joni said. "People who suffer from schizophrenia are often dependent and needy, so it seems strange to send them away. I mean, would I have sent Stuart away when he was a little kid? If I had sent him to a facility where the caretakers were disinterested, slovenly, and indifferent to their charges, I would have been a bad mother. The truth is, we send our mentally ill kids away because they are too difficult to be with."

A month or two later somebody died at the Hathaway Guest Home. Joni wondered how long they had been dead before anybody noticed.

After that they changed the name, as though that would alter everything. Joni knew that she could no longer let her son stay there. She felt that she had to find him a better place to live.

After much searching she did succeed in finding him a far better group home, but nothing would work out for very long. Stuart was considered uncooperative and unpleasant. He wouldn't keep appointments to see his psychiatrist. He wouldn't take his medicine. He was evicted from program after program.

"It's so crazy. These group homes are designed for people who are mentally ill, and yet as soon as these sick people get sicker or become difficult, they are kicked out."

Stuart got progressively worse. He had started drinking and this aggravated his illness. At about that time he met a very pretty young woman who was also mentally ill—she had a manic depressive disorder. Debby was the first woman that Stuart had had a sexual relationship with, and he became very attached to her. Unfortunately, the two of them together seemed to compound and exaggerate their individual diseases; they were a combustible and destructive combination.

But Joni, with her usual zip and goodwill, tried to behave as though everything were normal. Ruefully she remembers that on one occasion she invited Debby to come along on a camping trip with the family and close friends. The vacation exploded into disaster.

One evening, after a campfire supper, Debby took some of the younger children, who were along on the trip with their parents, down to a secluded spot on the riverbank. There she told them lurid stories. In melodramatic tones, alternately hushed and shrill, her eyes sparkling with excitement, Debby told frightening tales describing Joni as a werewolf in disguise. She predicted that Joni would swoop down in the dark of night and drink their blood. Adults would have realized that this was ridiculous, even funny. But the children were terrified and became hysterical. It was impossible to calm then. The camping trip was broken up that night, and everyone returned to the city.

Joni's efforts to keep her family's life as normal as possible seem only to boomerang. The more she tries to conventionalize the family gatherings, the more her project appears to elude her. Stuart's illness defies her efforts to integrate him into the regular life that her other children can enjoy.

Furthermore, Stuart's illness causes his sister, Daphne, and brother, Bob, to be embarrassed. They feel anxious and ill-at-ease whenever they are with him. His behavior makes them acutely self-conscious, and their discomfort is compounded by their fears that they too might become mentally ill.

Bob will no longer have anything to do with Stuart. Joni is anguished about this. She sees this as yet another failure, another rejection, for Stuart. She knows that her son already leads a very isolated and lonely life, and when his own family excludes him, she feels it to be unbearably cruel.

Stuart's father is no longer alive. Joni mentioned this in a low voice, scarcely above a whisper, as though she didn't wish to be heard. It is clear that her life has been very difficult. And now it is very hard to be the only responsible caretaker for her mentally ill child. Even though Joni has many supportive friends, she is the only person whom Stuart can rely on. Paradoxically, however, when Stuart is very ill and quite unaware of his needs, he often rejects his mother's efforts to care for him. He rejects her attentions precisely when he needs her the most.

"Now," Joni said, "Stuart has regressed so much, and he is living in another horrible group home." When Joni first visited this residence she was reminded of the Hathaway. But this "home" is the only place that would take him. The county, which previously was responsible for Stuart's housing, refused to find a place for him within their jurisdiction. Joni listed their reasons: "He doesn't take his meds, he is uncooperative, he molested a resident in a group home, he has a restraining order against him, he drinks, he doesn't participate in the day program."

Joni pursed her mouth tightly. "This county day program, at which unemployed mentally ill persons are supposed to spend their day, is unbearably dull. As far as I'm concerned, it's no different from that old-time underlying asylum reasoning that all mentally ill persons are unaware of their surroundings."

She stopped talking and tried to compose herself. Then she whispered, "I feel so helpless. And the worst thing is that he refuses to take his medication. Doesn't it seem strange that someone with a known chronic disease would be kicked out of a program at exactly the time when he clearly needs the most help?" Joni kept shaking her head in disbelief.

"In other words," Joni said, "he is very sick, and the county looks at him as though he has misbehaved, as though he has *intentionally* burned his bridges behind him." She paused. "So he has deteriorated a lot in the last year. He's just become more and more fragile."

Plaintively she asked, "How did he get this way? Sometimes I wonder how I manage with him at all.

"I suppose that I deal with it the way Stuart deals with it—with the ups and downs. I relive the grief with my son every time he has an episode. It is as though I mourn, over and over again, for the healthy young man who is no more.

"Last August, before he was forced to move out of that county's jurisdiction, he was asked to leave a group home called the Olive Branch. He had no place to go, so they relocated him into a home called The Oaks."

Joni's voice took on a painfully ironic tone. "The Oaks is the new name for the Hathaway Guest Home." She laughed wryly. "There are no women there any longer, and a few less residents. Stuart was only there for a couple of days when he and another young guy, who also has schizophrenia, decided to pack all their things and drive to Colorado. It was the beginning of the month, so they had their full Social Security checks, and Stuart had a beatup old jalopy."

Joni spread her hands wide and raised her eyebrows. "Well, that's what they did, without another thought, no idea of consequences—they just took off for Colorado.

"The next thing I knew I got a call while I was at work from Traveler's Aid in Colorado, saying that these kids had no money."

Joni wired just enough money for Stuart to make the return trip. The next time Joni heard from Stuart he was in jail. "Stuart had decided, so he told me, to get closer to God. So he parked his car on the side of a road, took off all his clothes, and started climbing a mountain in the Colorado Rockies."

Later Stuart told his mother that after he had been climbing for what seemed to be a very long time it got to be very cold, and that suddenly it was so dark, pitch black, that he couldn't see anything. He felt groggy, so he tried to lie down and go to sleep. Fortunately, he felt too miserably cold and frozen to stay still, so he stumbled down the mountain, groping his way through the underbrush and the trees—not knowing where he was except that he was going down—and lurched into a lake. The water was icy cold, but the muddy bottom seemed warm, and he remembers that it felt really good to him.

Miraculously, from there he was able to find his way to a road. He stood in the middle of the road, totally naked, with his arms spread out. Somebody actually stopped for him, put a blanket around him and drove him to a police station. The police booked him and put him in jail.

Joni didn't have enough money and couldn't afford to leave her work to go to Colorado to fetch him. The car had been found and towed by the police, but it was too expensive to retrieve, so, as she explained with a small shrug, "that was a complete loss." She sent him a bus ticket and wired him twenty-five dollars.

"The District Attorney," Joni said, "was wonderful. He found Stuart some clothes and scrounged up a pair of pants, a lightweight shirt, and some old tennis shoes. A nurse bandaged Stuart's feet because they had gotten so badly cut on the mountain. Then the DA put my son on the bus and sent him on his way."

Along the way he lost his bus ticket and Joni had to send him another. She has worked hard all her life and is now a secretary in a commercial bakery. A proud person, Joni doesn't consider that she has made sacrifices to be able to continue to care for her ill son. But her financial difficulties inevitably exacerbate the sadness caused by her son's chronic illness.

Joni recalls the Colorado District Attorney telling her that he didn't want to put Stuart in a mental hospital because he might end up being incarcerated there for years, and there was always the possibility that she might lose track of him, never knowing what had happened to him. The District Attorney's office made it clear that they thought it best if Stuart just went home.

"I didn't want him lost, and I certainly wanted him to be back in Portland," she said, "but I can't help wondering what they would have done if Stu had had something like acute appendicitis or even measles or whooping cough—I wonder if they would have shipped him off so quickly. After all, they did take care of his cut and bleeding feet. It is interesting that they did nothing for his severe mental illness."

When at last Stuart returned to Portland, his mother had to put him into the disreputable Oaks group home for a few days while she hunted for a place for him to live. Even though his behavior showed characteristic decompensating patterns (he was becoming more and more disordered), Joni was unable to hospitalize him. According to the state law, he was not considered sick enough for an involuntary admission. And as he became more irrational and incoherent, he also became quite adamant that he did not wish to be in a hospital.

The involuntary commitment laws stipulate that mentally ill persons must present a clear threat of serious harm to others or to themselves. Joni quietly litanized some of the legal reasons that preclude an involuntary hospitalization for Stuart: "He wasn't a threat to anyone—he wasn't going to kill anyone; he had a place to live; he was getting his medication . . ." Her voice trailed off.

"Even though he was picking up his meds, it didn't mean that he was taking them." Joni lowered her voice even more. "I would have preferred that he be locked up and medicated so that he had a fighting chance. I would have preferred that he was OK. I would have preferred that I had a restful day."

A very disoriented Stuart left the Oaks group home and moved into an acquaintance's apartment. After two dreadfully disruptive weeks, he was kicked out. With nowhere to go, he moved into his mother's home.

When Stuart moved in with his mother, it was the first time that they had lived together since his initial hospitalization for mental illness. Joni said, "It was awful. He wasn't taking his meds. He wasn't clean. He had nothing to do. His days and nights were turned around. He was scared to death. I didn't know what to do. And we didn't have a medical connection because the county refused to be responsible for him."

Joni stopped talking and tried to control herself. It was clearly difficult for her not to weep; she was overcome with feelings of both sadness and anger.

Pushing her short blond hair back from her forehead, slowly and very quietly she said, "Being mentally ill must be like always being backed into a corner. You don't know where to go, what to do, or what to say to make everything OK.

"You know that you can do things, but you also know that you cannot do them for very long. You know that the friends you had in school won't talk to you because they're scared of your illness. You know that people won't hire you because you haven't worked in a long time. You know that your mother is an independent person and that she lives alone and that you are now living at home—dependent on her—and you are twenty-eight years old.

"I do have a sense of hope that won't give up. Even though, at the same time, I feel so empty with loss. This loss doesn't become bearable." Joni held herself as though she were cold. "It's a continual ongoing loss.

"I realize that I feel as though I actually suffer my son's pain. I am bound to Stuart by the terror that I know he experiences. Schizophrenia is a terrifying disease. And I am also bound to him for the inhumane way that he has been treated. I cannot bear to see him be so unjustly dealt with. His survival has become my survival."

Stuart writes poetry, songs, and stories. His mother says that when he is able to he writes all the time. Recently, while he was staying with Joni, he had written a story which she offered to send to Joe, her daughter's husband, who is a printer. Stuart had put the story into an envelope and asked Joni to mail it. Joni picked it up and put it in her purse.

She remembers, "I had no idea that his story was in that envelope. Later in the evening, after dinner—we were still sitting in the kitchen—he asked me for his story. I looked puzzled. 'What do you mean?'

"He said that he knew that I had taken it. I told him, 'Stu, I didn't take your story.' He said, 'Yes, you did. I know you did.' He was getting more and more agitated and very angry, pacing around, swearing, and calling me names.

"With a quick and sudden movement he picked up a serrated bread knife that had been left on the kitchen counter. He held it up against my throat, bent my arm back, and screamed: 'If you don't give me my story, I'm going to slit your throat.'

"Believe me, I was absolutely terrified, I think I said something like: 'Why don't you release me and we'll look for it?' He did let me go, and we ransacked the apartment. Of course we couldn't find the story because it was in the envelope in my purse all the time.

"I was more than afraid, I was trembling. He was totally gone. He wanted it, it was his thing. I had taken it and he was clearly fixated on threatening me as the only way to get his written story back. Luckily the telephone rang and that proved to be enough of a distraction for me to be able to slip out of the apartment.

"I had been advised by Metro Crisis, in between Stuart's hospital stays, that if he ever got really out of hand I should call the police. They told me that if there was real trouble the police would pick him up and take him to the state mental hospital.

"I had often told Stuart that if he didn't take his medicine and he started acting bizarre and threatened somebody, the police would take him to the hospital. I know he understood this very clearly. But all the same he's told me, 'I'm not nuts. You want to send me to a mental hospital where there are crazy people and I am not nuts. I'm not sick.'

"I ran from the apartment to the corner drugstore, where there was a pay phone. I called the police, on the 911 line. It was a long hour before they got to my place. Stuart could have killed himself during that time. I stood and waited for them outside the apartment building. I remember it was damn cold.

"I kept darting in and out the entrance, trying to keep warm and also wanting to make sure that they wouldn't miss the building. I was shivering with both cold and fear. I was worried sick that Stuart might have done something to himself.

"When at last the police arrived, they explained that first they had to talk to my son to find out if he was a threat to himself or to anyone else. They told me that if he did not appear to be threatening anyone now— even though he had just threatened me—they would not be able to take him to the state hospital.

" 'This is the way it is,' they said, 'because if he calms down by the time we get him there, when the doc sees him he'll just tell us that he doesn't want him. They won't take him in unless he's acting up. And then we'll be stuck and have to drive him all the way back.' They made it quite clear to me that all they would be able to do would be to put him in jail for the night and let him go the next morning."

Joni and the two police officers walked up the stairs to her apartment. She opened the door. The lights were on and the kitchen was still messed up just as it was when she had rushed out. But now it was quiet. Joni anxiously led them through the sitting room, past the bathroom to Stuart's bedroom. He was there, fast asleep in his bed.

Joni felt like a fool. The officers were kind. They told her not to fret. This was their job and they preferred it when there was no trouble. All of this excitement, distress, and terror, all of this tumult, and Joni felt like *she* was the crazy lady, running to the store to make agitated phone calls to the police.

After this incident Stuart moved back into another group home. "He's very fragile now." Joni looked at her hands. "I'm not afraid to be around him. I don't think he'd really hurt me. But I'm very careful when I'm with him.

"I'm more afraid that I won't live my life. I'm afraid for me. I'm used up by Stuart's disease. It is hard for me to keep myself separated from him. Well, I don't expect to be totally separated, but separated enough that I am not worried about him all of the time."

She paused and quietly said, "I even have had the feeling that I wish he were not alive."

Joni spoke wistfully, "I find myself wondering, will it ever be possible for me to care for my son so that I can protect him? I want so much to both keep him from harm and give him at least something of a good life.

"And"—Joni paused, knitting and unknitting her slender fingers—"I wonder if I will ever be able to have some life of my own."

Commentary

BY

HARRIET P. LEFLEY, PH.D.

Dr. Lefley is Professor of Psychiatry at the University of Miami School of Medicine, a licensed psychologist, and former Director of the interdisciplinary Collaborative Family Training Project conducted at three universities. She was also Director of the National Forums on Training Mental Health Professionals to Work with Families of the Seriously Mentally Ill, sponsored by the National Institute of Mental Health and the National Alliance for the Mentally Ill. Her publications include five books and over 100 articles, monographs, and book chapters on community mental health, cultural issues in mental health service delivery, clinical training, and family support systems for persons with major mental illnesses. Dr. Lefley was named a National Switzer Scholar in 1988.

Support group experiences, self-reports, clinical observations, and empirical research findings all suggest that among the multiple burdens of families of persons with major mental illnesses, it is devastating for a parent or sibling to be alone with the problem, without the support of a mate or of other relatives. A study of burden-of-care for families of young persons with schizophrenia, conducted in 1992 by Carpentier and his associates, found that single mothers were especially vulnerable to stress. Single mothers most often lacked resources, they were less likely to have the energy to gather information about the illness and about available help, and were less able to be a support to the patient. Regardless of whether the major caregiver is male or female, parent or sibling, coping with major mental illness in the family, as Agnes Hatfield points out, "can lead to burnout for the one who shoulders the responsibility alone."

The story of Joni, Stuart, and his siblings, however, exemplifies many common themes in families' experience of major mental illness, regardless of family structure and composition. For this reason it is important to examine the basic elements of typical family experiences and then to see how they generate specific pressures on the single parent.

ONSET OF ILLNESS: BEWILDERMENT AND MYSTIFICATION

Like many family members, Joni accuses herself of having failed to recognize her son's slowly emerging decompensation (a breakdown in functioning), despite the fact that it is not unusual for parents to accept erratic behavior in adolescents as a normal stage of the development cycle. The boundaries between normative and deviant behaviors are diffuse at this point, and Stuart apparently was sufficiently functional to enter the state university and to conceal the illness until his sophomore year. The family's mystification was scarcely dispelled by their first contact with the mental health system. Joni's experience with Stuart's first psychiatrist is a familiar story to many family members, although she was probably luckier than most. In contrast to the hostile rejections reported by many other family members, this psychiatrist was kind and prescribed an appropriate medication. However, he followed a customary pattern by (a) refusing to define the disorder, thus deterring the patient's caregiver from learning about schizophrenia, and (b) raising undue hopes by emphasizing that he could help Stuart recover.

This part of Joni's story highlights the dilemma of the psychiatrist treating a first-break or early case of a major mental illness. Some parents have complained that under similar conditions their psychiatrist was unduly pessimistic, accompanying a diagnosis of schizophrenia with the warning that the patient was likely to deteriorate into a chronic state and holding out little hope for recovery. Joni's psychiatrist took the opposite approach. He refused to give Stuart's "emotional disorder" a name. In some cases of mixed features, a diagnosis is legitimately deferred. But in most situations diagnoses have been withheld from both patients and their relatives on the premise that this kind of "labeling" might influence familial reactions and the patient's prognosis. This was likely the rationale here, because of the psychiatrist's apparent conviction that he could help Stuart avoid hospitalization with what presumably was a major emphasis on psychotherapy during the six months prior to the first inpatient admission.

Joni thus felt victimized on two counts: as a working widow who had been influenced by what she viewed as psychiatric salesmanship into paying hard-earned dollars for unsatisfactory treatment, and as an unwitting contributor to her son's relapse. Joni obviously feels abused by the psychiatrist, who failed to recognize her son's accelerating psychosis—and from her description, the symptoms were indeed obvious—who delayed necessary inpatient treatment, and whose inaction led to a horrendous family situation and forced the mother to be the agent of admitting her psychotic son to the hospital. The psychiatrist, on the other hand, was undoubtedly acting in what he viewed as the best interests of the patient. Investing in outpatient treatment, he hoped to avoid the dual stigmatization of a diagnosis of schizophrenia and of psychiatric hospitalization.

Joni was very fortunate, of course, that Stuart went voluntarily and that the hospital admitted him. Unless there is adequate insurance, in many parts of the country patients with Stuart's symptoms are likely to be stabilized in a crisis emergency unit and released after a few days, rather than being maintained in treatment for two months. The hospital also offered an apparently competent and concerned social work staff, but their discharge planning was impeded by the lack of appropriate resources in the community.

Joni learned some hard lessons from her son's first hospital stay. First, she accepted the obvious lesson imparted by a concerned social worker that her son had an illness that precluded the fulfillment of former expectations. Second, she learned that parents sometimes have to contest the system in order to help their children attain an acceptable quality of life.

PARENTAL GUILT

Although Joni fortunately does not blame herself for her son's schizophrenia, like many parents she berates herself for having failed to recognize early-warning signals and wonders whether her acceptance of a six-month delay before hospitalization might have affected the course of illness. Family members are caught in the double-bind of feeling remiss if they do not follow professional advice and feeling remiss if following that advice produces an unsatisfactory outcome. In Joni's account there are multiple examples of self-recrimination. She "conveniently ignored" symptoms and waited too long to act; she felt that her son's illness meant she had failed as a mother; she selected a psychiatrist who failed to produce results; and she accepted professional discharge-planning that relegated her son to "fetid, filthy, slovenly" surroundings which may have exacerbated his illness.

Like many family members, Joni was caught in the dilemma of wanting to do the right thing, which operationally involved following professional directives, and letting her guilt interfere with an objective assessment of professional wisdom. She knew that it doesn't make much sense to send a "dependent and needy" young adult away from his family on the pretext that a dirty, disorganized board and care home will prepare him for independent living. She also recognized that the social worker's admonitions about avoiding dependency meshed very well with her own need to avoid living with a difficult and demanding adult child. Stuart's return to the family home might indeed have caused grief both to his mother and to his siblings. Joni thus followed the path of many parents—trying to find a better quality of life for her son, only to have him evicted from group homes and treatment programs because of his uncooperative behavior, failure to take medications, and occasional alcohol abuse. And as Stuart becomes progressively worse, Joni appears to feel guilty because she was unable to prevent his decompensations and to save her other children from their effects.

In Western culture, which places great stock in personal control and solutions for every problem, guilt seems to be a ubiquitous response to illness in a child. This is rarely the case in traditional cultures that have greater acceptance of external causality. Parents feel that if only they had done this, or not done that, the disorder might have been avoided. Psychiatrist Kenneth Terkelsen has described working with parents who cling to the notion that families cause schizophrenia because this explanation provides a means of expiation and approval from authority figures who then might be able to heal their child. The parent thinks, "If I am the bad one, then I can change my behavior and my child will get well." Guilt thus becomes a means of keeping hope alive. But today we know that schizophrenia is not caused by parents, and that symptoms can be exacerbated by a variety of stressors, particularly by the patient's own failure to take medications. With no basis in fact, the effect of guilt on the grieving parent and on the parent-child relationship can be highly destructive.

GRIEVING AND LOSS

Families often recall a premorbid history that contrasts sharply with the conventional clinical picture of the awkward, withdrawn loner who later becomes psychotic. In Joni's recollection, Stuart, the young man who developed schizophrenia, was the brightest of her three offspring, an outstanding athlete and student, a popular young man with many friends.

Many families report similar memories of seemingly highly functional adolescents, many of whom decompensate under the stress of university study, new jobs, and/or leaving the supports of home to live in another city. In all situations in which early psychotic episodes crystallize into long-term illness, there is an experience of dual loss—of the person who was, and of the person who might have been. In cases in which the young person showed exceptional capabilities, the feelings of loss may be felt even more keenly. Although parents inevitably grieve for unfulfilled promise, this is not an issue of the dashing of parental expectations. Rather, the parent shares empathic grief with a child who well realizes his past capabilities and mourns his own lost hopes and unfulfilled aspirations.

Young persons who have been incapacitated by mental illness are well aware of their lost developmental stages of learning and are acutely sensitive to their differences from age-mates and peers. They can see that others of their own age are completing their education, starting careers, getting married, and having families. Typically, they both desire and fear the demands of these social roles. It is not surprising that young persons with a diagnosis of schizophrenia and a history of hospitalization are reluctant to encounter generational peers or relatives from whom they are now experientially alienated and in whose presence they can only feel inferior and ill-at-ease.

It is also not surprising that among hospitalized patients, home visits often are followed by exacerbated symptoms and acting-out. Although such reactions have long been considered evidence of unhealthy family dynamics by insensitive professionals, the more obvious and parsimonious explanation is that exposure to ordinary family life in the outside world, followed by return to a mental hospital ward, simply reinforces the patient's feelings of separateness, alienation, and inferiority.

PROFESSIONALS' FAILURES TO COMMUNICATE AND EDUCATE

Professionals are often overalert to parental expectations and may misconstrue the sources of pressure on their patients. But professionals in many cases have relinquished their responsibilities in two important areas: to inform and to educate. Joni's experience with the psychiatrist who refused to give a diagnosis and offered no family education is fairly typical. She also appeared to receive no education from the hospital staff, beyond the advice that her son was unlikely to return to his former level of functioning but needed to be independent.

Many families do not receive even that level of information. Lacking knowledge of mental illness, and without specific instructions from hospital staff, families have no reason not to believe that there will be a speedy recovery from an initial psychotic episode. Indeed, many have anticipated an early return to school or work following their relative's discharge from hospitalization. A young person who has been released from the hospital but still sleeps all day, is withdrawn and reluctant to resume her former life, acts bizarrely, or refuses to maintain reasonable hygiene would be a source of exasperation to any ordinary family. Arguments and ultimatums may ensue, with a resultant cycle of decompensation and readmission. In other cases, a young person may be overeager to return to school or work and make up for lost time, oversubscribing to courses and activities with the enthusiastic encouragement of well-meaning family members. In both examples the patient's likely relapse might have been easily averted by family education on the nature and limitations of mental illness and by help with setting appropriate expectations and goals.

For many years, families were excluded from any contact with the therapists who diagnosed and served their loved ones. They were relegated to the role of providing information on background and denied any participation in the treatment process. In psychodynamic approaches, the rationale was and continues to be that any contact with family members contaminates transference, betrays confidentiality, and destroys the trust needed for the therapeutic alliance. However, family members never have been given any rationale for the evasiveness, deflection of questions, and often outright rejection they have encountered in their frantic search for information. Systems-oriented family therapies traditionally have been based on the premise that the patient is symptom bearer of the family's psychopathology. Even today some prominent family therapists, such as Matteo Selvini, dispute the biological basis of major mental illnesses and the need for antipsychotic medications, arguing instead that family therapy will "cure" schizophrenia.

Fortunately, families are learning more about the biological aspects of schizophrenia through the research and books of world experts. The role of the National Alliance for the Mentally Ill in publicizing and disseminating the latest research findings on schizophrenia has been a major factor in family education. With respect to the mental health system itself, however, it is only in recent years that families have been able sometimes (and not always) to obtain enough information so that they may establish appropriate expectations and learn the most beneficial ways of dealing with their ill relatives.

Practitioners who use psychoeducational intervention, supportive family counseling, family consultation, and family education have finally provided the type of interventions that families have long desired: support and understanding of the family's agony, education about the illnesses and medications, behavior management techniques, and problem-solving strategies.

THE AGONY OF THE SINGLE CAREGIVER

Studies of families of persons with mental illness demonstrate that even in two-parent families, the major caregiving tasks typically are fulfilled by one person, usually the mother. In a few cases the single caregiver task is fulfilled by a sibling; here the dynamics are somewhat different but the burden may be almost as great. Joni's task is exacerbated by not having another adult with whom to share the burden. She has no mate, and her other children offer little help and are even impediments. Joni tries to keep her family's life as normal as possible, to integrate Stuart and whatever friends he can find into family life, to keep a relationship going between Stuart and his siblings. But the harder she tries, the more she seems to fail.

The sibling patterns in this family are very common. Siblings suffer terribly from the experience of mental illness in the family. Julie Johnson, a professional social worker and founder of the NAMI Sibling and Adult Children Network, describes her peers as "hidden victims." Inevitably, siblings are embarrassed by the behavior of the person who is mentally ill, but sometimes this poses a real threat to their own stability and to the maintenance of friendships with others. Siblings can be stigmatized, alienated, and obstracized because of a brother's illness. In this family, Daphne has suffered the loss of an older brother, and Bob has suffered the loss of a younger brother who might have been his companion and friend. Stuart's former reputation as a popular athlete and an outstanding student adds to the loss.

The story mentions that the siblings have fears that they too might become mentally ill, another common theme in sibling accounts. In some families, siblings may feel they have to make up for their brother's or sister's illness by overachieving, by protecting the parent from too many life disappointments. They may fear that they will have to take over the caregiving role after the parent is gone. Many siblings find the bizarre or offensive behaviors and the family disruption too burdensome to bear, and distance themselves both emotionally and geographically from the problem. Bob's apparent rejection of Stuart is an example of this self-protective behavior, but it makes Joni's burden even harder to bear.

Joni's agony is also exacerbated by Stuart's pushing her away, particularly when he is very ill and needs her attention the most. Often a mentally ill young adult will resist parental caregiving in an effort to assert independence. Sometimes this is a positive coping mechanism. The effort to give the appearance of normalcy and autonomy is often adaptive, and carries the seeds of incentive. In Stuart's case, however, and given his lifestyle, his rejection of any help connotes illness denial and is concordant with his tendency toward self-destructive behaviors.

The multiple roles that the single parent is forced to play generate both physical and emotional stress. The single parent is much more likely to become emotionally overinvolved, and research on expressed emotion shows this is likely to be damaging to the patient as well as burdensome to the parent. Joni verbalizes her struggle with avoiding this kind of overinvolvement. She says, "I have become consumed by Stuart's disease. It is hard to keep myself separated from him." But she wants to be "separated enough that I am not worried about him all the time." The problem is that the system seems to offer her no way out. There is no evidence of a case manager, a knowledgeable contact person, or of any continuity of care in Stuart's long journey through the mental health system. It is Joni who always has to bail out Stuart and find appropriate care.

In many situations such as this, there is mutual overinvolvement that often takes a highly negative form. When one person assumes the entire burden, the patient is often more likely to project hostility onto the helper and to blame him or her for everything that goes wrong. The long-term dependency needs are both frustrating and frightening to psychiatrically disabled young adults. Since they cannot fulfill an age-appropriate social role, they continue to be enmeshed in the dependency-independence conflicts of adolescence. Thus a twenty-eight-year-old may respond to his mother as he did at fifteen—with moodiness, anger, and acting-out. They may idealize the missing or dead parent and blame the single parent for the loss of the other.

Psychodynamic patterns of these relationships also suggest that patients may blame the primary nurturers, the long-term sacrificers, for their inability to give the patient a better life. It is like a cumulative debt in which there is a positive linear relationship between giving and expectation; demand grows increasingly stronger from the debtor the more that is given.

The parent may respond with a range of coping strategies. A form of active coping may involve fighting with professionals about the best way to proceed. The parent views herself or himself as the only one who really cares about the patient and who knows her/his needs and suicidal potential. This may infuriate professionals and reinforce their prejudices, but it often brings needed services for the patient. A sister once proudly reported to her support group that she had screamed and carried on in a crisis emergency room precisely to elicit the staff's hostility so that they would feel sorry for her brother and admit him to inpatient care.

In maladaptive coping, there may be denial, excessive indulgence, or avoidance. Denial may burden the child with undue expectations and critical hostility (he is not really that sick), but he may be equally hampered by emotional overinvolvement and indulgence (he is too sick to be accountable). Both of these familial responses have been associated with a poor course of illness in patients. Some parents may respond by distancing themselves emotionally, or avoidance by drink or substance abuse, but this rarely happens. More often families learn a form of benign acceptance. In the best type of adaptive modes, they learn to convey a message of respect to their ill family members, hold them accountable for appropriate behavior, but do not burden them with undue performance demands that they cannot fulfill.

In some respects the psychological burden of the single parent can be less than that of two-parent families. When families lack education about mental illness and are unprepared for its multiple responsibilities, conflict is almost inevitable. Parents absorb frequently dubious psychological knowledge from the popular media, and are likely to believe that someone in the family caused the illness—usually the other parent. This conviction may even be reinforced by inappropriate psychodynamic or family therapies that view the patient's symptoms as a way of keeping the family together. Many couples respond with mutual blaming and recrimination, and too many marriages have been dissolved because of ignorance about the causes of schizophrenia and the attrition of energies needed to meet its demands. Although, as Joni's story shows, single parents are likely to blame themselves for not being perceptive enough or not having acted soon enough, recriminations from a mate are happily missing. Missing also in the single-caregiver situation are battles about treatment decisions and the best way to proceed. It is unlikely, however, that these issues counterbalance the pain of bearing the burden alone.

DILEMMAS AND DEFICITS OF THE SYSTEM

Stuart's experiences highlight basic deficits in the mental health system. Conditions in many group homes are deplorable, exacerbating the intolerable life situation of persons already suffering from private terrors and low self-esteem. Stuart is extruded from programs and moves from one setting to another because of his rejection of medications and aversive behaviors. In many systems it is the sickest persons with schizophrenia—precisely those who should not be subjected to destabilizing life surroundings—who are constantly being uprooted and moved from place to place when they start acting-out. Joni complains legitimately about the paradoxical aspects of a treatment system in which people with a known chronic disease are kicked out of a program at exactly the time when they clearly need the most help.

Some mental health systems have adopted no-eject, no-reject policies, but the dilemma remains of how to deal with grossly disruptive behaviors. As Joni points out, these behaviors are often manifested by the sickest patients who need the most help. Yet the behavior of these sick patients often disrupts programs and keeps them from fulfilling their treatment goals. One client's misbehavior may exacerbate the symptoms of many others, and in some cases the behavior is assaultive toward vulnerable peers.

The pattern of moving was repeated when Stuart decided to drive to Colorado, ending with a psychotic episode and incarceration. Although the Colorado District Attorney told Joni he didn't want to put Stuart in a mental hospital because he might be there for years, no state wants the expense and hassle of hospitalizing a nonresident. The pattern of getting rid of someone whom nobody wants to deal with by putting him on an interstate bus or a community mental health center van and moving him from here to there was repeated.

Finally, Joni's terrifying experience of Stuart's attack with the bread knife gives some inkling of the terrible ordeal of many family members and the failures of the system to provide preventive remedies against this happening again. Although people with schizophrenia actually commit few crimes beyond the harmless misdemeanors of the homeless mentally ill, violence is not unknown in families of the mentally ill. Studies of NAMI families indicate that in almost a quarter physical harm has been threatened or committed, and almost 40 percent report at least one suicidal attempt. The incident in which a terrified mother calls the police and they arrive only to find a calmed-down or sleeping patient is familiar to every family support group. The police cannot act unless they observe behavior that is dangerous to the self or others. In some cases the patient then turns on the family members who have called the police, initiating a cycle for which there is no apparent solution. In this case, as in many others, involuntary commitment is avoided at a heavy price to the family and presumably to the patient as well.

Would Stuart become stabilized, more at peace with himself and more functional, in a special kind of program with understanding, empathic, and accepting staff? This is what we like to tell ourselves with the design and implementation of model programs. Obviously he has not benefited from the programs in the community in which he lives. Would he become better, as some patients have done, in a peer-operated program run by role models who were once sick enough to have shared some of his experiences?

The end of this story is yet to come. Stuart has moved into yet another inadequate group home, where he may once again stop taking medications, become psychotic, and start the cycle all over again. Meanwhile, Joni wonders whether she will ever be able to have some life of her own.

HOW CAN JONI BE HELPED?

First of all, Joni needs a *support group*. She needs to share her feelings with people who have suffered through similar circumstances and who may be able to offer comfort, advice, and alternative solutions. Joni needs to work out her conflicting feelings of obligation, sorrow, and resentment. She could certainly benefit from psychotherapy, but often this can be done within the support group framework as well. In fact, when professionals conduct psychoeducational family interventions, research by McFarlane and his associates shows there is good empirical evidence that the multifamily group experience is superior to working with individual families. The sharing and support from others has intrinsic therapeutic value.

A good psychotherapist may be able to help Joni set limits both for herself and for Stuart. A support group can often speed this process along by teaching techniques that have worked in similar cases. In years of working with support groups, I have often found that very hard decisions can be reached through insight, but in some cases they are implemented only when the group insists that this is the right thing to do. Parents are often faced with decisions that go against their deepest nurturing instincts, such as getting a commitment order, extruding an abusive sick child from the home, or refusing to bail out someone who is finally taking medication in jail. These choices are much easier when others give encouragement. The essential message is this: "In order to be a good mother, you have to be a bad mother first."

Joni needs *respite*. The narrative gives little evidence of any alternative sources of support. Does Joni herself have a mother or father, siblings, or any other relatives who can give her a hand with Stuart? The narrative suggests that she has taken the problem entirely on her own shoulders, undoubtedly assuming that others will not understand or want to deal with someone as disruptive as her son. She speaks about a Christmas dinner to which she and her family invited guests, presumably relatives and friends. Stuart's bizarre behavior may have alienated others in the family network, and perhaps he has already suffered rejection. But our experience is that while some relatives distance themselves from the ill person and have even been taught by the popular media to blame the mother, other relatives are often willing to help but do not know how. Many parents suffer alone and shoulder the entire burden because they are embarrassed to discuss the problem openly and anticipate that others will be reluctant to become involved. Although stigma and social rejection are ubiquitous realities, we also find that social isolation is often unnecessarily self-imposed.

Joni's other children are now adults. Although they have certainly suffered as a result of Stuart's illness, they have observed their mother's ordeal as well. In an effort to spare them, Joni may have deprived them of their right as well as their obligation to be a support to their brother. Although Bob has openly distanced himself, he may yet feel a need to reach out and help, but does not know how. Joni needs to sit down with her children and allow them to help her share the burden. She needs to involve them in planning for her own future and for what will happen to

Stuart after she is gone. We assume that Stuart is receiving federal entitlements, but do not know whether Joni is representative payee, whether she has made a will or provisions for Stuart after she is gone, and what role her other children will play in the process. Even though the siblings are adults, Joni needs to reinstate her authority as parent to require them to fulfill their familial obligations. She is getting older and soon will be an aging parent, with diminishing physical and emotional strength to deal with her son's illness. Some siblings have their own resentments about the disruptions engendered by the illness and need to maintain their distance, but others are resentful because they have been excluded or "protected" by a parent overinvolved with the sick child. Joni may learn that her other children felt shut out from the problem and welcome the chance to help; she just never asked them in the right way before.

Joni needs to have some *feeling of control* of her life. Membership in a support group is tremendously important for psychological sustenance, but Joni's happiness will ultimately depend on having the resources in her community that can take Stuart off her hands and give him a decent life. For this she needs to join with others for public education and legislative advocacy. Systems do not develop on their own; they are created through the political process by influencing people in power.

When Stuart was discharged from his first hospital stay, it was to a board and care home with deplorable conditions. He wandered through a network of similarly bad situations. It was almost as if the system was designed to make his illness worse rather than better. Joni, like other parents, needs to become involved in monitoring, oversight, protection, and advocacy to make sure that the system becomes accountable for its case dispositions and that it regulates standards. She needs to make sure that the system develops good treatment programs that are rehabilitative rather than custodial and that are required to deal with heterogeneity rather than imposing a single program on all clients and extruding those who do not fit in. The system must be mandated to serve its sickest and most difficult patients and to make sure that they do not fall through the cracks.

Local NAMI affiliates, the local mental health association, and protection and advocacy committees are good channels for exerting these kinds of pressures on the system. In areas where there is no activity, families have often formed local AMI groups by placing ads in the paper or working with their local community mental health centers to form parent groups. This is hard work, but Joni already has given evidence of her energy and commitment, much of it dispersed to the winds in a vain effort to help her son. The same level of energy devoted to organization with other families might yield more concrete results. Research by Noh and Turner shows that a sense of mastery is the best way of alleviating family burden in mental illness. Political action to improve the mental health system is a very positive way of asserting mastery.

Finally, Joni needs *hope*. Stuart's story is a dismal one, but it is not unusual. Stuart keeps acting out and seemingly destroying every opportunity for rehabilitation, but this is his maladaptive way of coping. He is still flailing about for a sense of self and for a place in life, and refuses to accept the identity or limitations of a person with a mental illness.

Under the layers of schizophrenia, there is still Stuart the person. Many of his positive personal qualities and premorbid talents may still be intact and ready to be released under favorable circumstances. Like Joni, Stuart also needs a support group, but he needs one in which he can exert a sense of personhood rather than patienthood. Some psychosocial rehabilitation programs will give members a strong message of their value as human beings and will encourage the type of autonomy Stuart is so desperately seeking. Stuart could benefit even more from linking up with a consumer group—a group composed of psychiatric patients. The consumer movement has people in it who once were as sick as Stuart and who have been given new roles and opportunities for expression and for development of organizational talents. This is one avenue in which the anger and protest are often channeled into positive action.

Largely because of NAMI's efforts, government agencies and funding sources are now requiring family and consumer representation on governance and advisory boards, protection and advocacy committees, and mental health planning bodies. For the first time in history, mental health consumers now have some control over the decisions that affect their lives. If Stuart could be convinced to take part in consumer activity, he might have a role in this process. He might learn to value his identity rather than to reject it and to transcend its limitations by taking control of his own destiny.

But even if that does not take place, Stuart undoubtedly can have a better quality of life. He is still young, and there is evidence that for many people symptoms diminish and a higher level of functioning may be achieved over time. New medications are constantly being tested, and ultimately Stuart may find the right combination and be willing to take them. Even the most obdurate patients change as they become older and, hopefully, wiser about their lives.

3.

Slipping Through the Cracks:

Failure of the Mental Health System

SHIRLEY AND NEAL MATHEWS ARE KIND, gentle, and quiet, considerate not only with strangers and friends, but also with each other. They are both retired; he was a librarian and she a seamstress. Shirley sat down and turned to her husband, touching his arm. "I'm worried that I'll talk too much and you won't get a chance. You know how I can go on." Neal patted her hand. "I like to hear you talk, Shirl. You go on as much as you wish. I'll fill in when I want to." As it turned out, their conversation flowed from one to the other, almost as though with one voice. But despite their courtesy and apparent calm, it is transparent that the Mathews are suffering intolerable pain.

Anne, the second of their three daughters, is thirty-two years old. She is missing.

An exuberant, outgoing, and active girl in high school, Anne had a large circle of friends. A sunny young woman with a bubbling good nature, even as a little girl she had always been surrounded by chums. With her crinkly blue eyes and wiry red curls, fun-loving Anne was easy to love.

The first inkling that anything was wrong came when she dropped out of college during the spring quarter of her sophomore year. She came home and got a job. That in itself didn't seem to be something to worry about, but Shirley and Neal did notice a change in her personality. Vivacious Anne was unaccountably gloomy. She was subdued, and noticeably silent and private about her reasons for withdrawing from the university. Her parents concluded that she must have experienced some kind of stress while at school. Neal and Shirley are not the kind of people who would pry. They are patient and sensitive. It wouldn't occur to them to tamper with their daughter's privacy.

Anne worked through that summer and returned to school in the fall. But she didn't go back to the dormitory or her sorority, and she changed roommates. She stopped seeing most of her friends. Again, with very little to go on, Anne's parents had uneasy feelings about her.

Their concerns about her subsided, however, by the time she graduated from the university. That summer Anne went to Europe with two girl-friends. She seemed carefree and intent on having a good time. For the past few years Anne had squirreled away most of her job money, planning for this postgraduation summer trip. Happy and proud and relieved about her graduation, her parents made her dream possible by giving her the airfare as a graduation present.

Much of her summer was spent traveling with a young man from Sweden. Peter Ekstrom had been a fellow student of Anne's at the university; they met during their senior year. The two young people spent most of their time together, and Anne often brought him to her home. Both Shirley and Neal liked Peter, and they were pleased that their daughter was seeing Europe through the eyes of a European.

When Anne returned from Europe, Peter bombarded her with letters and phone calls. He asked her to marry him. He invited her to come to Stockholm and meet his family. He wrote a formal letter to Neal and Shirley telling them of his intentions. Anne decided "yes."

Shirley recollected that even though she was going to lose her daughter, it was a very exciting time. Peter's long-distance phone calls hummed through the house. Anne was alternately dreamlike or leaping around like a young gazelle. Tenderly, Neal remembers that his daughter never looked more beautiful.

But as her departure drew near, Anne prepared for her trip to Scandinavia in a very haphazard fashion. She was easily distracted. She had wildly fluctuating moods, often alternating between sullenness and irritability. Even though she was twenty-three years old, she seemed unable to get anything ready. Ultimately, her younger sister Cindy and her mother had to pack for her. And the Mathews thought it very peculiar when, on the day of her departure, she spent the morning in a puzzlingly desultory manner. She left things strewn about her room, she wandered irrationally in and out of the house, and periodically she strolled back and forth over to an elderly neighbor's home, a family with whom she had never been particularly friendly. Anne seemed amnesic.

"We were very worried," Neal said. "Even for a lovesick girl, Anne's behavior was odd, and certainly out of character for our middle girl. We didn't say it to each other then, but she did seem crazy. Of course we let her go. We just crossed our fingers and hoped that things would right themselves."

Anne had been in Sweden one week when the Mathews received a telephone call from her: "Mom and Dad, I'm coming home." Shirley and Neal were startled but not surprised. On the trip back from the airport, she said not a word; a crackling tension was palpable during the half-hour journey. Anne ignored their tentative attempts to make conversation. She stared out the window. When they arrived home, she grabbed her bags and strode to her room.

For the next few days she remained in her room, maintaining only minimal contact with her family. Finally, when she did emerge from her self-imposed isolation, her parents found their good-natured daughter transformed. She was unpleasant, sharp, curt and always angry. Anne was a distinctly altered young woman.

Even so, her parents again asked no questions. After many sleepless nights and long days, mulling over and rehashing Anne's every move, they came to the conclusion that her behavior was due to rejected love. Years later, by which time they knew that their daughter was mentally ill, Anne told her mother about her visit to Peter Ekstrom's family. She maintained that she had been tortured and drugged during the few days she had spent in Stockholm. By then, however, it was too late to pry apart delusion and reality.

Weeks passed and Anne made no effort to pull herself together. Neal felt very agitated. He told her that she had better put her life in order and get a job. "After all, Annie, whatever has occurred is over and done with." Neal was clear and firm.

Anne did find work. She got a good job in the accounting office at a local university. She appeared to be doing well enough when quite suddenly she quit. She had had a routine job evaluation and was told that she was giving a fair performance but needed to make certain improvements. Neal remembered, "I couldn't comprehend what was going on, but I certainly did understand one thing. It was that as far as Anne was concerned, whatever happened was always somebody else's fault." Both parents had become aware that they had to treat Anne with kid gloves. Their daughter could not stand any kind of criticism.

After that Anne had a series of jobs. She waited on tables, answered the phone for a small, sccdy law office, and was a box girl at a local grocery store. But she was fired from each job within a few weeks. The Mathews recalled that they felt very perplexed. Neal said, "Here we were still supporting her—with no light at the end of that tunnel—and not in any way understanding what the problem was."

Anne was leading a reclusive and isolated life; she had cut off all her friends; she didn't see anyone; she was quite alone. "Day after day, night after night, Anne would be in her room, all by herself. It was as though she had made herself her own prisoner. I ached for her," Shirley said.

The Mathews describe themselves as a close family; they feel disloyal when they talk about their family problems in public. Even now, after all that has happened, they feel shabby talking so openly about their daughter. "Even though we *now* know better, we still have nagging feelings that we are somehow at fault, that we did something wrong. We really felt blameworthy a lot during those early times, when we didn't understand what was going on. We had a deep sense of shame. And we felt confused because, you know—Neal and I—we knew that we've been caring parents."

Despite their wish not to expose Anne or themselves to public scrutiny, the Mathews asked Joanie, one of the young women who went to Europe with Anne, whether she had observed anything out of the ordinary on the trip. Joanie seemed puzzled at being questioned. "Anne was her regular good-guy self," she told Shirley and Neal. Either they had put the question to her in such a delicate manner that she misunderstood what they were talking about or she simply had not seen anything unusual in Anne's behavior.

Shirley said, "There was one odd little glitch in communication. Some girls from Anne's sorority told our younger daughter—quite some time after we came to know that Anne was mentally ill—that they believed Anne had had a nervous breakdown when she left school during her sophomore year. I've always wondered how it might have changed things if we had been told at the time. You know, we may be too careful about not imposing on other people's privacy. It looks like Anne has been more harmed than helped by our not wanting to butt in to her business."

When it became apparent that Anne was unable to hold a job, the Mathews began to feel very helpless. And this feeling of helplessness was to become all too familiar. Coincidental with Anne's inability to remain employed, she displayed what came to be an ongoing and continual concern about her health. Neal said, "Anne kept coming up with these ideas that she had various physical problems. I remember once calling the doctor to find out what the diagnosis was—we were paying for her medical care—and the nurse was very hostile. She said, 'We didn't know what to think of the way your daughter talked to the doctor. She used the most awful language.' Everybody saw all these manifestations of mental illness, but they just wanted to get her out of the office and be rid of her."

The medical whirligig did not let up. Anne complained about a whole litany of maladies with which she was certain she was afflicted. The list was long, including hypoglycemia, Epstein-Barr virus, and even AIDS. "By that time I didn't collapse because my daughter thought she was dying of AIDS. I was fairly certain that she had had no sexual contact, and anyway I thought she didn't look as though she had it.

"But there was no stopping Anne. She said she was sick and she couldn't work. We never told her she wasn't ill—after all, it's her body. I couldn't possibly know what was going on in her body. Yet when we tried to organize some health care for her, she refused. She insisted on calling all the shots.

"No matter what route we took to get medical attention for her, Anne would have nothing to do with it. Whenever she came up with one of her diseases, she would look up some doctor in the Yellow Pages and just take herself off to see him. She'd have all sorts of tests but inevitably she was found to be OK. She didn't have whatever disease she thought she had. Then she would be very angry and in a few months' time she would start the whole process again."

Gradually the Mathews faced the facts. They came to the conclusion that their daughter's odd behavior could no longer be easily explained away. Some close friends, Margie and Lewis, who had a mentally ill nephew, suggested that they attend a meeting for parents of mentally ill persons. This proved to be a watershed for them. While listening and talking to other parents, they recognized that Anne had many symptoms in common with other mentally ill young people.

"We felt so relieved," Neal said. "Now we knew what was wrong with our girl. Shirley and I were confident that now we could solve Anne's problems and—hallelujah—get our own lives back on track."

This heady time was short-lived. They decided to get some counseling. They presumed that a psychologist would be able to instruct them in ways to deal with Anne. But all too soon they realized that they had miscon-strued the situation. "Bluntly and in short order the psychologist told us, 'No point in your coming to counseling without Anne. It's Anne who needs the attention.' We felt like fools," Neal said.

Getting Anne to counseling was easier said than done. This goal proved to be a challenge that impelled them helter-skelter to mental health agen-cies, to hospitals, to law enforcement officials, and to still more doctors. They had been advised that if they wanted help for Anne, they needed a diagnosis or at least some agreement that she was mentally ill. It was implied that with a diagnosis in hand, some kind of hospital commitment and subsequent treatment would follow.

To their surprise, Shirley and Neal found their lives to be even more chaotic. Theatrical elements of chase and suspense now entered their everyday world. They had seen themselves as average people. They lived simply and modestly, enjoying the accomplishments of their three lively daughters. Now their lives had taken on a splintered, fragmented, and distraught character. Between them both they could not find a peaceful moment. The Mathews had become driven people.

"So many things were upsetting us," Neal said. "Our two other daugh-ters, Cindy and Jean, were beginning to feel jealous about the amount of time that we spent with Anne. Even though they no longer lived at home, they felt that we never had time for them, or when we did see them we just talked nonstop about Anne. They had always been close to Anne when they were younger, but now it was impossible for them to continue any kind of relationship with her. And there was no doubt that the sight of us pouring our resources into what had become a chronic situation was a source of extreme concern and irritation for them.

"We felt so frustrated. We cared as much about them as we did about Anne," Neal said. "We would try to explain to them that we had to look after Anne. She was sick. She had no one but us. We would tell them that we would do the same for them if they needed us. It didn't make any difference. One look at their faces and you knew they felt as though they were less important to us than she."

Shirley and Neal tried to persuade Anne to see a psychiatrist. "I ar-ranged for her to be admitted to the psychiatric unit at University Hospi-tal." Neal recalled that Anne laughed when he told her about the arrangements. "She was adamant that she was not mentally ill. She re-fused to cooperate in any way. I remember she said to me, 'Dad, I know

I have something wrong with me physically and that's all. You're just trying to upset me with all this talk about mental illness.' Then she would go back up to her room and refuse to talk with us.

"It was very hard for us to believe that she didn't recognize how peculiar she was. I guess none of us see ourselves as others see us, but we could scarcely believe that she had no insight at all. Her view of what was going on was so completely different from our view. That really shook us. She was so sure she was right and we were wrong. And she made such a big thing about our being the ones who were upsetting her."

Anne's obsession with her physical health continued. "We decided that we might be able to get her some psychiatric help if we cooperated with her 'medical forays,' as I used to call them," Neal said.

"One time when she said she had a pain in her head," Shirley remembered, "I drove her to the emergency room of a reputable downtown hospital. She had given up driving, so I used to drive her whenever I could. When she started to lose her jobs, she stopped driving of her own accord. Needless to say, we didn't urge her to use the car.

"I was hopeful that I might be able to get some help. I had heard that this hospital had a good mental health clinic. I parked the car and she went and signed herself in at the admitting desk. I joined her in the waiting room and sat with her until they called her name. She went in to see the doctor alone. When she went in to be examined, I walked over to the receptionist. I felt terribly embarrassed, but I forced myself to ask if she would be kind enough to alert the doctor that my daughter was very ill—mentally ill. I explained that I was desperate to get her some help.

"The receptionist looked at me coldly, as though I was a meddling old woman. Her voice was icy. 'Oh, they'll know what to do.' Then she turned back to her work. She ignored me. I remember walking slowly back to a seat and sitting there feeling enraged, ashamed, and helpless. In about fifteen minutes Anne returned and we just went home.

"We tried another tack. From time to time Anne had been to see an internist at that same hospital. So I called directly to the hospital's mental health clinic and explained to them our worries about our daughter. They put a social worker on the line and I told her the whole story over again, making it very clear that we could not persuade Anne to come into the clinic herself. I asked the social worker if it would be possible for her to call Anne's internist and alert him to our concerns about our daughter. The social worker sounded very sympathetic and kind. She assured me that she would do what she could to help me. She even told me that this internist had worked with some of her schizophrenic patients at the clinic. We never heard from any of them—just another dead end."

Neal and Shirley went to their local county mental health clinic, where they talked with Mike Unger, a social worker whom they found to be a "very understanding fellow." Neal said, "Remember, Shirley, how carefully he listened to us? He asked us the kind of questions which made us feel that we were on the right track; we really felt that these people would be able to help us. Mike spent a lot of time with us and took many detailed notes. Toward the end of the interview he suggested that he and another social worker come over to our house and see Anne for themselves."

Shirley nodded. "I was certain that things were going to be OK. After all, these social workers were in the business of dealing with the mentally ill. It seemed obvious to me that they would have the skills and know-how that would persuade Anne to get help. I actually thought while we were chatting with Mike that our problems were about to be solved."

"But what a fiasco it turned out to be." Neal smiled grimly. "Mike and another social worker were chatting with me in our family room. Shirl had gone upstairs to get Anne. Before I had time to say much of anything, Anne came swooshing down those stairs and, directly, she took right over as though *she* was conducting the interview. And she was very confrontational. 'Why are you folks drumming up business for your office?' Those were the first words out of her mouth.

"She never sat down. She stood there looking right at them with her arms akimbo. 'Whatever my parents have told you is not true. I'm not depressed, I have plenty of friends—and my life is just fine! She said it just like that. Her eyes were blazing with anger. Then she turned around and stalked out of the room and back upstairs.

"You could have heard a pin drop. We felt like fools. After the social workers left we couldn't help thinking that they must have thought that *we* were the ones who were crazy."

The social workers, however, did make a suggestion to the Mathews. "While we were standing by the front door saying goodbye, Mike and the young woman kind of mumbled to us that we might want to find Anne a place to live outside of the family home. They seemed to be telling us that it might help our daughter to learn to live more independently. I remember their saying something like, 'We all might get along better with that kind of arrangement.'

"Anne, of course, had no income," Neal said. "I was completely supporting her. She never received any welfare. Even so, Shirley and I agreed that it was worth a try. We figured it might be better for Anne, and also it might be better for us. We hoped that we would be able to tolerate our concerns for Anne if we had more space between her and us. Our worries about our daughter consumed us. We didn't think or talk about anything else. It seemed worth the chance even if we would be pinched for money."

"We found her," Shirley said, "a little dumpy studio apartment on the northwest side of town. Other than the fact that she had her own place, many things did not change. She would walk home, and even though it was a long haul that didn't put her off. Anne would come over and have her meals at our house. She came almost every day, and we would drop in over there all the time as well. We couldn't help ourselves—we were so worried about her.

"Anne did a marvelous job of furnishing this little apartment. I was proud of her." Shirley looked at Neal and they smiled at each other. Neal leaned over and gently took his wife's hand. He rubbed her hand, as though he were warming her. Shirley went on talking. "She took old chairs and a falling-apart trundle bed from our attic. I found her some pretty chintz—greens and blues, her favorite colors—and she re-covered the chairs and fixed up the bed so that it looked like a sofa. She was so neat, but nothing ever happened in this room.

"Everything was precisely in place, but it was as though it was completely empty—it sticks in my mind that there was nothing on the coffee table. It was as though no one lived there. Once it was all done, she always kept us standing by the front door. We never went beyond the front area, she would stand there in front of us blocking our way into the room. We kept hoping that this would all pass and that she would be like other girls. It was obvious that she never saw anyone but us. All this time she was completely alone."

Neal said, "Even so, Annie did have what you might call a job while she was in that apartment, she did do something. She always had been a very artistic girl. When she was young she was very creative with everything that she did. She could always make things look good, just like Shirl described when Annie fixed up her apartment.

"Her older sister, Jean, is the buyer for a string of airport gift shops. She is based in Los Angeles. When Anne made up some wildflower cards that were really beautiful we sent them to Jean, and she was able to sell them all. We were all pleased as punch. Jean gave her a really big order. Anne immediately started to work obsessively and"—Neal momentarily closed his eyes—"insisted on doing things all her way. She decided that this whole huge order of cards had to be sent at one time. Well, of course, it was impossible. The first cards came out pretty well, but then it was downhill all the way and the last ones were certainly not very sharp.

"I will never forget the mailing of those cards," Neal said. "I had given up arguing with Anne. There was no reasoning with her. She told me that everything she did was the way it should be— 'You don't know anything, Dad.' So we went along with her. We filled boxes and boxes with those cards and carted the whole lot down to the post office. I paid for the postage. Of course, Jean couldn't sell that many at one time, even if they had been well done. I believe Jean had to throw most of them away. I remember her saying to me, 'Daddy, I told Annie again and again not to send them in one batch.' Jean felt badly. She really had wanted to help. But Anne wouldn't budge an inch, it was all her way or nothing. After that it was pretty much nothing.

"For a while I thought that supporting Anne was going to be a temporary situation. It really never occurred to me that this was it. But we gradually became aware that this could go on forever. As long as we didn't make waves, it looked like the status quo would continue. Once or twice I broached the subject to Anne; she would kind of look away from me and say something like, 'All I want from you is food and shelter.' I didn't know how to deal with her. Here is my daughter, obviously not well, what am I to do? I wasn't going to let her go hungry.

"Anne was in charge of us. We were desperate to get help. But here we were again back at the starting line: no help for Anne without a diagnosis. So this time Shirl and I went to a different county mental health clinic. We went to one in the part of town where Anne had her apartment. They were very straightforward. They told us to file a complaint and then they would go over to Anne's place and check her out.

"It was the same story all over again. The social workers phoned us and said, 'As Anne is today there is no way that she will be committed. She will easily convince a judge that she is not mentally ill. Anne doesn't come near to fitting the criteria for commitment to a mental hospital: she's obviously not a danger to anyone and certainly not a danger to herself—she knows how to eat.' Huh." Neal paused. "I have heard since that unless a mentally ill person is a month away from starving to death, she doesn't get committed."

Shirley said, "But by now we were much more upset because we knew that Anne was really very ill. It wasn't just that she was an odd girl anymore. I was really afraid for her. She had started telling me the strangest stories, which I realized were too bizarre to be true. For eight hours one day—I was exhausted—I wrote notes copying down everything she said. She told me that she had been tortured by our neighbors and that it was all part of a conspiracy that had been going on since she was eight years old. I didn't act shocked. I just listened and wrote it all down. She saw all kinds of connections between people who didn't even know each other. That boy from Sweden, Peter Ekstrom, she told me that he and his family were also in on the plot. Well, by now we knew she was terribly ill and we felt frantic."

"Yes," Neal said, "it was very tough for us. We had no doubts that Anne was very seriously ill, but we were beginning to realize that nobody could do anything about it. It wasn't that the clinic people didn't listen to us. They were even sympathetic. But it seemed to me like a waste of money for them to even be operating when much of the time they couldn't really help. They said their hands were tied.

"As I see it, the reasoning behind the laws that impede a diagnosis and commitment for the mentally ill is cockeyed. All this garbage about harm to self or others: as though that is the only criterion for being crazy. You can say all you want about the American Civil Liberties Union wanting to be sure that somebody isn't wrongly committed, but to make so many people suffer seems to me to be a far greater wrong. My daughter is mentally ill. And they have interfered with my being able to help my child. I feel that I have been tortured. People don't realize what it is like to be forced to stand by and watch your child get sicker and sicker. I know what she needs and yet I'm forbidden to help her.

"Well, with no other options we listened to the so-called experts at the mental health clinic. They told us that we should stop taking care of Anne. 'The first step,' they said, 'is to discontinue paying her rent.' They said if we took away her underpinnings she would deteriorate faster and then they would be able to pick her up and get a hospital commitment for her. Shirl and I liked these people, these social workers, and we felt that they wanted to help us. They were mental health professionals and we felt assured that they knew what they were doing. We would never have taken such a drastic step without their advice."

Neal and Shirley told Anne that they were going to stop paying her rent. They suggested that she go over to the local clinic and that the social workers there might be able to help her out. They brought up the subject of jobs again. They explained to her that she should notify her landlady.

"The apartment manager was a very nice woman who cared and worried about Anne," Shirley said. "She was very upset that we were doing this to our daughter. I was so embarrassed. I tried to explain to her why we were taking this course of action, even then I thought it sounded crazy. I told her that the social workers expected Anne to 'act-out' when the sheriff came to evict her. In effect we were pushing her to become psychotic so that she would be taken to the hospital, where she could be properly cared for.

"So the manager gave Anne her notice. And with our help Anne did manage to pack up a few things, which we took back to our house and stored for her. I remember those weeks as being dreamlike, kind of fuzzy and unreal. I couldn't believe what I was doing to my daughter. The last few nights, just before her eviction, she slept on the floor with only a blanket to cover her. There she was, poor thing, sleeping with this single blanket when the sheriff came for her. And she just got up and went out with him, as peaceful and docile as can be. He was a kind and gentle man, he even helped her carry some boxes down. He asked her if she knew where she was going and she told him 'No.' We were there, standing on the street, we felt such anguish that we couldn't stay away. She gave us some more things to store for her and then she walked off with her little suitcase. We didn't see her for a week."

Awkwardly, Neal and Shirley turned from each other as though they could not bear to remember their grief. "That was the most horrible week of my life," Shirley said. "For some reason it was worse then than now—maybe you get used to things, but also maybe we felt so terrible because we were directly responsible. After all, we didn't have to do what the social workers had suggested. Even though we did it freely, we did feel that we were coerced by the situation. We were so desperate to get Anne some help. I guess we had hoped that by doing something unpleasant something good would come out of it."

"I don't think we slept much that week," Neal said. "We would lie in bed wondering if she was in a shelter or if she had jumped off a bridge. Our imaginations tortured us. Toward the end of the week, in the middle of the night—it must have been about three in the morning—we heard the scrape of the garden chairs on the patio, directly outside our bedroom windows. And there—thank goodness—was Anne. Dear, dear Annie, she was trying to sleep on the garden chairs so that she wouldn't disturb us in the middle of the night."

"Of course, after she came back we took her in," Shirley said. "We had no difficulty deciding that what the social workers had told us to do was not right. What they call social work has become a lot of complicated rules that have more to do with the law than with people. What they told us to do was outrageous. We wouldn't put our dog out. I don't think we'd turn a stranger away. To think that we could do that to our own daughter. I'm still ashamed, angry even, to think that I, Shirley Mathews, watched my very own daughter be evicted from her apartment and that I didn't lift a finger when she walked off all alone."

A few weeks after Anne had returned home, a family friend told the Mathews about an opportunity for shared housing. "There was an elderly woman, a Mrs. O'Brien, who had had cancer surgery, she lived alone in a nice big house. Doug, her son, wanted someone to live in the house with her," Shirley said. "It sounded like a perfect situation for Anne. The job requirements were minimal, Anne's duties were to be simple: some cooking and a little cleaning. There was a woman who came in once a week to do the heavy cleaning and the son, Doug, did all the marketing. Mrs. O'Brien just wanted to be quiet and left alone. Since Doug was obviously a responsible person, he checked in with his mother every day, we felt that as so little was required of Anne, she probably could manage this pretty well. We were even hopeful that it might help her. She was only there for a short time, however, because toward the end of the second month Mrs. O'Brien died.

"Anne had told me that Mrs. O'Brien would go into the bathroom and sit there doing crossword puzzles. And that's where she was the day that she died. After she had been in the bathroom for a very long time, Anne knocked on the door and asked her if she was all right. Anne told me later she thought she heard Mrs. O'Brien say she was fine. A short time later when Doug telephoned, he told Anne to open the bathroom door and make sure his mother was OK. Anne went into the bathroom and found that she was dead."

"Anne was amazing," Neal remembered. "She didn't panic. She actually didn't show any emotion. First she telephoned Doug and then she called the police. After that she called me. All she said was, 'Daddy, will you come and get me? Mrs. O'Brien is dead.' I went right over. When I got there she seemed almost placid. I helped her gather her things and brought her back home.

"While I was helping her pack, I picked up off her dresser two old uncashed checks that had been made out to her by Doug O'Brien. They were the small, agreed-upon recompense for her work. I remember feeling bewildered. Annie was unable to do what seemed so simple. She hadn't gone and cashed these checks. She never did get her money. She was incapable of organizing something as simple as cashing a check. And she refused to make the checks out to us so that we could cash them for her. It was an education for us. She had been able to do some work for two months, but still couldn't understand how to care for herself."

"But even worse than that, within a few hours of Anne's return, we were shocked to see that she was in a gravely deteriorated condition," Shirley said. "When she had been at the O'Briens', we only saw her for maybe a half hour at a time. We realized when she came home that she could keep herself sort of pulled together if there was only time for a hello and a goodbye. But now we both knew we were looking at a terribly ill young woman."

Anne joined her parents at mealtimes. She would sit picking at her food; she ate scarcely anything. She rarely spoke, and when she did, what she said was clearly delusional. She was certain that their neighbors were coming in at night and poisoning the family's food. This was the reason she gave for her finicky eating habits. The dinner hour had become a time of unbearable tension. Shirley and Neal ate silently because they feared that they might upset Anne. Most of the time she appeared to be self-absorbed, almost locked into herself, unaware of her parents' presence. Gradually she came to the family meals less and less. The Mathews felt very conflicted. "It was such a relief to eat together without her being there," Shirley said. "But at the same time we were consumed with apprehension and worry about Anne.

"It was a very strange time. Anne's room and bathroom are upstairs on the second floor. Our bedroom is downstairs. Neal and I tried to go on with our lives as though things were normal. Of course there was nothing normal about the way we were living. Our daughter lived in our house, and it was as though she were a ghost. Sometimes whole days would go by and we never saw her. She rarely went out. Most of the time we heard no sound from her bedroom. Oh, it was obvious that she was using the bathroom, we could hear the water running, but we had no idea whether she was still in her pajamas or dressed.

"We knew that she slipped down to the kitchen to eat. I would put things out for her, and I wrote little notes on the refrigerator trying to tempt her to eat something that I had made especially for her. So we could see that she wasn't starving herself. Once or twice I would come upon her in the kitchen. She would look startled but she didn't run away. She would finish what she was doing. When I actually saw her eating something, that was shocking in itself. It was the way she ate. She would practically inhale a loaf of bread. I have never seen anyone eat so quickly."

"Shirley and I decided this couldn't go on," Neal said. "We had to make another attempt to get Anne some help. We had heard that there was a very good mental health clinic quite close to where we lived, one that we had not yet tried. The problem, we were told, was that they took only a limited number of patients. Even so, we thought they might be helpful and by now we didn't have much to lose.

"Right away we liked these folks. They were a very sensitive group. A young fellow, Jack Watson, talked with us and he said, 'Look—I really can't help unless I come over and see Anne.' We told him about all our other experiences with mental health clinics, how we had become suspicious that they might make things get worse. We stressed that we didn't want to spook Anne. We talked at length about whether or not we should tell Anne that he was coming to see her. He felt that was the right thing to do.

"That evening I went up the stairs and knocked on Anne's door. She barely opened her door. I could hardly see her face. I stood in the hall and told her that the next afternoon a counselor from a work clinic was coming to chat with her. I remember saying that they had a job-placement program—I didn't want to mention anything about mental health.

"I went on to tell her that this was a very positive program and I explained to her what was involved: that a counselor would learn a job with her so that if she became ill her counselor could take over until she felt better. I think I stressed that this meant that she wouldn't lose her job. Maybe I didn't go into all that detail, but I certainly did tell her that they had terrific counselors. 'No,' Anne said, 'I won't have anything to do with it.' And then she said something like this being the last time. I didn't understand what she was talking about."

Neal paused and took a deep breath, "Then she told me that I was very defensive—by now I really didn't know what was going on. She was very excited and angry. I hadn't seen her like this in a long time. Almost incoherently she rambled on and on, blaming Shirley and me and her sisters for all her problems.

"Unfortunately, I got really mad," Neal said. "Before I could stop myself I was telling her, 'Soon you'll have to quit accusing everybody for being the cause of your difficulties. It's not our fault that you are the way you are. Anne,' I said, 'you are going to have to start to take a little responsibility for your own well-being.' After that she just looked at me—I remember so well her little pale face—and after a long silence she whispered what might have been 'oh.' But maybe it was just a sigh."

Neal spoke quietly. "If I could take it all back, I would."

Early the next morning, at about six-thirty, when Shirley walked into her kitchen she was startled to see Anne fully dressed and going out the back door. "Normally," Shirley said, "we are not early risers, but I had an appointment that morning and was trying to get the house in order before I left. I was surprised to see her leaving the house. I called out to her—very sharply—that we expected to see her that afternoon. I even told her that we were tired of her running our lives and that she better be back on time. I remember repeating myself and insisting that she be back on time. I can't bear to think that I spoke to her like that. Without giving me a glance she said, 'No way,' and slammed the door."

Anne did not return during the day. But the Mathews didn't give it a second thought. They felt confident that she would come home when she knew there was no chance of the counselor being there. That evening they had been invited to a party and they came home around ten-thirty. They were sure that they would find her sitting out on the patio chairs.

Shirley and Neal sat in their kitchen. They drank many cups of tea. The hours ticked by. The house grew chilly. They sat up all night. Anne never came home.

"We reported her missing to the police the next morning," Neal said. "We felt sick. We could only think of all the crime going on, people are abducted all the time—some poor women disappear for months if not forever. Everybody gave us advice and we did everything that anyone suggested. We sent about seventy pictures of Anne to all kinds of agencies all over Portland.

"Two months to the day of her disappearance we got a call from Detective Ellis—he was in charge of the Portland Bureau for Missing Persons—telling us to call the Tacoma sheriff's department immediately. 'It looks like your daughter is sitting in the Tacoma police station right now. The officer there told us she says the KGB are after her and she wants help in tracking them down.' "

"We called right away." Shirley's voice broke momentarily. She paused and caught her breath. "The officer in Tacoma seemed to be really considerate. It was such a relief at last to talk with an official who seemed to be caring. I have become so sick of all this talk about laws, it's always talk, talk, talk about the law and they ignore the people. My daughter is a real, warm, flesh-and-blood human being. But the humanness of these poor sick crazy people is ignored. It's always a matter of do they or don't they comply with the law. As though the law could take their temperature or tuck them into a cozy bed or bring them some hot soup. It's due to the law that my poor Anne is out there in the cold." Shirley's eyes filled with tears.

"The officer in Tacoma was kind. And I really give him credit, he was very insightful when Anne came into the station and started talking about the KGB. He asked her her name. He spoke to her very gently and told her to sit down and that he would look after her. Then he went directly to the computer and brought up her name, which was listed under the missing persons file.

"He immediately called Detective Ellis and told him that Anne Mathews—listed as missing and fitting the description—was in his station. Within a few minutes of Detective Ellis's call to us, we were on the line to Tacoma. It seemed amazing to me that for once they had got it right. I was delirious with happiness when this officer told me that Anne was sitting there as calm as can be and she looked healthy and clean. Anne told him that she was staying at a shelter there in Tacoma. So somehow she had managed to care for herself for two months without one penny. Knowing this was a gift in itself.

"The officer told me that he had already called for someone to come over from Mental Health. He assured me that they would probably take her to the Washington Mental Hospital, where they would put her on a seventy-two-hour hold until they arranged for a court hearing."

"That was the best news we had had in years," Neal said. "We were so happy—we were jubilant—to hear that she was alive. And now it seemed at long last that she would be getting some proper treatment. For two months our lives had been completely on hold. We were incapable of doing anything but think about what we could do to find our girl. And we agonized over everything we felt we had done wrong which might have caused her to leave. Believe me, we went over and over our last few words with her, and how we wished we could take them back!"

The Mathews' joy was of a poignantly short duration. Tragically for Anne and for her parents, the social worker from the Tacoma Mental Health Clinic spoke to Anne for a mere few minutes. Finding that she intended harm neither to others nor to herself, and that she was clean, well fed, and had shelter, the social worker told Anne Mathews that she was free to leave.

Before she left the police station, Anne went to the desk. She was clearly perplexed. She asked the kindly officer at the desk if the man who had been talking with her was from the KGB.

Anne Mathews did not return to the Tacoma City Shelter. Other than a rumor of a possible sighting in Seattle, this is the last concrete account that Shirley and Neal Mathews have heard about their daughter.

Subsequently the Mathews called the Metro Crisis line in Seattle and asked for the names and addresses of the shelters in that city. They wrote letters to all of them, enclosing a photograph of Anne. They included a brief note for her—written on one of her own hand-painted cards: "We realize you have the right to do what you wish to do, but we want you to know that we miss you and would like you to come home. Your Dad and Mom and sisters still love you. We love you and wish you a happy birthday." (By happenstance the date coincided with her thirty-second birthday.) They sent the note unsealed within a cover letter that explained how long Anne had been missing and contained as many pertinent details about their daughter as they could think of.

They received only one reply:

September 8, 1988
Dear Mr. & Mrs. Mathews,
   Recently we received your letter of concern about your daughter's safety. We are sad to hear of your daughter's dissappearance [sic]. Since we are strictly bound by confidentiality, we regret that we will not be able to provide you with any information, either positive or negative regarding the where-abouts of your daughter. We did feel that a response from our program was appropriate, however. Our hearts extend to your family in this difficult time.

Commentary

BY

MARSHA MARTIN, D.S.W.

Dr. Martin is the Director of the Mayor's Office on Homelessness and SRO Housing, New York City. She is on a leave of absence from her position as

*Associate Professor at the Hunter College School of Social Work. Dr. Martin is a
former director of the Midtown Outreach Program, an innovative program designed
to reach the homeless mentally ill in the greater Midtown area. She is a past board
member of the Coalition for the Homeless, Women in Need, the Coalition of
Voluntary Mental Health and Alcoholism Agencies, and the Council of Family and
Child Caring Agencies. Dr. Martin authored the first study on homeless people who
use the NYC subway system as an alternative shelter.*

During the late 1970s it was customary to see the following caption
appear on t.v. screens in living rooms across America minutes before the
late-night news: PARENTS, IT'S TEN P.M. DO YOU KNOW WHERE YOUR CHIL-
DREN ARE?

That caption predated the current crisis of homelessness in America and
at the time was meant as a reminder to parents and, some would add, to
children as well, to check in, to make sure that everyone was accounted
for. Today, for many families in America, that question is a particularly
poignant one. And the answer is a painful no.

On any given night, more than 600,000 Americans are literally homeless, living and sleeping on our streets, in parks, in shelters, or in darkened
corners of public transportation settings. These men and women are
America's missing people—men and women whose whereabouts are unknown except to the passersby. These men and women have left their
homes, their families, their relationships, and their sources of support.
Some vignettes from case records illustrate the varied characteristics of the
homeless.

Fantasy and reality merge in Emily's world. She rattles on endlessly, with
elaborate plans to feed and house the homeless. "I'm one of the most allergic
persons in the U.S.," she says. "Put me in jail and I can't last more than fifty
hours, even in the very nice jails they have here. I couldn't take the food. I
eat three pounds of vegetables a day." But sometimes she scrounges scraps
from a fast food outlet. "Recycling," she calls it. Medication makes her ill.
"I gain fifty pounds every time I'm in the hospital." For more than a year
she has slept in an abandoned building with no electricity.

Mary, a middle-aged woman who looked much older than her age, had
been hospitalized on several occasions by the neighborhood police department. Her hospitalizations were characterized by bizarre delusions: people
putting parts of animals into her body and spirits controlling her mind.

Diagnosed with paranoid schizophrenia, Mary set up residence on a street corner adjacent to a small grocery/delicatessen where she continually panhandled the customers for spare change and yelled at the passersby to leave her alone.

Rosa is a survivor. At 55, she has lived on skid row for more than 20 years and slept in cheap hotels until none would have her. Rosa has delusions. She imagines that her sons, taken from her years ago, are in danger. She can be hard to handle then. Barred from hotels, Rosa moved into the area's parking lots.

Homelessness and mental illness represent problems of immense proportions, as illustrated by the vignettes. When combined with related needs and unpredictable circumstances, as it often is, the effects can be devastating. There is consensus nationwide that one-third of the men and women observed sleeping in parks, on the streets, in transportation stations, and in shelters are suffering from severe mental illnesses such as schizophrenia and manic depressive disorder. And while estimates vary by locality from 20 to 60 percent, there can be no debate about the fact that the men and women observed on the streets, and those seeking emergency shelter, safety, and food, belonged to someone. Perhaps that person sitting huddled in the doorway is John's uncle, Carole's mother, Billy's niece, Dottie's cousin, Ruth's brother, Oscar's son, or Mary's daughter. Maybe it is Jack's brother-in-law or Reverend Townsend's former wife. Or maybe it's Anne Mathews. Government programs, entitlements, and community and mental health programs have been expanded to increase the size of the safety net, yet many Americans continue to fall through the cracks. There are twice as many seriously mentally ill individuals living on the streets and in shelters as there are in public mental hospitals. Anne may be one.

While it is possible to review and discuss in detail the events leading up to Anne's change in mental status, the departure from her family, and her subsequent designation as "missing," it will not explain what happened. No one would or could imagine that any of Shirley and Neal Mathews' daughters would end up homeless. But as Anne's story concludes, the likely hypothesis is that she has fallen through the safety net, become one of America's missing persons, and entered the homeless service system.

Reviewing Anne's situation, it is very easy to ask, couldn't something have been done to help? Couldn't the social workers have done something to help the Mathews? To help Anne get the necessary treatment and services? Why did her family wait so long? And why didn't her friends raise questions about her behavior earlier? Anne could have benefited from a complete medical and psychiatric assessment and evaluation. At some point she might have benefited from hospitalization. However, as many families quickly learn, arranging help is not so easy. In fact, it is a complex, tedious, and all-consuming process.

If a family member with schizophrenia is willing to accept mental health services, it can be less complicated. However, it is still necessary to monitor the quality and delivery of those services. If the relative is unwilling or unable to accept services, as is often the case, there are many questions that must be answered, conditions that must exist, and criteria that must be met before involuntary actions can be taken. There are questions such as: What are the symptoms or present behaviors? Are they extreme, severe? Has the behavior changed significantly in the recent past? Is the person in danger of harming self or others? The answers are important because the steps mental health professionals take will depend on the answers. Anne was unwilling to accept care. Anne did not perceive a need for mental health services. Anne did not present a serious enough risk to herself or anyone else necessary for invoking involuntary procedures. And even if Anne lacked or lost the skills necessary for self-care, she remained coherent and able to communicate with her family and the mental health professionals who made their way to the Mathews' home.

Every state has a legal definition of mental illness that usually contains references to the "danger to self and others" and "disability" criteria. These criteria, in combination with psychotic symptoms, indicate a level of incapacity that severely affects the individual's ability to care for self and satisfy basic survival needs. The legal definitions assist in the determination of who is eligible for and receives emergency treatment and who does not. The mental health system does not have sufficient resources to provide care for everyone who needs it. Accordingly, it is necessary to evaluate everyone who may appear to need treatment for the severity of need. Even then, the system cannot guarantee the level of care and treatment necessary. Finally, men and women who have a serious mental illness have a legal right to refuse treatment, even when treatment is available to them and when it is clearly in the individual's best interest. Consequently, many individuals, like Anne, do not receive treatment that could benefit them. Instead, they fall through the cracks and join the ranks of the homeless.

Finding a mentally ill family member who is missing and may be homeless is a very difficult but not impossible task. In addition to knowledge of mental illness, homelessness, the mental health and homeless service system, and local and state laws, finding a family member requires a degree of hopefulness, patience, creativity, persistence, and common sense. And as the Mathews discovered very early in their search for Anne, even then the outcome may not always lead to immediate success. This chapter will explore the nature of homelessness within the population of mentally ill adults who suffer from schizophrenia by describing a process of adaptation that emerges the longer the individual remains homeless. A snapshot of the homeless service system will be presented in order to familiarize families with program names, program frameworks, and ideologies. Finally, suggestions will be presented that families may consider when trying to find a missing relative.

STREET LIFE: BECOMING HOMELESS

For most Americans it is difficult to fully understand and accept the circumstances that result in homelessness for anyone they know. It may happen to other people, but it is impossible for most of us to imagine it happening to someone we know, a close friend, or relative. Homelessness, for most people and especially for those with schizophrenia, often results not from a single event or episode but from the culmination of several stressful experiences. Anne's story typifies the process. As Anne's intellectual functioning changed from clear to confused, as her behavioral reactions changed from cooperative to resistive, and her emotional relatedness shifted from involvement to aloofness, she lost the resources, skills, and attachments necessary for remaining connected. Although she was able to complete some limited tasks, the activities necessary for living indoors, in a home, were too demanding, too challenging. As Anne's behavior changed, the Mathews did seek professional assistance. That assistance was not particularly helpful. In fact, families across America report similar stories in trying to get help for their mentally ill members. In the absence of real help from the mental health and social welfare systems, as is illustrated in the preceding accounts, many men and women manage to bypass this system and eventually end up on the street.

For most Americans it is also very difficult if not impossible to comprehend how anyone, regardless of mental status, would appear to "choose" to remain homeless when family support and/or institutional resources are available. However, without insight, and perhaps a fresh understanding of the dynamic interaction between homelessness and schizophrenia, the effort to find a family member and invite him or her back home will be futile. Although the overall picture of homelessness looks discouraging, closer analysis shows that some homeless men and women suffering from schizophrenia have shown unexpected strengths—ones that are often masked by the illness. The fact that so many people have survived a period of homelessness under appalling circumstances should be seen as clear evidence of their capacities and resources which, if understood, might be built upon.

Homelessness is more than being without a home; it is being without the relationships that link most of us to a network of social supports. It is being without the supports, resources, competencies, and connections essential for meeting the basic human needs required to maintain relationships and participate in a household. To be suffering from schizophrenia, which is a debilitating and disabling illness associated with the loss of the mind, and then to become homeless, is to be without the requisite internal and external resources necessary for optimal self-care and community living. Homelessness for someone with schizophrenia can represent an extreme and bewildering condition of disaffiliation, marginalization, loss of identification with the community, and, finally, the loss of a sense of self. With limited mental energy and no home, a person with schizophrenia has no structure or foundation on which to ground, no source of emotional nurturance and nourishment, and no stability. Being homeless means no bathroom door to close, no evening meal at the end of the day, no one with whom to share stories.

Homelessness is a process that occurs over time, and adaptation to it also takes place over time. While the adaptation is under way, persons with schizophrenia make various accommodations to their changing affiliations and fluctuating mental status. What once would have seemed bizarre is no longer experienced as such. Relationships are experienced and viewed differently than before. The skills necessary for completion of tasks and the activities of daily living diminish over time as the perceived and disordered needs of the victim change. Anne's participation in household chores altered dramatically on her return from Europe. She retreated into her bedroom and dramatically altered her participation at home from helping to being helped; from participating with her parents in household chores to becoming almost a chore herself.

ADAPTING TO HOMELESSNESS

Paradoxically, homelessness presents a challenge to anyone who undergoes it and can represent an opportunity for mastery and competence. Very often persons with serious mental illness, especially those suffering from schizophrenia, are justifiably excluded from participating in the routine activities of daily living for fear that "something terrible" could happen, as is illustrated in the case of Anne. Her parents never stopped worrying about her. In fact they tried to limit her exposure to stress in order to support their daughter's efforts to make it on her own. Understandably so. Whether it was living in the "dumpy studio," taking care of Mrs. O'Brien, or making and mailing the cards to her sister in Arizona, they never stopped worrying about Anne's competence, nor did they stop being there to help. The experience of being supervised, supported, and cared for, even with the best of intentions, combined with feelings of paranoia (being watched), persecution (being controlled), and psychic malaise (being emotionally exhausted) can result in a forced and necessary retreat from the activities of daily living.

Homelessness, or more accurately stated, walking away from familial resources or institutional care for a person who misinterprets reality and has very strong convictions that his or her thoughts and actions are being controlled by others, can represent an opportunity to get away, to enjoy freedom from persecution. Anne, without mental health treatment and the help of her parents, tried to continue living on her own. She tried to keep up with the demands of working and meeting deadlines and to maintain social ties. She failed. Instead of seeking treatment or professional help, Anne left her home. She had become overwhelmed, excited, and frightened very easily. Fleeing from something rather than fleeing toward some place, she disappeared.

In a very bizarre twist, some of the behaviors considered maladaptive and inappropriate for indoor living, behaviors that are a byproduct of the illness, become useful as a means of protection for outdoor living. Being a little paranoid can be useful; one can never be too trusting of the person sleeping in the next cot over. Talking or yelling at imaginary persecutors and poor hygiene can keep people at a safe distance. Evidence of confused, disordered thinking and a heightened sense of vulnerability can result in increased assistance: handouts from passersby or "friendly visitors" of sorts. This assistance can take the form of meals, money, conversation, opportunities to bathe, clothing, telephone use, and tickets back home.

For homeless adults, especially those with serious mental illness, living on the street represents a survival strategy, not just a temporary solution to a situational problem. Most schizophrenia victims do not make an eccentric or idiosyncratic choice to be homeless; they do it to survive. When they walk out the door, it is an attempt to escape and survive. This fright/flight survival drive sparks a process of adaptation that continues the longer the homeless person with schizophrenia remains on the street. He or she evolves strategies and develops routines in order to meet basic needs, alleviate the stress of homelessness, and maintain a little sense of self-worth and dignity.

Efforts to reach homeless adults suffering from schizophrenia must be coupled with an understanding that they create personalized methods, albeit often bizarre ones, for acquiring necessities such as food, clothing, showers, shelter, and financial support. These ad hoc strategies for meeting basic needs and acquiring essential resources grow out of a disordered thinking pattern and must be understood as essential components of the individual's repertoire of skills. They become the protective outer layer much like a roof over one's head or a thick wool overcoat in the dead of winter.

Additionally, maintenance strategies that include defense mechanisms such as denial, rationalization, fantasies, and self-entertainment, along with basic survival skills such as the ability to eat virtually anything, select discarded food carefully, sleep sitting up, locate sheltering materials with good insulation qualities (newspapers and cardboard boxes), bathe in sinks, secure safe places to rest, stand in line for hours on end, and live life in the public view combine to form an effective armament against the world.

For some persons with schizophrenia, homelessness may be the first and only arena in which they feel a sense of efficacy and mastery. Although homelessness is a frightening reality, more confusing than not, more dangerous than not, it can allow even the most disordered individuals to attempt to take care of their needs. Unfortunately, no one *is* watching; no one *seems* to care. Consequently, the person's felt experience of competence, combined with coping with the illness itself, serves as reinforcement for the behavior and lifestyle. It is the felt sense of efficacy, achieved outside of familial or institutional supports, that sustains homeless mentally ill men and women. This can in part explain the resistance of the person with schizophrenia when challenged to give up various elements of the homeless lifestyle.

For someone like Anne, living in this new outdoor world, it becomes much easier to accept help from a stranger than from family or friends, who may be perceived as being part of the group controlling everything, real or imagined. As scary as the street or shelter may be, schizophrenia often makes leaving home, wandering the streets, sleeping in shelters with strangers appear to be the only valid choice.

Families and service program staffs must understand the process of adaptation to homelessness and the perceived opportunities and choices it offers people who have schizophrenia. Efforts to communicate with adults with schizophrenia should demonstrate an understanding of the nature of the adaptation and match the skills and competencies of the formerly homeless family member with the tasks and challenges of living indoors. This does not mean that families and services should live without rules, structures, or expectations. Nor is it meant to suggest that families be forced to arrange their lives to accommodate a person's needs developed during a psychotic process. It does suggest, however, that flexibility, creativity, challenges, and autonomy be included in all opportunities for family members to return home or to other residential settings. Fortunately, in many municipalities there are programs for homeless mentally ill adults that help families and their missing members to reconnect. After relocation to housing, many programs continue to provide the necessary support to keep the relationship going. These programs may be found in the telephone book under the heading: "Government and County Services." Usually they are listed as "Health and Social Outreach" or "Homeless Social Services."

THE HOMELESS SOCIAL SERVICE SYSTEM

The homeless service system has had to adapt itself to compensate for the absence of a comprehensive system of care. Homelessness and mental illness present startling challenges to the human service and mental health systems. It is no longer enough to offer the homeless mentally ill emergency care, shelter, clothing, or hot meals. As is illustrated in Anne's story, the men and women who are homeless or are at risk of being homeless have a multiplicity of problems, possess a complex array of needs, and have developed repertoires of skills with which to attempt to address those needs. Anne's problems did not begin with her homelessness and will not end with her becoming domiciled. The problem is that most mental health and social service systems are not organized to respond to this level of problem or need.

Persons with serious mental illness, especially those on the street, require a comprehensive, coordinated, and accessible system of basic and specialized services to establish and maintain themselves in the community. These services include outreach, assistance meeting basic needs, mental health care, 24-hour crisis assistance, housing, primary medical care, education, family support and counseling, employment and vocational services, case management services, the development of natural support networks, and someone who cares. Since the community mental health movement of the 1960s, municipalities have struggled to provide services to the mentally ill. Unfortunately, this struggle is long from over. Thousands of mentally ill adults have become homeless in the absence of such a comprehensive system, and most of them suffer from schizophrenia.

Recognizing the crisis of homelessness among the mentally ill, the National Institute of Mental Health began a rigorous program of research, service innovation, demonstration, and evaluation in the area of homelessness and mental illness. Since the 1980s, the NIMH Office of Programs for the Homeless Mentally Ill has worked with state and local governments, mental health professionals, and consumers of mental health services to develop an effective service and housing program for the homeless mentally ill. Much of what exists in the form of services and programs nationwide developed out of activities and advocacy at NIMH.

In addition to the NIMH program, the passage of the Stewart B. McKinney Homeless Assistance Act (PL 100-77) made available federal dollars to states and municipalities for emergency and some long-term relief. The act created a variety of funding streams for programs such as community mental health, primary health care, housing, emergency food and shelter, job training, and education for the homeless and those at risk for homelessness. The act also authorized expansion of some existing programs: veterans' job training, community service block grants, food stamps and so on, to ensure eligibility for homeless persons.

With support from the McKinney Act, states and localities have been able to expand existing services and develop new ones. Almost every major city in the United States has a program designed to bring relief to the homeless. Most cities have one, some, or all of the following: outreach, drop-in center, health care, and emergency and transitional housing services. Most of these services provide a chair or bed to sit or sleep on, a hot meal, health assessment and screening, and a refuge from inclement weather. Thus far, services for the homeless mentally ill have clustered around three program models: outreach services, drop-in centers, and emergency and transitional shelters. Taken together with case management, these program models comprise the essential components of a good emergency relief system of care for the homeless mentally ill.

In order to find a missing family member, it is necessary to know what type of service system exists and how that system works. Because there has been national leadership on the issue of homelessness and mental illness, many programs have been developed across the country that attempt to provide comprehensive services to persons with serious mental illness, alcohol, and drug problems. The result: many very good programs operated by innovative nonprofit agencies that have been effective in connecting persons with schizophrenia to services, families, and housing. What follows is a brief overview of the homeless service system.

OUTREACH SERVICES

A variety of outreach services and programs have been designed to work with the homeless mentally ill. Some programs provide access to community-based services designed to meet basic needs; others represent satellite offices, a kind of outposting of essential services in areas where homeless men and women congregate. Regardless of the approach, outreach programs are very often the first step toward indoor living for most homeless individuals. While the intent of the programs is to link the homeless to community-based services, very often it is necessary to provide concrete services and ongoing case management to facilitate movement from the street and/or public-transportation facilities. While many outreach programs may not offer physical spaces, they can provide a psychological space that may help a person with schizophrenia reconnect with social services.

The clients targeted by outreach programs are those who are disaffiliated, reject the services offered by traditional mental health clinics or social service offices, and require a flexible, patient approach. Even when first approached by outreach staff, they may resist offers of assistance. Outreach teams have developed a sequence of techniques for gradually engaging the hard-to-reach, most resistant clients. They include offering a brown-bag snack; providing minimal material services such as food and clothing; using multiple, repeated contacts to establish familiarity and trust; and providing assessment, referral, and supportive counseling and other services.

Outreach programs become, in essence, the testing ground for the reestablishment of relationships. Fear of rejection, fear of inadequacy, or just plain paranoia will in all likelihood keep a homeless person with schizophrenia at a distance initially: refusing assistance, insisting that everything is all right. However, it is important to note that safety and care may be perceived to be more accessible from random passersby and police officers on patrol than in an isolated room, a board-and-care home, or even from family members, who may have become part of a delusional system.

Outreach and engagement services can be effective if the approach limits the sense of invasion of privacy and affirms the skills and mastery of the homeless person, thereby not destroying the organization of his or her world. Approaching homeless mentally ill men and women over time, with the recognition that they have wants, needs, and a sense of self, however disorganized, based on a life of varied and valuable experiences, will result in their desire to reconnect and move from homelessness toward affiliation and perhaps even treatment.

DROP-IN CENTER SERVICES

Drop-in center services are designed to meet the survival needs of mentally ill homeless individuals. They often require no formal commitment or affiliation. They offer accessibility and acceptability. They provide basic services, including food, clothing, respite, showers, delousing, psychiatric and medical attention, socialization, and safety, in an atmosphere that respects the individual's desire and need for anonymity, autonomy, and competence.

After a given period of time (usually defined by the homeless person in consultation with the staff), allowing the reluctant and usually paranoid person to adapt to the drop-in center ambience and routine, some centers provide opportunities for work and rehabilitation through the development of groups, day programming, and vocational rehabilitation–type activities.

Outreach and drop-in center services provide the much needed first invitation to return to indoor living. These two basic pretreatment services permit homeless mentally ill adults to reaffiliate through a slow-developing process. Depending on the length of time a homeless mentally ill adult has been without ongoing treatment and supervision, it may be months or years before he or she is able to regain the sense of self, self-sufficiency, and trust necessary to exchange life outdoors for life indoors. Even with treatment, including hospitalization and psychopharmacology, the residual aspects of the psychotic process very often remain. Some of these effects are difficulty in learning, blunted affect, difficulty with interpersonal relationships, decreased mobility, and increased vulnerability. Once the shift begins, however, transitional shelter and housing can provide the structure in which to complete the adaptation back to indoor living.

EMERGENCY HOUSING AND TRANSITIONAL HOUSING SERVICES

As Baxter and Hopper write: "There is not a woman on the street who does not want shelter. It's just that they are afraid. One woman used to ring the doorbell but would refuse to come inside. We used to give her food on the doorstep. Eventually, she agreed to come in and sit on the bench in the foyer. Three months later, she came up the stairs and slept in a chair in the living room. Now she sleeps in a bed. . . . It's a matter of gaining their trust."

Emergency shelter provides the physical space necessary for trust to develop. Unfortunately, many homeless mentally ill adults will have experienced a variety of emotional and physical assaults, resulting in a lack of trust, as well as the absence of a well-defended exterior. Understanding this, emergency shelter and transitional housing programs try to provide sensitive and creative rehabilitative programs. The demands placed on the patient cannot be so severe, as perceived by the patient, to require too much. Homeless mentally ill men and women learn to live by their own rules, based on their experience of reality and their own assessment of needs. Emergency shelter and transitional housing program staffs understand that the rules must be flexible and negotiable. They also understand that everyone needs some structure and rules to live by if he or she is going to live successfully in the community. How well a shelter or housing program helps a homeless person readjust to indoor living will be based on its rules and their application. An example of this might be the response to personal hygiene needs.

In some shelters, showers and attention to cleanliness on a daily basis are priorities and requirements for prolonged stays. In others, hygiene is not a requirement for services at all. The variability given to the issue of hygiene reflects the needs of the homeless adult for privacy and protection. Asking a homeless mentally ill person, who may be suffering from a paranoid psychotic process, to shower is asking him or her to become completely defenseless. The clothes on his or her back represent the only real protection/shelter from assault and the elements. To remove this protective layer is assuming and asking too much. Taking a shower is not as important to mentally ill adults as food and the feeling of safety and trust. Assisting the homeless person with schizophrenia to regain a sense of trust is the priority at most shelter and transitional housing programs.

Case management is also key to the successful adaptation to residential living. The purpose of case management is to provide services simultaneously and sequentially over time to ensure a good fit between the housing and the resident. Case managers make certain that the individual has all of the services and supports, including ongoing mental health care and treatment, necessary in order for him or her to remain housed. If the family member needs services, the case manager may provide them or obtain them from the community. Case managers provide ongoing assessment of needs based on the nature of the family member's impairments and disabilities, assesses the service system for resources, and arranges for the delivery of services to meet the family member's needs.

Following the development of the trusting relationship, most shelter and transitional housing programs try to assist the homeless mentally ill adult to reestablish relationships with community agencies and families. Very often the first efforts are directed toward family. One of the first questions asked, during both informal and formal intake processes, is whether there are family members who could be contacted. Initially the answer is no; however, over time it sometimes changes to yes.

The abovementioned components of a service program are essential in taking the first step out of homelessness. These components will assist in providing immediate and short-term relief, but they will not provide the necessary ongoing structural support that is needed to curb homelessness. They are, as the Mathews family learned, an important place to check when looking for a family member.

WHERE TO GO, WHAT TO DO: LOOKING FOR A FAMILY MEMBER

Knowledge of the service system for adults with mental disorders who are homeless, and of the dynamics of homelessness, is essential in trying to find a family member and inviting her or him to return home. After becoming familiar with the homeless service system, and before attempting to find a family member, it is important to raise questions like: Can the family provide the real and perceived opportunities, choices, and freedoms experienced by the family member while he or she was homeless? Will he or she be returning to the "you need treatment, I don't need treatment" familial and familiar merry-go-round?

The return of someone who has spent time homeless will challenge even the most sophisticated family: the coping mechanisms and strategies of adaptation utilized by homeless people with schizophrenia will inevitably be trying as the transition takes place. The skills and competencies developed, based on self-identified needs, and the most effective way, as perceived by the mentally ill person, of meeting them, may no longer be necessary once back at home. However, asking the mentally ill person to surrender methods that have proven useful during days and nights of homelessness and perceived independence is like asking him to give up the job he has been successfully coping with.

Many communities have agencies that provide specialized services for homeless individuals and families, and most large communities have special programs or services for homeless individuals and families with mental health needs. If there are no services listed in your local telephone directory, look for the six national resources that can provide information about homeless programs nationwide.

HEALTH AND MENTAL HEALTH INFORMATION

The National Resource Center on Homelessness and Mental Illness in Delmar, New York, the Center for Mental Health Services in Rockville, Maryland, and the National Health Care for the Homeless Council in Nashville, Tennessee, can assist with the names, addresses, and telephone numbers of outreach, drop-in center, transitional, and permanent housing programs across the country.

ADVOCACY INFORMATION

There are three national advocacy organizations located in Washington, D.C., which can provide additional information. They are: the National Alliance to End Homelessness, the National Coalition for the Homeless, and the National Center on Homelessness and the Law. These organizations can direct you to local initiatives to end homelessness through advocacy, services, and coalition-building. Each organization works with a network of agencies and individuals that are knowledgeable about homelessness and local resources.

In addition to the abovementioned national organizations, the Social Security Administration will send a letter to the missing person, providing the purpose of the search is humanitarian. Through the letter-forwarding services, the SSA will include one letter a year, assuming the individual is receiving SSA/SSDA/SSI benefits or is listed through his or her Social Security employment-tax deduction. The agency will not reveal the person's whereabouts or verify that the letter was received. It simply acts as an intermediary. Any Social Security office can assist a family with the letter-forwarding process. A word of caution. If the missing family member is suffering from feelings of persecution and/or from paranoia, receiving a letter in the mail from parents or relatives may do more harm than good.

The National Alliance for the Mentally Ill has established a Homeless and Missing Mentally Ill Network that actively assists families in locating missing relatives throughout the 50 states. NAMI recommends the following steps if your missing relative is 21 years of age or older:

1. You must give NAMI legal authority to proceed with the search before the case can be opened and worked. In doing this, provide the following information:
   - Photograph of the missing person.
   - Full description and age.
   - Social Security number.
   - The last place he or she was seen.
   - Description of clothing.
   - Address, if possible, of nearest relatives and friends and their phone numbers.
2. The moment you determine that your relative is definitely missing, immediately list his or her name with your local police. Request that he

or she be placed on the nationwide missing persons list. (NAMI legally cannot do this for you.)

3. Provide NAMI with the police case number.

4. If and when NAMI locates your missing relative, have in your possession one of the two following legal documents so you can ask NAMI, the police, or other relevant organizations to hold the person until you can get there:

- A court order from a local judge authorizing this action, if the judge believes that the person is dangerous to herself or himself or to others.
- Proof of legal guardianship over the missing person, authorizing you to act with full authority to protect your relative who is unable to help herself or himself.

5. To obtain one of the above two documents, you must have the full support of your missing relative's physician and possibly some of your neighbors who know your family member.

6. If you already have either of the above documents when you make your request to NAMI, attach a copy along with the other information so NAMI can act swiftly in your behalf if it is notified that your family member has been found.

Families that cope most effectively with their mentally ill members are characterized by greater acceptance, less intrusiveness or rigid attitudes, a better ability to listen, lack of fear, and a generally positive attitude. Those who do poorly have limited tolerance for the annoying symptoms, the stress, and the attendant turmoil caused by bizarre, intrusive, and agitated behavior.

The role played by social workers, psychologists, nurses, and psychiatrists is crucial in reconnecting with indoor living. Unfortunately, most mental health professionals have not been trained to provide needed services to persons with serious mental illness or to their families. The reason is that most professionals seek prompt gratification from their work and find coping with persons who are severely and chronically mentally ill, whose behavior is detached from day-to-day reality, extremely unattractive. In addition, because of the dependent nature of an effective therapeutic relationship, many professionals find people with schizophrenia too difficult to work with. As the Mathews quickly learned, the system does not offer much help or hope for persons like Anne. Instead, it searches for patients who will show dramatic signs of improvement and capacity for social adjustment. Instead of reorganizing services to reach the most vulnerable and needy, services tend to be reduced and/or redirected toward those with the greatest potential for successful rehabilitation.

If you are looking for a relative, the homeless service system has had some success in working with persons with severe mental illness and is probably the best equipped to respond to their needs. Most workers in this system welcome the chance to work with families.

Should Anne Mathews return home, unless she receives mental health treatment, she will soon be right back where she was when she fled to the street: very ill and unable to care for herself. And, under the best of circumstances—that is, with treatment and housing—she will still suffer from a disability. Even though there is potential for rehabilitation in several key areas, most people with schizophrenia will always need psychiatric care, assistance, and support.

Improvement in the system of care for individuals with schizophrenia and their families is not likely to occur until the need to care for persons with any type of severe mental disorder is taken seriously.

WHAT FAMILIES CAN DO

The homeless mentally ill need your ongoing support if they are someday to lead lives of stability, health, and dignity. By participating in the following ways, you will assist not only your ill family member, but untold numbers of other families and patients.

1. Visit a program that serves homeless individuals and families. Familiarize yourself with local efforts to end homelessness.

2. Visit a program that services mentally ill adults and their families. Familiarize yourself with what mental health treatment is and is not.

3. Volunteer for an indefinite period of time at a mental health or homeless program. Learn from the clients/patients/guests themselves about homelessness.

4. Join the local chapter of the Alliance for the Mentally Ill or the local Coalition for the Homeless. Participate in advocacy efforts and self-help activities.

5. Develop a list of resources and individuals who can provide professional assistance to the homeless. Get to know what services they offer and the eligibility criteria. Be persistent: stay on the phone until you are satisfied with the information they have given you.

6. Volunteer to speak at the local mental health center and professional

educational institutions responsible for training mental health professionals. You have a great deal of information to share.

7. Familiarize yourself with entitlement programs: things like payments, mailing cycles, and certification procedures.

8. Participate in drives for food, clothing, and money for shelters, special mental health programs, and rehabilitation programs. Join with others who care and dare to make a difference.

9. Read books and articles on mental illness, mental health systems, psychoeducation, psychosocial rehabilitation, psychopharmacology, and community mental health. Your librarian can help you find the right ones.

4.

Whereabouts Unknown:

Searching for a Missing Family Member

EIGHTEEN MONTHS PASSED BEFORE SHIRLEY AND Neal Mathews were reunited with their daughter. Save for a few straws in the wind which came early on, they had had no news at all. The days dragged by interminably, and the memory of the telephone call from the police officer in Tacoma, Washington, took on the hazy outlines of a mirage.

That tantalizing phone call had told them that their missing daughter was sitting on the other side of the officer's desk. As if they were present, they could envision Anne, darting quick glances toward the officer, twisting her fingers nervously as she anxiously perched on a bench, always on the lookout for her nemesis, the KGB. But the miracle of almost being able to touch her was short-lived. As they savored the anticipated joy of hugging her, Anne slipped through their fingers.

But all this was in the past. Anne was safely back home. As the Mathews reminisced about their harrowing year and a half, their relief was tempered by the ongoing daily reality of their daughter's chronic disease.

"It seems they take care of the homeless people in New York City," Shirley said. She was fingering a wallet-sized identity card that bore a photograph of Anne's face seen against a warm red background. Anne's eyes stared out blankly; her hair looked limp and dirty. A statement on the card indicated it was to be used for food coupons and/or public assistance.

"Anne was going to toss it. I asked her if I could keep it." Carefully,

Shirley replaced the card in her purse. "You see, I don't want to forget. Maybe we can help others. There were so many people who tried to help us. And some who helped Anne, too."

"But there were others just the opposite," Neal said. "People who used the excuse of confidentiality to do nothing, who followed the letter of the law and wouldn't open their eyes to see what was really going on. And certain people who willingly let a young woman sleep night after night in a public park, when they *knew* that she had frantic parents trying to get their mentally ill daughter returned home."

"Even so," Shirley interjected gently, "I can't get the little kindnesses out of my mind."

Anne had described a freezing cold night in a small town near the continental divide. Shivering and without money, she had walked into a homey and brightly lit twenty-four-hour cafe. The owner, a big blowsy woman with a booming voice, looked Anne over and just sat her down and gave her a full-course hot meal—free. When Anne had finished eating, the woman placed a chair in the restaurant's warm vestibule and said to her, "Honey, go ahead, you're welcome to spend the night in here."

"The next morning Anne hitched a ride. There must have been a lot of kind and helpful folk. She also tells of two nuns in New York who spent hours driving her all over the city looking for a women's shelter that would take her in."

"That's one side," Neal said. "But in Trenton, New Jersey, they gave her 'bus therapy.' You know what that is—a one-way bus ticket out of state. They shipped her to New York City." He drew in his breath sharply.

There had been no clue too fragile for the Mathews to follow. One evening, shortly after the Tacoma episode, they received a late-night telephone call from a friend, Wayne Lambert, who lived in Seattle. Wayne sounded strained and apologetic. He was pretty sure he had seen Anne on a downtown Seattle street that morning around seven. He was rushing to an early meeting, and wasn't a hundred percent sure it was Anne, so he hadn't approached her. "You know, it might have looked like I was making advances to a strange young woman." Thinking it over, he realized it must have been Anne and was ashamed that he hadn't done the right thing. Being a decent man, he had phoned Shirley and Neal to tell them about his sighting.

"Another near miss," Neal said. "Of course, we drove right up to Seattle. We went to all the shelters. Nothing, absolutely nothing. That darn confidentiality business would always crop up. 'Sorry, we can't help you. We're not allowed. Confidentiality laws, you know.' Always the same story, and they mouthed it just as nice as pie. All the while, we were eating our hearts out with worry and fear about our Annie."

"We even found out," Shirley said, "when Anne was back home, she'd actually spent a month in one of the shelters we'd gone to visit. We discovered, only after it was way too late, how to get around the confidentiality thing. You don't ask if so-and-so is there. You say, 'I want to speak to so-and-so,' or, 'I want to leave a message for so-and-so.' As if you *know* that the person you are looking for is there."

The Mathews drove up to British Columbia. An envelope had arrived at their house for Anne from the Cathedral in Victoria. They opened it, hoping for some news of their daughter, and found that it contained a check made out to her, from the telephone company, in the amount of 50 cents. There was also a neatly penned note, written on the Cathedral's stationery, regretting that the church was unable to use the unendorsed check, which had been left as an offering in their collection plate. Later, they were to find out from Anne that while they were in Victoria, searching for her, she was there, spending her nights sleeping under the bushes, directly across from the police station. Anne had believed she was safe from her imaginary pursuers, the KGB, if she kept the police station in sight.

The Mathews listed Anne on the Canadian missing persons' computer file. "Now, that was really interesting," Neal said. "The officer took all our data about Anne and right after her name, he typed in 'Hospitalize Immediately.' I was astounded. 'Boy, we couldn't do that in the United States,' I told him. 'We do it differently in Canada,' he replied. 'Here, people with mental disorders are considered to be a medical problem. It's the doctors who make the medical decisions, not the judges.' "

Anne's paranoia propelled her across the breadth of the United States. She was tormented by fears, quite real to her, that the KGB, the Nazis, and the Mormons were out to get her. Without resources, often cold, usually hungry, she walked and hitched rides across the country. She had become obsessed with reaching the Pentagon.

"Somehow Anne got herself all the way to Washington, D.C.," Shirley said. "She says that she met with some official at a parking lot on the north side of the Pentagon and told him she wanted the KGB and all that crowd brought to justice. He told her that he would fix everything."

Neal winced, "Who knows what really happened? She might have just spoken to a parking attendant. There are lots of things about Annie's journey that we'll never get a handle on. It's a miracle to me that she wasn't molested or really harmed. According to Annie, the worst thing that happened was when she dozed off in a New York subway. Some young punk grabbed her handbag and took off with all her food stamps and welfare money."

"At a certain level," Shirley said, "Anne was able to care for herself. She'd get her clothes, for instance, at the Salvation Army. Sometimes, she says, she did go to shelters, but if it was warm enough, she preferred to sleep in the open. Anne was afraid in the shelters. She was afraid to be around so many people. I've been told that this can be typical of people with paranoid schizophrenia.

"What I can never understand is that in all those months, with all that information we sent out, none of those agencies, shelters—or even the Salvation Army—checked her against the missing person file. She always used her correct name and our home address. That's how we got on her trail in Victoria. She'd given the phone company our telephone number."

Even so, it was through the National Crime Information Center— NCIC computer file—that Anne Mathews was finally found. At five-thirty A.M., on a balmy spring morning in a peaceful suburban community in a southeast coastal state, the police got a call from an agitated local resident who reported that a disheveled and ragged young woman was sleeping on his carefully manicured front lawn. Within five minutes two police officers responded to the call. The young woman stood up and obediently answered their questions. Her name, she said, was Anne Mathews, and she gave them her home address in Portland, Oregon.

While Anne waited quietly, one of the officers returned to the patrol car and reported her identification to his precinct. They checked her name on the NCIC computer file and found she was listed as an endangered adult. But she had broken no laws, so the police didn't book her. Nor did they take her into protective custody and keep her until her parents could be notified. They had no warrant; there had been no criminal behavior. She was merely an inadvertent trespasser. Even though the young woman was unkempt and bedraggled, she was polite and surprisingly articulate. The two young officers, courteous and gentle, took her to a downtown center that dispensed services for homeless people.

When the Portland police were notified that Anne Mathews had been picked up, they immediately contacted her parents. "It was the first we knew that Annie was on the east coast," Neal said. "We figured that if she was alive . . ." He stopped talking and shook his head. "We had never once spoken of our greatest fear—that she could be dead." Neal paused again. "Anyway, we had figured that she had to be somewhere on the west coast."

The Mathews' first reaction was to get on a plane and go directly to pick up their daughter, but they were apprehensive that they might scare her away. Now, only too well, they understood that one false move could jeopardize this chance. So much depended on doing this right. They decided they would have to rely on others—people they didn't know—to rescue their daughter. As each day passed, however, with Anne still on the streets, it became more difficult for them to let strangers do the job of recovering their adult child.

"It was nine long weeks before we got her back home. But it took almost a whole month just to get her hospitalized. For us, that was the worst time of all. We knew where she was. We actually knew her approximate whereabouts. It would have killed us to have her slip away again."

"It might have killed her too," Shirley added quietly.

"We were on the phone every day," Shirley said. "We called everybody in our state and over there too. We were unashamed. We begged and wheedled, pleading with anyone who might help us rescue our girl. But it was the other families—families who also had mentally ill relatives—who came through. I called AMI, the Alliance for the Mentally Ill, and if it hadn't been for their missing person network in Virginia, we might have lost our Anne forever. A really kind woman at the Virginia office knew of an AMI member, a nurse—an RN—called Martha Golden, who worked at a hospital in the same town where Anne was sleeping out in the downtown city park."

"Can you believe it?" Neal broke in, "My daughter was living in a public park and the police did nothing to bring her into a safe place. 'This young woman can care for herself,' is what they said. What they really meant is that this bag lady would occasionally go to a laundromat and wash her stuff. Annie liked to be clean, and for them that was the equivalent of her being able to care for herself. That took them off the hook—she didn't fit the legal criteria to be picked up and hospitalized. What kind of person would think that a young woman was able to care for herself when she was sleeping night after night in an open public place where all kinds of appalling things could have happened?"

Twenty-one days had passed since Shirley and Neal had received the news of their daughter's whereabouts. They were clearly at their wits' end when they spoke by telephone to Martha Golden. Tensely, they told Martha how they had tried every avenue they could think of, and how every possibility had ended in frustration. They had badgered mental health administrators, sometimes going to the very top. They had spoken to the police, to social workers, to caseworkers. Occasionally someone would offer them some hope—even assurances that all would be well—and then they'd never hear from that person again. Other times they would be told flat-out that nothing could be done, that the laws precluded and would stymie any rescue operation. Martha was very sympathetic. She had, she told them, a sister with schizophrenia.

"Martha heard us out," Shirley remembered. "She was so patient. When we had spent ourselves, there was a long hushed silence on the line. I wondered if we had been disconnected. All of a sudden Martha shouted, 'For God's sake, where's common sense?' "

Martha Golden went straight to work. She got in touch with the local mental health social services, and she contacted the sheriff's office. She located Anne. She went to the park and saw how pathetic, thin, grubby, and worn-out Anne was. But she did not approach her. Martha knew enough not to scare her off.

Taking full responsibility, Martha authorized the preparation of commitment papers, even though it meant laying her own job on the line. The trick was to pinpoint Anne and have the papers served before the timing on the documents ran out. When Anne broke her glasses and went to the downtown center, where they coordinated services for the homeless, the chance circumstance that Martha had been counting on seemed to be in the making.

The social worker at the center made an appointment for Anne to go to an eye clinic. Martha was alerted immediately. This was the break they were all waiting for. Everything was put in place. The sheriff, with the commitment papers, was waiting at the eye clinic at the appointed time. Anne never arrived.

Neal almost exploded at the memory. "By now, Annie had been sleeping in that park for more than three weeks. I was sure we were going to lose her. I was ready to get on a plane and grab her myself, and to hell with the law."

Two days later, Anne returned to the center and made another appointment. This time she showed up at the eye clinic. Fortunately, the sheriff made a second trip; he was waiting for her with the commitment papers—and handcuffs.

"Anne says she'll never forget the sheriff grabbing her and shoving the handcuffs around her wrists. 'Momma,' she told me, 'he never said a word, he never explained, and he was so rough.' That poor girl must have been terribly scared. She couldn't have understood what was going on. Her mind had played so many tricks on her, and here was something terrifying actually happening to her. Even now, it pains me so to think of it. When they got her to the hospital she was completely crazed. They said she was jumping around and screaming obscenities, she was biting and striking out at anyone who was nearby. They told us that she was so unmanageable that they had to pin her down on the floor. She was so uncontrollable that they put her in isolation."

Shirley paused and raised her hand to her face, which had flushed to a soft pink. "They stripped off her upper garments. They were afraid she might try to commit suicide. Apparently some women have used bras to hang themselves. Anne remembers the details to this day. You see, there were men present."

Other than this initial trauma, however, Anne was treated with kindness and sympathy. She quickly responded to the medication. Within five weeks she was released from the hospital, and with a hospital escort, she flew back to Oregon and was reunited with her parents.

"Annie is grateful now that she was committed," Neal said. "She's especially grateful for the medicine, even though we hear that she was shrieking and kicking when they first gave it to her by injection. Now she takes full responsibility for taking her own medicine. Poor Annie, for years she's had no peace. She says she never wants to be driven by those crazy thoughts again.

"So now my daughter has an official diagnosis of schizophrenia, and there's no more problem about getting the social services for her. But she just sits around the house all day doing nothing. The doctors say she has—what they call—the negative symptoms." Neal sounded tired.

"Looks like, for Shirley and me, our journey with mental illness is just beginning."

Commentary

BY JUDITH B. KRAUSS, R.N., M.S.N., AND DIANE M. GOURLEY, R.N., B.A.

Judith Krauss has been a member of the Yale University School of Nursing faculty for twenty-two years and is currently Dean and Professor of Nursing. Dean Krauss is a noted authority on the care of people with serious mental disorders, as evidenced by her numerous publications, including an award-winning American Journal of Nursing *"Book of the Year,"* The Chronically Ill Psychiatric Patient and the Community *(co-authored with Ann Slavinsky, 1982). She is currently editor in chief of* Archives of Psychiatric Nursing, *which emphasizes clinical research, practice, education, and policy issues. The Dean has received recent awards from the Connecticut Nurses Association for distinguished contributions to nursing education and the American Nurses Association Council for Psychiatric-Mental Health Nursing for distinguished contributions to psychiatric nursing.*

Diane M. Gourley is a nurse clinician at River Valley Services, Community Support Program, Middletown, Connecticut, where she co-designed and teaches the family education program. She has cared for the seriously mentally ill in the community for over twenty years as primary clinician and community liaison nurse.

"Whereabouts Unknown" and the companion chapter, "Slipping Through the Cracks," are about the onset of a serious mental disorder, the need for families to have a bridge between the medical diagnosis and management of the disease, and the day-to-day realities of coping with the illness, and the recovery process. This story is a tragic illustration of how people can slip through the cracks of a failed mental health system. Yet it is also a story of caring and perseverance, the resiliency of the human spirit, and the uniting of common goals with common sense which, finally, resulted in appropriate treatment and care for Anne Mathews and reuniting her with her family.

THE IMPACT OF SCHIZOPHRENIA

The diagnosis of a serious and persistent mental disorder like schizophrenia launches a family into a world characterized by tumult, confusion, loss, grief, and conflict. Schizophrenia is definitely a "dread disease." What makes it so is that most people fail to understand its neurobiological origins, preferring to think of it less as a disease and more as some basic human flaw or mental defect that is the result of bad habits, bad parents, or lack of will. Jeanette Keil eloquently describes her reaction upon first hearing her own diagnosis: "Distorted and confused as my thoughts and feelings were, when first diagnosed, the very word 'schizophrenia' was momentous enough to account for the cataclysmic tremors I experienced inside. It rang in my ears, a death toll for the life I had once known."

No sooner had she been diagnosed than Keil began to grieve the loss of her former self before schizophrenia.

The manifestation of the disease is different for each individual. This is partly why it has been so difficult for society to accept it as a disease and what makes the experience so confusing for family members, delaying the realization that a relative is seriously ill. In "Slipping Through the Cracks," Anne Mathews was subtly transformed over a period of eighteen months from a bubbly, outgoing, active high school girl to a homeless young woman who believed that she was being tortured and poisoned by the neighbors and pursued by the KGB. It wasn't that her parents were so unconcerned about her that they didn't respond to the signs and symptoms of her disease but, as Kessler suggests, there is no blueprint for the disease, no list of the seven warning signs of schizophrenia as there is for heart disease. So her parents responded issue by issue, crisis by crisis, increasingly certain that something was gravely wrong. Yet family members are not likely to think of schizophrenia as they wonder what could be the problem. In this society people touched by the disease are so stigmatized that it is the last thing you think of until, like the Mathews family, you are so confused and in such pain that you accept the diagnosis with relief and with the hope that you will finally find some solutions.

In her well-known book *Illness as Metaphor,* Susan Sontag characterizes illness as: ". . . the nightside of life, a more onerous citizenship. Everyone who is born holds dual citizenship in the kingdom of the well and the kingdom of the sick. Although we all prefer to use only the good passport, sooner or later each of us is obliged, at least for a spell, to identify ourselves as citizens of that other place."

Keil echoed those sentiments in observing that once people accept the diagnosis of schizophrenia they realize that they are citizens, not tourists, in the kingdom of mental illness. The problem is, without a passport it is difficult to travel this new land with its new language, new customs, and very foreign culture. The passport comes in the form of information, education, advocacy, and adaptation to individual needs. It can be obtained from a confusing array of mental health professionals, self-help groups, friends, family, and inner resources. One only need navigate the maze that will lead to the path of recovery.

It is in navigating this maze that families early and often may come into conflict with the communities in which they live, work, and play and with the very mental health care system that they need to help them. It is often at this juncture that common sense and common goals collide with the common laws of the system, such as confidentiality. "Slipping Through the Cracks" provides a poignant illustration of how confidentiality, a perfectly well intentioned concept, can become operationalized in a way that obstructs helpful family involvement in care. There is no common sense when a homeless shelter, in the name of confidentiality, "protects" the identity of a psychotic, seriously ill resident from parents who would take her home and ensure that she receive appropriate treatment. There is no common sense when the local police would choose to ignore an obviously psychotic, ill-kempt young woman who sleeps in a public park rather than assist her commitment to treatment. Had Anne Mathews been a young child, or even a stray dog, she might have been better taken care of because our laws are less conflicted about invoking dependency on helpless children or pets.

LESSONS FROM "SLIPPING THROUGH THE CRACKS" AND "WHEREABOUTS UNKNOWN"

Virtually all of the chapters in this book provide a family view of the people, treatments, and systems that help or hinder families in their efforts to cope with the diagnosis of schizophrenia, the clinical and behavioral manifestations of the illness, and the general life disruption which results when a relative is stricken. We believe these stories illuminate five major areas which deserve further consideration:

- The need for early diagnosis and education
- The need for inclusive treatment planning
- The needs of siblings
- The need for respite
- The need for system reform

Early Diagnosis and Education. A traveler in unfamiliar territory will have great difficulty getting from one place to another without benefit of a road map. Similarly, families will experience great difficulty managing schizophrenia without benefit of a diagnostic map. While it is true that psychiatric diagnoses carry the burden of stigma, it is also true that they are associated with a growing wealth of scientific and clinical information that is critical to proper treatment and management of the disease. Schizophrenia is not a homogeneous concept. There are variations and subtypes of the disease, differences that matter when it comes to choosing proper medication or understanding the long-term prognosis related to daily functioning. Regrettably, the Mathews family went a very long time without benefit of a diagnostic map.

Patients and families need to have as much information as possible in order to be equipped with the proper tools for coping with the illness. The more the family knows, the more effective they can be in assisting the treatment team and their relative. In our view, information about the illness not only enables the family to be of practical help but also gives the family hope   hope that we will increase what we know and eventually discover a cure, and that we can use what we know now to make a reasonable adaptation to the disease and improve quality of life in the absence of a cure.

Of course, families need to be taught about a lot more than the diagnosis and symptoms. They need to be alerted to the known and likely side effects of treatment, in particular medications. For instance, awareness of normal and abnormal effects of medication will decrease alarm over the dulling and blunting effects of certain medications on behavior and increase the family's ability to communicate with the treatment team. Families need to know that not all symptoms are amenable to medication and that sometimes no medication is the right treatment. They need to know about the effects of overstimulating and understimulating environments and they need to know when to ask and whom to ask for help if symptom management is becoming a real problem at home and in the community. Early in the illness, when symptom management is likely to be most difficult, families deserve to be told that something as painful as calling the police to have a relative taken to the hospital is the kindest thing they will be able to do—far kinder than tolerating disruptive and destructive behavior in their unprotected home setting.

And, finally, they need to know where they can turn for help. There are a growing number of national consumer groups, most of which have local chapters, that provide a resource for families and support—much like what the Mathews found through the National Alliance for the Mentally Ill. There is certain help and information that can come only from people who have experienced the trauma of mental illness and the frustration of dealing with a cumbersome system of care. Local treatment settings and mental health boards should have listings of organizations available in their area.

In addition to individualized education, "Slipping Through the Cracks" highlights the need for more and better public education. This happens in two ways: through formal programs targeted to the general public and run by local mental health agencies, boards, and self-help groups and through more public disclosure by families like the Mathews family. It is only through public education and personal disclosure that we will ever be successful in destigmatizing psychiatric disorders.

Those of us in the helping professions who care for people with severe and persistent disorders need to make a more personal commitment to monitor and conduct public education seminars. Are we getting the latest information about biomedical markers and the neurobiological origins of schizophrenia out to our local publics in ways they can understand it? Do we take opportunities in our day-to-day social lives to educate friends, family, and neighbors? Are we free of stigmatizing attitudes and behaviors ourselves? Do we press the clinical agencies where we work to invest time and money in public education? Do we volunteer time with local self-help groups, and do we extend to these groups an invitation to provide education to our staff?

Families need guidance and encouragement in the area of self-disclosure. It is important to be able to say to relatives and friends who have contact with the family, "Anne has been diagnosed with schizophrenia. It is a neurobiological disorder which affects the way she perceives reality and how she thinks. We expect she will be able to get symptoms under control with medication, but you shouldn't be alarmed if her emotions seem a little blunt—that's one of the side effects of medication."Disclosing means the family doesn't have to behave as if there is some horrible secret. Keeping secrets is stressful, and families who are coping with schizophrenia don't have room for unnecessary stress. Besides, treating a psychiatric diagnosis as a secret simply reinforces the stigma associated with it. There's nothing like knowing that a relative or close friend has a psychiatric illness to broaden someone's attitude! Disclosing also means that it will be easier, in the long run, to manage embarrassing situations—and whenever someone is psychotic or symptomatic you can count on an embarrassing situation.

Disclosing early and often makes it more likely that the family and the relative can exit gracefully when symptoms demand it. By the way, we do not mean to imply that families should disclose their personal business to just anyone. But, much as you would inform a circle of friends, close colleagues, and relatives that a member of the family has cancer or heart disease, we advocate the same principle when someone has a psychiatric disease. In our view, careful disclosure has a normalizing effect on everyone and serves an important public education function, which cannot be achieved through more formal programs. The Mathews were fortunate to have a friend like Wayne Lambert who called them to say he had seen Anne, even though he was ashamed that he had not approached her. His concern that he might have been misperceived as making advances to a strange young woman is normal in a culture like ours that is so concerned with proper, polite behavior. There is little doubt that had he approached Anne she would have "made a scene." We have a long way to go in our public education mission before such a "scene" would be considered an acceptable price to pay for getting someone the psychiatric care that they needed.

Inclusive Treatment Planning. If there was a single theme that permeated these chapters it was the lack of systematic treatment planning and the systematic exclusion of the Mathews family from what random plans were made. Even at the end of the story, one had the impression that the Mathews and Anne were left sitting at home wondering how to cope with so-called negative symptoms (symptoms not amenable to medication and that lead to social withdrawal, lack of emotional range, and general apathy). We found ourselves wishing that Martha Golden had been sent home with Anne.

Assessment and diagnosis should lead to a plan for treatment. The plan is usually more specific in the short term and more general in the long term, but should address the future and have some goals set out over a reasonable time frame—reasonable being defined by the diagnosis, the symptoms, and the predicted trajectory of the disease. Most importantly, the treatment plan should be shared with the family.

There is an abiding truth about persistent and severe disorders like schizophrenia. The illness and the recovery unfold over a period of many years, and the only constant is the patient and the family. Since the health providers and the treatment change often, it makes no sense to exclude the only constants from treatment planning.

If the Mathews were part of a comprehensive treatment planning effort on Anne's behalf, they might be able to put her negative symptoms into some kind of perspective. It will be no more pleasant to deal with them, but it might be a lot more tolerable to have an idea about how long they might continue and what can be done about them over time.

Patients and families are the exclusive source of valuable data about the progression of the illness and the progress of recovery and about the effects of treatment. If they are part of a plan, they will be more likely to observe these data and report them to the treatment team. Over time, patients and families are the experts on what works and what doesn't and may offer valuable advice that can be shared with others in similar circumstances.

It is often the case that, in the name of confidentiality, families are excluded from care. In our view, there is a vast difference between protecting the private disclosures of patients and denying basic information to families concerning the disease, symptom management, the treatment plan, and day-to-day living. Yet, all too often, no information is shared in order to avoid the remote possibility that a real confidence might be violated.

Siblings. At some point in their seemingly endless journey with Anne down the path of schizophrenia, the Mathews took note that Anne's sisters were being affected by her illness and by their all-consuming efforts to get her treated.

Diane Marsh writes of siblings, especially adult siblings, as the "forgotten family members." She recounts the emotional burden of anger, guilt, grief, and shame that many siblings carry and reminds us that, in addition to the emotional baggage, siblings often have many reality demands. They have to cope with the behavior of their ill brother or sister and may be called upon, as in the case of Anne's sister Jean, to provide an opportunity for a brother or sister where there might otherwise be none. They frequently must do without parental support and advice because their parents are so exhausted by the effort of caring for their brother or sister. Marsh cautions us that there is the risk of "parentification" when siblings assume too much responsibility, but she also implies that there is equal risk when siblings attempt to totally distance themselves from the family and the illness. She recommends referral to self-help groups, many of which have special meetings for siblings. She suggests that assertive education and intervention with siblings might help them identify and cope with feelings that otherwise remain out of awareness, yet still affect their own lives and development.

Siblings also need to be educated about the genetic risks associated with schizophrenia and other disorders. There is nothing so tragic as the genetic potential that a neurobiological disorder will repeat itself in subsequent generations—except maybe the possibility that a sibling would not be forewarned.

And, there is the necessity to anticipate the future. Many adults who are diagnosed with schizophrenia are able to live independent from their family. However, some will require more care and supervision and may be unable to live in full independence. If for no other reason, siblings should be fully informed about the illness and the progress of recovery at regular intervals. Even if they are not directly involved in care, down the road they may need to assume increased responsibility as parents age, or become ill, or die. Not all siblings will feel able to consider taking on such responsibility. It helps if parents and siblings discuss these eventualities well in advance so that plans can be made for substitute care, so that no one is left in the dark about expectations and intentions.

Respite. Patients and families alike need to take a break from the twenty-four-hour-a-day involvement with illness in order to gain a little perspective and peace and to restore energy. One hopes that someone will help Shirley and Neal Mathews get past the trauma of having lost their daughter to homelessness for eighteen months, so that they will feel able to gain some respite for themselves. We can only imagine that the Mathews would be afraid to let Anne out of their sight for fear of losing her again. Yet, they will surely lose her and themselves if they don't purposefully interrupt the intensity with which they have cared for her over the last few years.

Again, local mental health agencies and boards should have information concerning formal respite programs. It can often be therapeutic for family members and patients to take an agreed-upon time-out. Sometimes one party needs the time-out while the other isn't ready, and that's where the treatment team can be of help in deciding when and how to separate. Respite is synonymous with a reprieve, lull, letup, or rest. All of us require lulls in our lives, times of relative calm and quiet, when we can take care of ourselves with a minimum of responsibility for others. Such lulls often illuminate new insights into problems left behind and definitely recharge the batteries for the inevitable return to "real life." A good treatment plan will address respite early on and set goals for achieving it on a regular basis.

System Reform. A whole book could be written on the need for reform of our mental health system. It is often observed that we have a non-system of care, and the stories in this book certainly bear witness to that observation. We will emphasize three observations about the need for system reform.

First, it is obvious that we must find a way to create centralized clinical, administrative, and fiscal authority for care if patients and families are to survive our decentralized system. The Robert Wood Johnson Foundation has just concluded a five-year program in nine major cities in the U.S. in which they tested various models for a central authority. Under this program a single central authority had to be organized from among the many authorities for various aspects of service in a given city. The new entity had fiscal, administrative, and clinical responsibility for care that was delivered to a population of patients with serious and persistent mental disorders. The services included inpatient and outpatient treatment, rehabilitation, housing, and case management, and the central authority was required to include consumer organizations.

While the evaluation of the project has not yet been published, early results published by Shore and Cohen indicate that patients being treated in these systems had easier access to a wide array of services and did not so often become "lost to treatment." As a site visitor to several of these projects, Krauss observed active participation on the part of consumers and families which actually resulted in changed service delivery. Without a central authority, it is not clear who is in charge and it is too easy for no one to be in charge while families and patients get lost in the treatment maze in search of assistance.

Second, there needs to be an increased focus on housing alternatives and living skills. The Robert Wood Johnson (RWJ) project quickly discovered that there were not sufficient supervised housing programs for people with serious mental disorders. In too many instances the only choices were to live at home with mom and dad or to live on the streets. During the five-year period of the project, RWJ and the U.S. Department of Housing and Urban Development (HUD) collaborated to provide loan money and housing vouchers to cities as a way of leveraging creative relationships between mental health departments and businesses to develop housing starts and supervised programs. As one might expect, these projects got a community response that was not all positive. However, the mental health department was in a position of strength due to its well-formed partnership with business. Together they were much better able to fight the "not in my backyard" (NIMBY) syndrome and make real headway on behalf of the mentally ill. Local media cooperated in printing the many success stories associated with these new housing opportunities. And, most importantly, living options were finally created that supported independence to the extent possible while providing a necessary level of supervision.

Third, it is apparent that the time is past due to reexamine a number of laws that affect mental health services delivery. For the most part, these laws have been on the books since the days leading up to deinstitutionalization. Now that community-based treatment and treatment in the "least restrictive" setting is the norm, we must examine those laws to see if they still serve the people they were intended to protect. In the past, protection meant extracting patients from so-called "treatment" so that they could live in less restricted ways in the community. Now protection means seeing that treatment is mandated for people who are sick to ensure that jail or a shelter don't become a substitute for psychiatric care.

Confidentiality is another example. While we would never advocate abolishing confidentiality, it may be time to loosen or broaden its definition. Anne Mathews was done great harm, repeatedly, in the name of confidentiality. Consumers, families, and providers should unite in their efforts to understand and study current laws and regulations with an eye toward useful reform.

A PSYCHIATRIC NURSING PERSPECTIVE

When the helping professions allow a person to suffer the ravages of schizophrenia for fear of being accused of coercion or violation of confidentiality, it is a sign that the system is getting in the way of the common goals of health professionals and families:

1. to properly diagnose, understand, and treat the disease;

2. manage the illness;

3. promote recovery; and

4. marshal the necessary resources to foster independence and quality of life.

That is why Martha Golden, the nurse who helped get Anne Mathews home, finally cried, "For God's sake, where's common sense?" The fact that Martha Golden is a nurse is not surprising. Psychiatric nurses, indeed nurses in general, are equally as conversant with the language of diagnosis and disease as they are with the language of everyday realities. The primary mission of the nurse is to care for individuals and for the environments (the hospital, outpatient clinic, community, home) in which care is delivered. Henderson formulated the internationally accepted definition of nursing: "The unique function of the nurse is to assist the individual, sick or well, in the performance of those activities contributing to health or its recovery (or to peaceful death) that he would perform unaided if he had the necessary strength, will or knowledge. And to do this in such a way as to help him gain independence as rapidly as possible."

The focus of the nurse is not the disease, but the experience of the illness and the interaction between person and environment. While the nurse hopes for a cure and administers potentially curative treatments s/he concentrates more on recovery.

Anthony has observed that most of what we know about recovery from mental illness comes from the consumer literature, which describes it as a deeply personal process of changing one's attitudes, values, feelings, goals, skills, and/or roles, which leads to a way of living a hopeful, satisfying, and contributing life even with illness-caused limitations. He notes: "Recovery from mental illness involves much more than recovery from the illness itself. People with mental illness may have to recover from the stigma they have incorporated into their very being; from the iatrogenic effects of treatment settings; from lack of recent opportunities for self-determination; from the negative side-effects of unemployment; and from crushed dreams."

Recovery from schizophrenia, or any severe mental disorder, is a difficult job. Being a family member of someone with schizophrenia is a difficult job. No one ever applies for these jobs and there is no standard job description. But it is guaranteed that with no orientation, job training, or education, patients and family members will not succeed at the job.

The psychiatric nurse can and does assist in this process of orientation, education, and training. The psychiatric nurse is the bridge between diagnosis and treatment of the disease and recovery from the illness— between clinical management and day-to-day community living. Psychiatric nurses, through education and experience, have knowledge about the assessment and diagnosis of mental disorders, medical treatment, managing long-term illness, the recovery process, the community, daily living needs, and the health care system. Nurses can be found in inpatient, day treatment, outpatient, and community-based treatment facilities. Their services are characterized by twenty-four-hour, seven-day-per-week responsibility, a holistic view of mind and body, and a "careative" rather than a curative focus, with an emphasis on health, strengths, and adaptation.

They are a good source of information about the disorder and treatment, expected main effects and side effects of medication, symptom management (from both a patient and a family perspective), and how to navigate the system. They have been trained to assist people with problem-solving and decision-making with the goal of maintaining as much autonomy for the individual as possible but allowing dependence and interdependence when necessary; and they know a lot about day-to-day behavior problems and the difficulty of maintaining personal boundaries and structure in the midst of madness. Since they tend to accumulate a continuum of data about the patient over time, psychiatric nurses assume the coordinating function for the treatment team and can provide a vital communication link between the team and the family.

A psychiatric nursing perspective can be helpful at any time in the course of an illness and recovery. However, there are certain junctures at which such a perspective is essential. At the time of assessment and diagnosis the family would be well advised to ask whether a nurse could be assigned to help them understand and process the information they will be receiving from the treatment team. At this time, the nurse can translate scientific and psychiatric jargon into understandable terms and she can help the patient and the family identify and cope with the emotions that go along with learning more about the disorder. If a patient is admitted to an inpatient facility it will be virtually guaranteed that a psychiatric nurse will be part of the care. Families should not hesitate to ask who the primary nurse is that will be assigned to their relative. Unfortunately, if a patient is first treated in an outpatient facility, it is not guaranteed that a nurse will be involved. But, families can ask for such involvement, if only on a temporary basis while they adjust to the illness and treatment.

Another juncture at which a psychiatric nursing perspective is useful is during any major treatment transition, whether it be discharge from an inpatient facility, transfer to day treatment, halfway house, or vocational rehabilitation, or a major change in medications. These are periods when symptoms can worsen, or new symptoms might develop, and there is often a need for someone to be sure that information is properly communicated and coordinated—something that nurses know how to do very well.

Psychiatric nurses are often available during relatively quiet treatment maintenance periods when one might require general oversight of medication and occasional symptom monitoring. Many model case-management systems make use of nurse supervisors or coordinators to consult with the primary case manager, who may have day-to-day community contact with the patient.

Patients who have other serious health problems, such as diabetes, heart disease, cancer, or other chronic conditions, might benefit from the care of a psychiatric nurse because the nurse has education and experience in general health conditions and can address possible interactions between treatment for the psychiatric disorder and the other condition and act as a liaison between the mental health team and other treatment teams.

In the ideal world, everyone with a diagnosed severe psychiatric disorder, like schizophrenia, should be assigned a psychiatric nurse as part of the treatment team. These days, the reality is that everyone is more likely to be assigned a case manager who may or may not be a nurse and who may or may not be part of a team that includes a nurse.

Case Management and Nursing. In the past decade, the case management model has evolved as a way of extending the reach of mental health services into the community where people with psychiatric disorders must learn to live, work, and play. Case management was invented because our post-deinstitutionalization mental health system was not working. One of the few benefits of long-term hospitalization back in the sixties was that the state psychiatric hospital served as the central clearinghouse for all of a patient's needs—food, clothing, housing, useful occupation, health care. It took us almost a quarter of a century beyond deinstitutionalization to realize that we had so decentralized services as to make it impossible for patients and families to gain access. Thus, case management was invented as a way to provide each patient with one person who would broker services and be a primary community contact.

We believe that the concept of case management is sound and, at its best, a way to ensure that everyone is working toward common goals with common sense. But, families and mental health professionals should not confuse case management with clinical management or other services (rehabilitation, residential, vocational). Case managers may be social workers, caseworkers, mental health workers, nurses, psychologists, or psychiatrists. In any given system case management may be defined as a broad array of services or more narrowly restricted, for example, to community living skills. Good case-management systems are well anchored to a larger treatment system, and the case managers are part of a team of mental health professionals, any and all of whom should be available to the patient for direct care or to the case manager for consultation and supervision. Families should not hesitate to ask about the background of a case manager and to inquire about the composition and workings of the larger team. We believe that families have a right to know who is in charge and that, ideally, every team should have a psychiatric nurse.

In our increasingly decentralized and nondifferentiated mental health system we have moved pretty far from the ideal. Witness how long it took Anne Mathews and her family to encounter Martha Golden, a psychiatric nurse who understood the disease and the illness, knew how to make the system work, how to give support to frantic family members, and how to set things in motion that would eventually get Anne into treatment. And, if it weren't for the Virginia Alliance for the Mentally Ill the Mathews might never have found Martha Golden. For that matter, they might never have found their daughter because they were never really viewed as part of the solution to Anne's problems.

As this book attests, it is time for a paradigm shift in our view of families. It is not enough that we have given up the schizophrenogenic theories that so damaged and alienated families. We must replace these blaming explanations of mental illness with something new, a vision of families as full partners in care. Families will know that they are valued when our systems include them at all policy levels, our clinicians involve them in treatment planning, our services reach out to them to provide support, and we take their self-help organizations seriously. Families will know that they are valued when it is the rule, not the exception, that common sense prevails and common goals are achieved.

5

Dial 911:

Schizophrenia and the Police Response

LUCILLE SCHMIDT IS A SLENDER, CAREFULLY dressed woman. She speaks quietly and with composuré. A woman who has mustered a wealth of self-control, she strives to establish a distance between her delicate sensitivity and her public persona. Lucille Schmidt is a brave woman. She is unaware that her hard-won fortitude and courage reveal her sensibility.

Lucille and her husband, Jack, have two children: a daughter, Gillian, who is in her late thirties, and a son, Anthony (Tony), who is thirty. Tony suffers from paranoid schizophrenia and has been in the forensic ward of the state mental hospital for the past seven years.

Gillian, the Schmidts' daughter, is married. Her husband, Roger, is a lawyer and she is a high school math teacher. They have no children. Lucille and her daughter are very fond of each other; they have an easy and comfortable relationship. It becomes evident as she discloses the recent family history that the Schmidts are—and always have been—a family who cherish a delicate intimacy with each other.

Throughout the difficult and painful narration about Tony's illness and the consequences of his disease, Lucille maintains an apparent tranquillity. The degree of serenity that she is able to keep in place seems almost preternatural. However, when she inadvertently mentions her daughter's recent cancer and mastectomy her calmness is pierced. Sitting quietly, scarcely moving, she begins to weep copiously. The suppressed sadness and agitation caused by her son's tragic life are suddenly revealed. An offhand remark about her daughter's brush with death and subsequent recovery exposes not only her current anxiety but also her long years of cumulative pain.

When Tony Schmidt was nineteen he was a tall, lean, and handsome young man. Dark hair, long-lashed hazel eyes, and classically chiseled features gave him a matinee idol appearance. Even at nineteen Tony could be described as having an unselfconscious personal style that one could almost call elegant without being effete. He had always been a serious scholar and a fine and sensitive musician. He played the clarinet. Tony enjoyed being a good student, and it was important to him that he excel. His achievements brought him pleasure. It would have been impossible to conceive, let alone predict that this careful, quiet, and consistently high-achieving nineteen-year-old young man would four years later end up in the jail ward—the forensic ward—of the state mental hospital.

Sitting with her hands carefully folded in her lap and her ankles neatly crossed, Lucille Schmidt spoke cautiously and quietly. "My husband Jack and I have a son with paranoid schizophrenia, who is now thirty years old. He is in the forensic ward of the state mental hospital, and he has been there for seven years."

Lucille recited her story as though she were coming from a great distance, as though this were some other mother and son that she was talking about. Her voice was hushed, and the timbre was such that one listened to her with an intense concentration.

"The illness started—or rather I should say we noticed that something was irregular—when Tony was nineteen years old. He was in his first year at the state university and his first semester had appeared to be normal and satisfactory. He had graduated from high school with many honors, including being a presidential scholar. Tony had a surfeit of gifts: not only was he a fine student but he also was an accomplished and skilled musician with a love of jazz. He had decided on a chemistry major with a minor in music. Gradually, however, during the second and third semester, things seemed to be falling apart.

"We noticed that he kept changing roommates. This was odd, because Tony had always been consistent in his friendships. It was his fashion to choose his friends with care and caution, the consequence being that he usually had loyal and long-term relationships. As a boy, Tony had led a life that was remarkably free of impulse." Lucille paused. "I don't mean that he wasn't a spontaneous person; I don't mean that at all. What I intend to imply is that Tony was thoughtful; he wasn't frivolous."

But now Tony had lost interest in his schoolwork. Tony had lost interest in his friends. As his mother put it, "Tony had lost interest in just about everything." Concurrently the Schmidts started to receive very distressing phone calls from their son. Tony would telephone them as he sat in the emergency waiting room of a hospital near the university. Apparently he was appearing at the emergency room almost daily and presenting an ever-changing list of ailments. At one time he thought he had had an acute attack of appendicitis; another time it was a brain tumor. If he had a slight cold, he feared that he had diphtheria; if he nicked himself while shaving he became certain that the cut was becoming septic and gangrenous. The list was inventive and growing. So were the hospital bills. Even though none of Tony's complaints was ever verified as an actual illness or disease, even though he appeared at the hospital regularly for nearly three months, no one from the hospital suggested to the Schmidts that their son might be mentally ill.

"Tony came home for the summer vacation. We have our own business. We own and run a hardware store. My husband suggested that Tony might want to work for him, but it was quickly apparent that wouldn't be possible. Jack, my husband, is a very quiet man, he doesn't like to impose himself on anyone. And Tony, who had always been very cooperative, was suddenly truculent and difficult. Jack suggested to Tony that he find a summer job outside of the family business. But that was also unsuccessful. He would go to various job interviews and inevitably he would be hired, but within two weeks he would be asked to leave. It wasn't only that he was what one might call irritable; in addition he didn't seem to be able to concentrate on any matter at hand."

One evening while Lucille was preparing dinner—she was cooking lasagna, Tony's favorite food—Tony walked into the kitchen and sat down. He bent over the table and cradled his head in his arms. "Tony seemed to be rocking his body and he spoke to me in a very strained thin voice. He said: 'I think something is wrong with me. I think I'm different from other people. Mom.' At this point his voice almost broke. 'Mom,' he repeated, 'I need help, I'm afraid. Things are happening to my mind and I'm scared.'

"I called our children's pediatrician for advice. He had followed our children since they were very young. We had a lot of respect for him. He knew our children very well and we knew him very well. He suggested three psychiatrists to us and we interviewed each of them. We were very pleased with the doctor whom we chose."

Tony did not return to the university. His mother said, "Little did I realize then that our dreams for Tony's future were to be just that: dreams." He remained at his parents' home and started seeing Dr. John Reid, a psychiatrist. "Tony was tested and Dr. Reid diagnosed Tony as having paranoid schizophrenia. Immediately Tony was started on a course of medicine. I believe the medication was Prolixin. Tony's behavior improved, but he continued to be very irritable. He would say: 'Don't touch me, don't touch me,' that kind of thing, which indicated to me that he was hypersensitive. I felt as though I was dealing with a burn victim, but it wasn't just his body that I couldn't touch: it was the person, it was Tony himself.

"And it was very difficult for him to get up in the morning. I thought that he should be on some kind of schedule. It worried me that he didn't seem to have any goals. But Dr. Reid told me not to argue needlessly with Tony, that I could be firm, but I should try to 'let him be' as much as possible." Lucille felt that she and Jack were very fortunate to have worked with a psychiatrist who explained their son's disease to them so carefully. "He was honest with us, he was very realistic," she said. He not only told them how to comport themselves on a daily basis with Tony, but also described in detail what they might expect.

"Dr. Reid told us what we could anticipate as Tony's untreated schizophrenia ran its course: things like rocking in his bed or taking off his clothes and walking down the street. He tried to prepare us for all sorts of bizarre behavior. Importantly, he told us to contact our local mental health center, and he did not neglect to tell us that we could expect little help from them as long as Tony neither endangered himself nor others.

"We did call our mental health center, and Dr. Reid was right: they were kind but they said, 'Unless your son harms others or himself there is nothing we can do.' " Lucille shook her head: " 'There is nothing we can do' really stuck in my mind."

As things worsened, the Schmidts considered themselves fortunate to have had the advice of a doctor who prepared them for the worst-case scenarios. Had they not been so well prepared, they would have been more easily shocked and horrified by the gradual and appalling disintegration of their beloved son. Because they were not as surprised as they might otherwise have been, when the situation deteriorated and became more and more horrific and outlandish, they were able to retain some self-control. They remained responsible parents and never completely threw up their hands in despair.

Unfortunately, Tony did not continue to see Dr. Reid. He would take the family car ostensibly to go to his appointments, but he would drive off and disappear for hours, sometimes not returning until very late at night. Even more seriously, he stopped taking his medicine. Lucille remembered that Dr. Reid called; he told her that as long as Tony wouldn't take the medicine and wouldn't go to counseling that there was nothing more that he could do.

"Jack and I really appreciated the way he handled Tony's case because we have been told some terrible tales about therapists leading people astray. Now that we have come to know so many other families who have children with this disease, we have heard a number of horror stories about doctors continuing all kinds of useless treatment. And many of these people have paid a great deal of money only to find that they have simply been gypped. If a person with schizophrenia doesn't take some kind of neuroleptic medicine, all the 'talking cures' in the world won't be worth a row of beans.

"Gradually Tony became more and more strange. We had given up all hope of his having a job. He could still get a job, but it was impossible for him to keep it. Two or three days seemed to be his limit. Sometimes he was asked to leave and sometimes he just walked away and didn't return. None of these were important jobs: he worked at a gas station or a food store, that kind of thing.

"At home he was becoming more difficult and more withdrawn. He had stopped seeing any of his friends and he was very solitary. I remember one evening when his grandmother [Jack's mother] was visiting. It was after dinner and we were all sitting in the living room playing cards. We were playing gin rummy, when Tony sprung up and threw all his cards in the air. He screamed at us as though we had injured him: 'I can't take it anymore, I can't take it anymore.' He ran off to his bedroom and we sat there quite stunned. We had no idea what had happened. Nobody had said or done anything untoward. At the time it was very unnerving, but much worse was to come."

One of Lucille's friends, Emily, who was a nurse, came over to dinner at their house and quickly grasped that both the Schimidts were at the end of their tether. As Lucille remembers: "We simply did not know what to do." Emily arranged for Jack and Lucille to attend a meeting of a support group that was attached to the Oregon Alliance for the Mentally Ill. "We found out that we were not alone, that there were others going through the same thing. It isn't only the stigma which makes a family feel as isolated as their mentally ill relative appears to be, but we also realized that we were becoming as frozen in our absorption with Tony as he was with his illness.

"Jack and I had been carefully educated about schizophrenia not only by Dr. Reid but also by our daughter, Gillian. She was taking her masters degree at that time, and she had taken a course in abnormal psychology. She photocopied the pertinent pages from her textbook for us. Despite this familiarity with the disease, we still felt as though our experiences were unique.

"What was happening in our home was so peculiar that we simply couldn't imagine that it could occur anywhere else. I think that in those early stages what was really paralyzing is that even though Tony's behavior was obviously not 'right,' it was not outrageously crazy. The total effect was that we always felt as though we were in some kind of muddle. All the time we were constantly questioning, we were always evaluating how Tony's behavior fitted into what we called normal and what we called abnormal."

Lucille and Jack Schmidt were able to find a great deal of comfort in the support group. As they chatted with other families, they realized that they had been fortunate in finding—straightaway, with no fuss, no time lost—a kind and conscientious psychiatrist who was able to give them (so quickly) a clear diagnosis. And of equal importance, they came to know that their daughter and her husband were unusual in their consistent and unflagging emotional assistance. With the passage of years and Tony's progressive degeneration, the Schmidts understood that their daughter and son-in-law's continued loving and tangible support was a rare treasure.

For a few months Lucille and Jack felt a thin ray of hope. Tony decided that he would like to go back to school. Happily, ecstatically, Lucille enrolled him at a local university. He took some music courses. For a short time he returned to seeing Dr. Reid, kept regular appointments, took his medicine. Lucille remembered feeling giddy with euphoria. Perhaps they would beat this after all. Perhaps a good outcome was possible. Perhaps they were to be different from the other families whom they had met at the support group.

Concurrent with his mounting success, Tony became certain that there was nothing wrong with him. He stopped going to see his doctor. He stopped taking any medication. His deterioration was dramatic in its speed. He was intensely hostile, irritable, and surly. His parents experienced an acute sense of panic as their optimism slipped away. They felt themselves to be standing on the edge of an abyss. It was as though they were watching their son hurtling through space. And equally as terrifying, they felt themselves to be losing their grip. At any moment they sensed that they too might be out there with nothing to secure them, nothing onto which they could grasp.

Again Jack and Lucille went to visit their local county mental health agency, and again the agency told them that there was nothing that they could do to assist them. "I hate this term 'system,' " Lucille said. "But that is the word that is used, and the mental health agency made it quite clear to us that Tony was not in the system. It wasn't only that they couldn't hospitalize Tony but they couldn't help us in any way. Even though Tony had been diagnosed by a psychiatrist as having paranoid schizophrenia, he did not qualify to be in the 'system.' It was a Catch-22 situation: for Tony to be eligible for state and national benefits for the mentally ill, he first had to be hospitalized, and to be hospitalized he had to show a clear indication that he would harm others or himself."

Her voice lowered and hushed, Lucille spoke as though to herself. "We have no health insurance because my husband and I are self-employed. We have always prided ourselves that we pay all our bills on time. We are not people who owe money. We now realized, in a way that we had not faced before, that Tony's illness was to be difficult and long term, and we were afraid."

Tony became increasingly agitated and difficult to live with. He was sure that he was dying, and again he made almost daily trips to emergency rooms around the city. His imaginary illnesses were burgeoning. Lucille remembered that "in one month he went to forty emergency rooms, thinking he was dying from one ailment or another. I paid the bills and then Roger [Gillian's husband] said to me, 'Tony is over eighteen. You don't have to pay those bills.'' I never thought I would ever do such a thing. But I did it. By then I knew there was no other alternative. I would call the hospitals and tell them that Tony couldn't pay his bills because he had a mental illness.

"I did receive a call from one of the big downtown hospitals. They inquired if I knew that there was a problem with Anthony Schmidt because he had been there so many times. I told them I knew only too well that there was a problem. I asked them if they could suggest how I could get Tony hospitalized. I asked them if they could help me. But they gave me the same answer that the county mental health had given to me. They all knew he was very ill, but all they could do was tell me what I already knew. I knew because I lived with him."

With alarming irregularity, bizarre and frightening episodes erupted around Jack and Lucille. They had always seen themselves as ordinary citizens who led ordinary lives. Now they lived like people who had set up house in a minefield. "One time," Lucille said, "I remember Tony walking into the kitchen and asking for a glass of milk. I poured it for him and he grabbed it from me—I'd scarcely finished filling the glass. He took that full glass of milk and slammed it so hard on the counter that the glass shattered. There were milk and splinters of glass all over that kitchen. But that wasn't the worst. I said to him, 'Oh, Tony,' and he retorted: 'I meant to do that.'

"It was a miserable time. Always, we have eaten our dinners together. Tony continued to join us, but he invariably seemed to be angry. Sometimes he just shouted loud, ugly words, sometimes he would throw things: bits of food, a spoon, his napkin. One time he sat down and Jack said: 'How was your day, Tony?' Tony didn't answer; he just took his arm and swept everything—everything—off the table onto the floor. Food, dishes, and cutlery were strewn every which way all over the kitchen. Jack and I"—Lucille shook her head—"we both wept.

"One evening we came home from the movies around ten thirty. Just as Jack was turning the key in the front door, a chair came flying out of Tony's second-floor window. He had hurled his desk chair right through his closed window. The street lights lit up the sparkling shards of glass which were everywhere, all over the front yard. Tony told us that we had disturbed him, that we had come home too late and that we had woken him up. We felt as though we were his hostages.

"We tried everything. It's silly when I think back. We even tried flute lessons. We kept hoping we could distract him from himself and get him re-interested in something positive. Of course, nothing worked. And slowly we were becoming aware that Tony's behavior was changing from being just bizarre to being dangerous. Even though we realized this, we had become almost paralyzed. We were exhausted. It was rather like being hypnotized by a snake charmer. Everything was becoming so horrific that in retrospect I believe that we too were losing touch with reality.

"There was an incident with a car which we should have done something about but we let it go. Tony got into an argument with an old schoolmate. Martin was his one remaining friend who, out of kindness, would occasionally drop over and see him. Martin told me that they were standing and chatting by the curb in front of our house. My car, which at that time we still let Tony use, was parked just in front of Martin's car. They had been talking about a certain tennis player, and Tony angrily had disagreed with Martin's estimation of this particular player's ability. Without any warning Tony suddenly ran to our car, jumped in, and attempted to back the car into Martin. As Martin explained it, there was no real danger. He thought Tony was just acting like a young kid who had lost his temper. Martin was easily able to get into his own car and drive away. He telephoned to tell us about it because he wanted to explain why he wasn't coming to see Tony anymore."

Lucille said that she and Jack talked to Tony about this, but "we couldn't reason with him. It was like talking to a wall." But a few months later the Schmidts were no longer able to avoid doing something about the tumult that was occurring in their house. "Tony had just gotten another of his temporary jobs near our house," Lucille recalled. "He walked home, and I was in the kitchen beginning preparations for our dinner. Tony was slicing some cheese for a sandwich, and I turned toward him and asked him how his day had gone. He lunged forward with this sharp knife in his hand and waved it around my face. All the time he was shrieking at me to leave him alone. I didn't scream or yell, I just stood there very quietly.

"Dr. Reid had warned me, early on, that I should always be very cautious. He had said that he didn't think that Tony would harm anyone, but that Tony did have visions of doing something with a knife. Dr. Reid had also suggested that I practice calling 911. Tony left the kitchen and went up to his room. I must have been shaking because it was a few minutes before I could control myself enough to go to the telephone. I didn't call 911, I called my daughter and then went over to her house. Gillian lives nearby. I stayed with her until my husband came home from work.

"I told Jack what had happened, and I said that we had to call the county mental health agency. Jack couldn't do it. He said to me: 'I just cannot do it.' We didn't call that evening. I wish we had. We stayed close together. Neither of us was ever by ourself, and Tony didn't come out of his room. The next day my daughter interceded and she called Dr. Reid. He saw her immediately, and he carefully explained to her that we couldn't permit Tony to live at the house anymore.

"Dr. Reid telephoned me and told me that he had just seen Gillian and he wanted to know—from me—what had happened. Then he said, 'I want you to get on that phone right now and call the county mental health and start a police hold on him.' I said: 'I'll wait until Jack gets home.' And he said, very sharply, 'No, you are going to do it right now.' So I had to be the strong one.

"I called the county mental health; by now they knew us, we had phoned them so often. They told me we had to go out there to fill out some forms. Jack picked me up and we drove out together. When we got to the bottom of the hill that is about a half mile from the agency, Jack turned to me. 'Lucy,' he said, 'Lucy, I can't drive anymore, I just can't do this.' I got behind the wheel and completed the drive to the agency. I knew that Dr. Reid was right and that we had to go through with this business. I knew that Tony needed us to do this. And I was certain that this was the only way we had to ensure him some appropriate care."

Lucille sat quietly and looked down at her hands. "The woman at mental health who wrote down our report didn't seem to believe us. We had to convince her that we were sincere. We had to convince her that we were afraid of Tony. That made us feel very cheap.

"They did, however, agree to do a police hold," Lucille said. "The police came the next morning to pick him up. They were kind and peaceful and seemed very sensitive to the situation. They suggested that Lucille go into another room, but Tony was so bewildered she felt she couldn't completely abandon him. He cried out to his father: "What are you doing to me, Dad? What's going on?" Lucille's composure almost fragmented as she remembered that morning. "He couldn't understand what we were doing to him. And for that instant I couldn't either."

Tony was taken to the state mental hospital. It was a Friday morning, so it wasn't until Monday that the Schmidts heard from the investigator. There is a routine examination and investigation of all purportedly mentally ill persons brought into hospital. The investigator called Jack and told him that they didn't really think there was anything wrong with Tony. Lucille wondered if the investigator was so persuaded because Tony was clean and neatly dressed. At this time she recalled, "Tony's symptoms were not yet so flagrant. On the other hand," she said, suddenly cupping her face in her hands, "he was so clearly mad."

On Tuesday evening Tony simply walked away from the hospital. The staff notified the Schmidts. Lucille went to stay with a friend. Jack and Lucille were afraid, but Jack went back to the house. They reasoned that someone should be there if Tony decided to go home. Tony hitchhiked into the city. He went straight home and Jack was there waiting for him. Jack called the police, as he had been directed by the hospital staff. Tony seemed pathetic and distraught. Later Jack told his wife that he had an overwhelming desire to scoop his son up and hold him safe. But it was not to be so.

The police arrived. They were a different crew from the first lot. This time they were not kind and gentle even though, as Lucille said, "they knew they were dealing with someone who was sick. These two hulking men came in and slammed into Tony, knocking him to the floor. Tony struggled ineptly and even started spitting like a small child. My husband was near tears, especially when Tony yelled: 'Dad, don't let them do this to me. Help me, Dad, help me.' " Lucille's voice had dropped to a whisper.

The police took him back to the hospital. The hospital investigator reconsidered his earlier opinion and ordered a twenty-one-day hospital treatment for Tony. Tony was sent to a small local hospital that ran a crisis ward for the county. Tony refused treatment. The county initiated a commitment hearing. Lucille and Jack went to the hearing. They were asked to describe what had occurred before Tony's hospitalization. The judge listened and quickly terminated the proceedings. He said, "There is nothing wrong with this boy. He is a spoiled brat."

"That was that," said Lucille. "The threat of harm was not enough. If Tony had actually stabbed me, I suppose they might have considered him to be ill. It seems strange that they would make that the criterion of illness." Almost imperceptibly Lucille shook her head.

"The next few months were worse than ever. We knew we couldn't have Tony live at home anymore, so we found him an apartment, and an apartment, and an apartment." Lucille smiled. "I can smile about it now, but then it was hell. We would get an apartment, pay for the first and last month's rent, get him all settled, and after about a week he would do something and he would be kicked out. Sometimes he would just be an incessant nuisance and call the fire department when there wasn't any fire, or he would call the gas company and say there was a smell of gas. But more seriously, he would knock on the apartment manager's door, at all times of the day and night, complaining about noises in the apartment building, complaining about other tenants, complaining that it was too hot, that it was too cold. So they kicked him out, over and over again."

Tony was starting to look very unkempt. His madness had become public. People were looking at him strangely. He was glassy-eyed and hallucinating, mumbling about aliens and space ships and creatures in the light bulbs. Soon the only places the Schmidts could find for their son to live in were the cheap and dilapidated downtown hotels, where they paid the rent one week at a time. These were horrible places: places frequented by pimps and prostitutes, by drunks, by drug pushers and users—places where Jack and Lucille would never have ventured had it not been for Tony. In these places the Schmidts were fearful not only for their son but for themselves as well.

"Always, Tony wanted to come back home. He didn't like any of the arrangements we made for him," Lucille remembered. "We felt quite desperate. We were worried about Tony when he wasn't with us and we were afraid of him when he was with us. We told him that when we were both home he could come and do his laundry, and that he could eat with us whenever he wished. By then his thinking was so poor. It seemed as though he was either withdrawn or violent. There didn't seem to be much middle ground. He would telephone us at all hours of the night, wanting to talk about his difficulties, and my husband would always get up and go and meet him. Jack never turned Tony down if Tony said he needed him. Poor Jack, he was so exhausted. He still believed that he would be able to reason with our son."

One evening Tony, now a strangely disconnected and unclean figure, walked into the emergency room of the county hospital. When the woman behind the admitting desk told him he would have to sit down and wait his turn before she could talk to him, he lunged forward, screaming, "You bitch," and tried to grab her by the neck. Fortunately there was a security guard standing nearby. He was able to subdue Tony, who was taken to the psychiatric-crisis ward, where he was put on a "two-doctor hold." This is a legal maneuver that enables the medical staff to keep a mentally ill, usually psychotic person in the crisis ward until a hearing can be arranged.

The Schmidts had no idea of Tony's whereabouts until the next day, when, much to their surprise and relief, he telephoned them. He demanded that they come immediately and get him out of the hospital. They did not. They were overjoyed to hear that their son was in a safe place. They could scarcely believe their and Tony's good fortune. The psychiatrist on the crisis unit spoke to them and informed them that there would be a commitment hearing in the county courthouse. The investigator on the case also spoke to them and explained how they could be helpful.

By now Tony was so evidently psychotic that his parents were sure that he couldn't be denied appropriate care. "There was a careful and well-prepared two-hour hearing," Lucille recollected. "I felt quite certain that there would be no trouble in getting Tony committed this time. Both Jack and I were on the stand, and two psychiatrists testified that in their opinion Tony should be hospitalized. After the judge had listened to everybody speak he said, 'There is no doubt in my mind that Tony Schmidt is mentally ill, but under the current laws I cannot commit him.' So he was out on the street again."

The same old routine reasserted itself. The Schmidts would rent a place for Tony and then he would be evicted; sometimes within a few days, sometimes—when they were lucky—a few weeks. More and more Tony was a pathetic sight, a shambling disheveled creature. Early one foggy and drizzling morning he was found wandering on a runway at the airport. He said he was waiting for the spaceships so that he could be "rejuvenated." His parents doggedly and stubbornly went on caring for their son. But now they admitted to themselves that they were in a hopeless situation.

Almost four years had passed since the summer that Tony had left the university. During this time he had remained friendly with an older man, Bill Watson, who owned a record store downtown, and was very tolerant of Tony's bizarre ways. He understood that the boy was ill, and his feelings of compassion overrode his uneasiness about Tony's behavior. It was music that enabled the two men to have a common ground. Even though Tony himself and the world—as it appeared to him—had been profoundly distorted by his illness, Tony's interest in music had remained unabated. Music seemed to draw him to a kind of sanity, almost as though it were a language immune to the distortions that madness had imposed.

One wintry afternoon, Lucille received a telephone call from Bill Watson. Bill often phoned Jack and Lucille. He was very concerned about his young friend. Initially, he hadn't understood why Tony's parents were unable to procure medical care for their obviously ill son. In time he came to comprehend that the Schmidts had tried every avenue in pursuit of attention and protection for Tony. So instead of berating them he joined them in his own way. He too offered Tony kindness and patience.

Following what had become an ingrained pattern of kindness, he telephoned Lucille on this chill December afternoon. "I knew something was wrong as soon as Bill spoke my name. His voice had a strange strangulated sound. 'Lucille,' he said, and he repeated himself, 'Lucille, Lucille. Tony has just wrecked my store and the gallery next door and the coffee shop across the street. Now he is sitting in a police car outside my broken window and'—Bill stopped talking and I thought he was going to weep—'he's sitting there with his funny smirking smile. Damn it, what is going to become of him?' " Lucille sat quite quietly, unaware that she was shaking her head.

About forty minutes before Bill telephoned Lucille, Tony Schmidt had walked into the coffee shop that was catty-corner across from his friend's record store. If a friend of Tony's from his university days had passed by, he would have been hard pressed to recognize in this unclean and peculiar man any resemblance to the younger, handsome, and earnest Tony Schmidt. Tony sat down and ordered a cup of coffee. A young waitress reluctantly took the order. She was discomfited by Tony's piercing gaze. When she returned, he asked her if she would go with him for a fuck. She was startled and trembled as she put the coffee on the table. It spilled. She ran away. Tony screamed, "You bitch," and swept the cup and saucer to the floor. Then, screeching and laughing, weeping and yelling, Tony Schmidt went berserk. He hurled chairs through the windows, he pushed tables over, he grabbed plates full of food and tossed them into the air, he scooped up knives and forks and spoons and threw them at the few remaining customers who scattered in their attempt to make a quick exit, he took glasses, brimming with water, and flung them up against the light bulbs—the red filaments sizzled like firecrackers. And then he ran out of the cafe.

He darted across the street and ran into the art gallery, which was beside Bill Watson's record store. He raced alongside the walls, pulling the paintings to the ground. His hands were bleeding from the shards of broken glass but he appeared not to notice. Swinging into Bill's store, he grabbed a stool and jabbed a hole in the window. With the same stool in his hand he danced around the store, smashing the light fixtures. Then he grabbed handfuls of recordings—records, cassettes, compact discs—and threw them through the open jagged circle in the shop window, as though they were darts and he was aiming for the bull's-eye. Just as suddenly as he had started on this rampage, he stopped. He stood quite still. He was quite docile; an idiotic giggle was his only sound. By then the police had arrived. They easily handcuffed him and placed him in their car. He sat there smiling. Tony Schmidt was utterly mad.

Later that Saturday afternoon Tony was taken to jail. The next morning, when the Schmidts received a phone call asking if they would come down to the county jail and bail out their son, they refused. Jack and Lucille had not slept. The previous evening they had made phone calls to their lawyer and to friends who were members of the Alliance for the Mentally Ill. The general consensus pointed to leaving Tony in jail for the legal processes to take place. Any other route might yet again deny him the hospital care that he desperately had needed for so long. For Tony's parents to achieve humane results it appeared that they would need to submit their son to inhumane procedures. It was not an easy choice.

"We stood firm," Lucille said. She sighed almost imperceptibly. "Tony was transferred to an old and disgusting jail which has since been torn down. It was like a dungeon. The court appointed him two attorneys. They were nice young fellows. Jack and I stayed in close contact with them. One of them knew a little about schizophrenia, at least he said he did. We realized that they really didn't know much when they said they didn't think that it would be good for Tony to be in a mental hospital. They thought that a group home would be more appropriate. Fortunately when they started to inquire around at group homes they found that none of them would take Tony." Lucille made a slight move as if to straighten her back. "We have reached a point where we simply wait for people to come to an understanding of the problems—of the difficulties that are inflicted on mentally ill people. We have learned to be patient and we don't expect much.

"The jail rules were very strict. We visited him as often as we were permitted. I talked with the nurse at the facility so that they knew Tony had people who cared—at least they knew we were there. Tony was kept in a basement cell. It was dark and damp and it was filthy. I believe that medieval prisons must have been like this. One time the guard started chatting with us as he escorted us down to the little glassed-in room where we could to talk to Tony. 'You know,' he said, 'he doesn't belong here, he belongs in a hospital.' I replied that we knew."

Tony made a pathetic attempt to commit suicide. He broke his glasses but made only faint scratches on his wrists.

The Schmidts had to urge the owners of the cafe and gallery to press charges. Nobody wanted to bother to complain. The damage costs were covered by their insurance and the suit was seen as a nuisance and a waste of time. But if Tony was not charged he would be released back to the streets. This time, however, good fortune came to Tony Schmidt and his parents. His friend Bill Watson understood the implications involved if he and the other complainants did not pursue the case. Charges were pressed. The pretrial hearing took place in January. Tony had already been in jail—and untreated—for a month.

The trial was set for February. Jack and Lucille had to make sure that Tony's attorneys would put in an insanity plea. The Schmidts jumped through hoop after hoop. "It was as though we were on a treadmill which at the same time was an obstacle course," said Lucille. Nothing was made easy for them. At every turn they were confronted by petty difficulties and misunderstandings. Yet again they found themselves painfully aware that they are part of a community that remains stubbornly ignorant about schizophrenia.

"We are very grateful that the store owners pressed charges. The trial took place in February. Tony had been in jail for more than two months and he was pathetically delusional and psychotic. He was always talking aloud to that mass murderer Charles Manson. It was awful. When they brought him into the courtroom people gasped aloud. They brought him in in shackles. He looked so dreadful. He was dressed in soiled prison clothes, his hair was long and dirty and matted, and his skin was pustulated. He was wild-eyed and plainly deranged."

The trial was short. Since it was a stipulated trial in which the facts were not in dispute, there was no jury. The prosecution and defense were in agreement before the trial that Tony Schmidt was mentally ill, so there was no contest. The judge sentenced him to eleven years in the forensic ward at the state hospital, under the supervision of the Psychiatric Security Review Board. "Tony got the same sentence that he would have had if he had been found guilty in a straight criminal case," Lucille said.

"I suppose I felt relieved. I thought that perhaps at last Tony would be safe. And he has been safe." Lucille paused and cleared her throat. "I want to be fair. I think that the hospital does the very best that they can. And I have nothing but good to say about the Psychiatric Security Review Board; they are like a parole board, only kind and understanding of what they are doing.

"I'm very involved in trying to make things better for the patients in the forensic wards. Right now there are about 340 people in those wards. So many people and so little money. The forensic wards are the stepchild of the mental health system. If anything is to be funded, it will be before the forensic wards. I am very angry when I think that if only Tony had had some attention and follow-up early on, all this would have been unnecessary. If only people accepted mental illness like any other illness, Tony and others like him would not be subjected to such a nightmare. To say nothing about the families or even the rest of the community."

Initially Tony Schmidt did not respond to any medication. He continued to be delusional until very recently, when he was one of a small group of people with chronic schizophrenia to be treated with a new drug called clozapine. So far Tony appears to be among the lucky ones who have responded favorably to this drug.

Lucille and Jack are concerned about Tony's release. In about four years he will be considered for a discharge from the forensic ward of the hospital. They are worried that they will find themselves back where they were before his commitment. "There are so many loopholes in the laws," Lucille said. "Once Tony is released, if he should refuse again to take medicine, we could be right back to where we were. Of course, he may be fine, this new medicine may help him. But we don't count on anything."

Commentary

BY RICHARD K. JAMES, PH.D.

Richard K. James, Ph.D., is a Professor of Counseling in the Division of Counseling, Educational Psychology, and Research at Memphis State University. He has worked as a school counselor and a director of a Title III ESEA innovative education program for socially maladjusted/emotionally disturbed children. He has been a consultant and a group therapist for the Federal Bureau of Corrections. He has written numerous articles in the field of child counseling and crisis intervention therapy and has co-authored two books in the field. He presently serves as a consultant and trainer for the Memphis Police Department's Crisis Intervention Team and Family Trouble Center Programs and has received the Human Service award from the Memphis Chapter of the Alliance for the Mentally Ill for his work in training police officers to deal with the mentally ill.

Tony and his parents could be cloned over and over in any metropolis, town, or country crossroads in the United States. Their unending nightmare is played out day after day across the country.

In a very real sense, Tony is lucky. His first encounter with the police was benign—almost considerate. His second encounter resulted only in being roughed up a little as he was forceably constrained. In both instances the action of the officers was more the exception than the rule when the police are called on to deal with a mentally ill person who is acting-out.

In general, police response to a person with schizophrenia who is delusional, hallucinating, and out of control is far different. Tony, especially if he had been armed, might well have been met with a hail of gunfire or a severe enough beating with nightsticks to cause serious bodily injury. The story of Tony only lightly touches the extent of the problems of reasonable, ethical, and moral confinement of the mentally ill in the current morass of the various state legal systems. It does not touch at all the severe problems that the mentally ill are likely to encounter with law-enforcement agencies. Why is this so?

INSTRUMENTAL VERSUS EXPRESSIVE CRIME

Criminal actions can be classified in two broad categories. A crime is *instrumental* when there is some identifiable material gain for the perpetrator. A crime is *expressive* when there is no material gain but a great deal of cathartic and violent energy released. Police are trained very specifically and at length to deal with instrumental crimes, as is the criminal justice system. These crimes and their perpetrators have a logical end to their means, and they are pursued and prosecuted in the same way. Instrumental crime is what most police officers go into law enforcement for—it is simply hunting down and catching the bad guy.

Expressive crime is the curse of every police officer as well as the judicial system. Domestic quarrels, barroom brawls, neighbor disputes, drug-induced rages, and mental disturbances are typical of these calls. They take up tremendous amounts of officer time, they are not logical or linear in their outcomes, they happen over and over again, and they are extremely frustrating. They are also the most potentially dangerous situations police officers face, and are perceived as such by them. Officers' actions tend to follow directly from their perception of such expressive crimes. One comment of a Memphis officer captures the essence of the problem. After a tremendously violent struggle to control a psychotic adolescent, he turned to the hysterical mother and said, "Sorry, lady, but we just aren't trained for this."

It makes little difference that the mentally ill person may be even more terrified of the police. It is the perception of the officer that matters. When confronted with a wild-eyed, hallucinating, pumped-up person with paranoid schizophrenia, and further agitated by frightened relatives and neighbors who are demanding action, police officers who, for the most part have had no training in dealing with the mentally disturbed, are likely to act from their own fears. They may match the mentally ill person's actions step-by-frightened-step in a rapidly escalating situation. This often happens in front of horrified friends and relatives who called the police because they were afraid the individual might hurt himself or herself and who then see the police doing exactly what they didn't want to have happen in the first place.

LEGAL ISSUES

Police officers are further frustrated by the inability of the judicial or mental health system to deal effectively with chronic mentally ill people. These people are often well known to officers because they continually "go off meds," become delusional and violent, and must be transported again and again to a mental health or judicial system that not only has little space or help for them, but also little understanding. The unheard pleas of Tony's parents and the immobility of the judicial system to do anything about the severely mentally ill are too often the rule. Picked up for wrecking their parents' house, people with schizophrenia like Tony may be back on the street within twenty-four hours unless felony charges are lodged against them.

In many states, mentally ill individuals must have a criminal complaint lodged against them or commit a criminal act before the police can take them into custody. While well-meaning laws have been instituted to safeguard the rights of the mentally ill, these same laws have hamstrung police officers. In many states, police cannot take mentally ill individuals who are seen as representing a danger to themselves or others into protective custody and transport them to a place of safety such as a hospital. Their only recourse is to take them to jail, even though a jail is about the last place a person with chronic schizophrenia who is suffering a psychotic episode needs to be.

Many officers are sensitive to the needs of mentally ill persons and are well aware of the bad things that jail has to offer. Yet, when confronted by demands to "do something about that crazy person," they are put in a double bind. As an act of desperate kindness, officers whose jurisdictions border states that have protective-custody laws have invented a creative strategy with their neighboring officers. They pick up a mentally ill person in their state, call the neighboring state's police, and tell them that they are going to drop the person across the state line. Once the person is put across the border, the other police department will take him or her into custody and transport him or her to the hospital. Clearly, this is a desperate, ad hoc solution that does not begin to address the problem.

Even in states such as Tennessee that have laws allowing police officers to take mentally disturbed individuals into protective custody, another problem arises. Jail may be the only alternative because there is no mental health facility in the immediate area to send the person to for observation or care. Few watch commanders would allow a patrol officer to drive an individual who is severely psychotic over a hundred miles to a mental health facility equipped to deal with him or her. The only solution to this logistical problem is to lodge a criminal complaint against such persons and put them in jail.

THE MEMPHIS RESPONSE

Given this extremely pessimistic picture of typical crisis care for a severely psychotic individual, is there anything that can be done? The answer to that question is a qualified yes. Yes, if advocates for changing legal procedures with the mentally ill become politically active in doing so. Yes, if the local political administration feels enough heat to make some changes in its provision of mental health service for the severely disturbed. Yes, if the police department is forward thinking enough to make some dramatic shifts in training on how to respond to mental disturbance calls. Yes, if mental health systems are willing to become closely involved with law-enforcement agencies to help train police officers, coordinate crisis and emergency care for the severely psychotic, and follow up with effective long-term case management. While a tall order by any set of standards, the following illustration of what happened in Memphis shows how those actions can occur.

Until 1987, Memphis pretty much characterized what would happen to a mentally ill individual such as Tony when the police became involved.

Sadly, like most significant changes, it took a tragedy to change things. Police were summoned to a housing project, where an individual armed with a butcher knife had been cutting himself and making threatening statements and gestures to his neighbors. He was clearly out of touch with reality, and the first officers on the scene were confronted with an extremely agitated and deranged middle-age male. They called for backup, and then even more backup was called as they were unable to gain control of the individual. Finally, after a brief standoff, as the man made a lunge with his knife toward the police, he was met by a barrage of fire from service revolvers and died on the scene.

In the months prior to this occurrence, two members of the local Alliance for the Mentally Ill chapter, Ann Dino and Helen Adamo, witnessed the police attempt to control Ann's schizophrenic son. Nightsticks were finally used to subdue him, much to the horror of the two women who had called the police for help. They immediately mobilized the local chapter into action and began an intensive lobbying campaign with the mayor's office to change police procedure in handling the mentally ill— with little effect.

However, the shooting death that later followed and a lawsuit heaped a tremendous amount of criticism on the police department. As a result, it was instructed by the mayor's office to plan and implement procedures to avert such tragedies. After a good deal of research, questionnaires on dealing with the mentally ill were sent to 41 major law-enforcement agencies throughout the United States and Europe. A thorough review of these programs indicated that none of them responded immediately to a mental-disturbance call with a "specialist." It was decided that since the police were the initial point-of-contact agency, their personnel needed to have the expertise to do crisis intervention. It was also decided that the "experts" would be regular patrol officers trained in a specialist/generalist approach. This novel concept would train enough uniformed patrol officers so that an officer with specialized skills in handling mentally ill individuals could be placed on the scene within minutes of the dispatcher receiving a call. Enough officers were to be trained so that every shift and every precinct would have at least one officer on duty. These officers were screened by a selection committee on the basis of personality tests, interviews, records, and watch commander recommendations. Although assigned to their regular ward beat, they would be on call throughout their precinct when their specialized skills were needed to calm and contain an out-of-control individual. Enough officers were to be trained so that all four shifts in all precincts would have at least one specially trained officer on duty seven days a week.

Memphis is fortunate in that it has many facilities that provide psychiatric services, including a state hospital and a VA hospital. It is also home to the University of Tennessee Health Sciences and Memphis State University—two large and sophisticated training centers for psychiatrists, clinical and counseling psychologists, mental health counselors, psychiatric nurses, and psychiatric social workers. It also has comprehensive community mental health centers with specific geographical service areas that cover the city, and the Crisis Stabilization Unit, a short-term inpatient psychiatric facility that provides immediate emergency care for the severely emotionally disturbed. In other words, the city has a comprehensive mental health system and excellent mental health professionals that can serve as teaching staff on virtually any aspect of mental illness and its treatment.

Through the lobbying efforts of the local AMI chapter, many of these institutions were persuaded to contribute staff to a joint police/mental health committee that would plan a training program for police officers in defusing and controlling mentally disturbed individuals by verbal rather than physical intervention. In a memorandum of agreement, the mayor's office agreed to provide the necessary police support to ensure that a cadre of these officers would be trained. Numerous social service and mental health agencies also signed the agreement to provide support personnel to the program. Because there was no extra money available to pay trainers, several mental health professionals committed to conduct training as a community service. In retrospect, this point has become very significant because it not only enhances the professionals' credibility with the police, but also gives them a great deal of continuing investment in the program.

TRAINING OF OFFICERS

Officers on the MPD Crisis Intervention Team undergo an initial 40-hour training program and receive both classroom and field instruction in the following:

1. Diagnostic and clinical issues of the dangerous mentally ill.

2. Diagnostic and clinical issues of Posttraumatic Stress Disorder.

3. Basic crisis-intervention verbal responses for controlling aggressive behavior.

4. Suicide-intervention techniques.

5. Treatment strategies using crisis-intervention techniques.

6. Simulation activities that include videotaped role play and critique of officer performance.

7. Patients' rights and legal aspects of crisis intervention.

8. Psychotropic medications and their side effects.

9. Alcohol and drug behavior in the mentally ill.

10. Articulation and coordination of police/caseworker roles.

11. Specialized training in nonlethal forms of physical containment such as the Taser electric stun device.

12. Face-to-face discussions with patients at a local mental hospital about their perceptions of police officers.

Number 12 is a thorny problem because of the possible legal ramifications and confidentiality issues involved. However, these dialogues are extremely important in giving officers insight into the fears that mentally ill people have of the police and what they can do to alleviate them. At the same time, many of their own fears of "crazy" people are cast aside.

Simulation activities are one of the most critical components of the training. Officers engage in role plays in attempting to control different types of mentally ill individuals. There are no scripts, and officers must use the techniques they have learned as they try to obtain compliance from a variety of difficult clients played by mental health professionals and veteran CIT officers. These role plays are conducted in front of the trainees, videotaped, and carefully critiqued with each officer. Although there is a good deal of stage fright, this training is critical in showing officers what they are doing right or wrong while in the safety of the classroom.

A critical cross-training component is merged into instruction. To obtain as accurate a picture as possible of the real and often chaotic world of the uniformed patrol officer, all mental health professionals who serve as trainers ride with patrol officers on a regular basis so that they can observe first hand the problems with which they are faced and structure learning activities accordingly. Regular follow-up sessions and an intradepartmental newsletter are provided for the officers as part of an ongoing continuing education in more effective ways of handling the mentally ill.

RESULTS

As of 1992, the MPD CIT had 95 trained officers on duty seven days a week in every precinct on all four shifts plus numerous other officers who have been promoted to other bureaus. Subjective reports and empirical evidence would seem to indicate that the program is extremely effective. People have come to depend on and trust the MPD officers with the little silver and blue CIT pin on their uniform blouse. Follow-up reports from AMI members shower accolades on the officers and indicate unanimous support for the program.

The same is true of some very cynical mental health workers in the community. One comment from a psychologist at the Memphis State University Counseling Center sums the professional view of the CIT program. "I never thought I'd say this about the cops, but that CIT officer who came to the dorm was really good. I didn't think that situation was going to get anything but worse, but he cooled it off. Frankly, I'm kind of envious, I don't know that I could have done as well." It is noteworthy that every year, at its chapter awards banquet, Memphis AMI recognizes the top CIT officers from each precinct and the outstanding CIT officer for the whole department. One CIT officer-of-the-year attributed the verbal skills he learned in his CIT training to saving his life when a fleeing felon wrestled his gun away from him and was preparing to shoot him.

Self-reports, however, are often the psychological equivalent of buying the king's clothes and tend to become self-fulfilling prophecies of what people want to believe. Hard data in the form of statistics are the bottom line of program effectiveness. In its first sixteen months of operation in 1987–88, MPD CIT officers responded to 5,831 mental-disturbance calls and transported 3,424 cases to mental health facilities without any patient fatalities. In the latest sixteen months, these figures have increased to 7,330 calls and 4,490 transports with no fatalities. Both calls and transports have risen significantly, which indicates that the public is aware of and is using the program. Approximately six out of every ten recipients of service are transported to a place of safety, which means a large increase in mental health services for the community. While there are no figures to adequately determine how many recipients are injured due to police intervention, one indicator of the overall decrease in violence is the number of police officers injured on duty. Injuries are significantly less than what normally would be expected since the program has come into operation. In other words, police officers themselves are safer for using these techniques.

Another interesting statistic is the significant reduction of barricade situations since the start of the program. One of the members of the MPD hostage-negotiation team stated that, "By the time we get there, the CIT officers have the situation under control." Techniques used to calm and control the mentally ill have spread and are now used in dealing with domestic disputes and other crises. Thus, CIT training has sent a strong message that every individual who resorts to calling the police should be treated as a person in crisis.

From a police perspective, such a program is not easy to sell. In the beginning, many officers scoffed at the ideas that were being promoted as "headshrink" stuff, and CIT officers caught a great deal of flak from fellow officers. However, as the CIT program became successful, many other officers started to ask questions about CIT operating tactics as they saw CIT officers defuse hot situations. Presently in Memphis there are far more applicants for CIT training slots than there are positions available.

COORDINATING SERVICES

Police officers and mental health providers tend to look balefully at one another over some very strong professional fences. On one side the police see the mental health system as a bunch of softhearted social worker types or fuzzy-headed shrinks who don't have the remotest notion of the reality of the mean streets they patrol. On the other side, mental health providers often view the police as heavy-handed Gestapo agents who hit first and ask questions later and don't have the remotest notion about how to deal with people.

Historically, these professions seldom have had close working relationships, and have often been at cross-purposes. Yet it is clear that with the tremendous numbers of mentally ill men and women who either go off their medication or have no one to care for them, the police officer will invariably be the initial point of contact when these persons get out-of-control. Therefore, the professional fences need to come down, and attitudes must change. By training police to deal with mentally ill people, the mental health system can form an extremely strong alliance and rapid-response system.

In Memphis, close professional working relationships have been developed between the police and mental health workers in the various clinics and hospitals. If a recipient of services has a caseworker, it is more than likely that the CIT officer will know the caseworker and already have a close working relationship with him or her. As a result, the philosophy of the program is that caseworkers will provide close follow-up through home visits, monitoring of medicine, and other necessary health and environmental functions to keep the patient stabilized. While that approach has been pretty much followed, questions arise as to its effectiveness.

One nagging statistic is bothersome and we are not sure what to make of it: the repeat call. Repeat calls have risen in a highly significant manner since the program's inception. Does this mean that citizens are now more confident that police will handle calls effectively? Does it mean that they know they can get temporary relief from their stressful life situation by getting the mentally ill person removed from the home for a little while? Or does it mean that follow-up activities by the mental health system have failed to provide long-term solutions? Currently, we don't know. The answers are not easy to ascertain, but are critically important because one of the major goals of the program is to provide close coordination and follow-up services by mental health providers once a patient is identified through the MPD. This problem is typical of the rest of the country and is currently under investigation in our city.

THE CRITICAL INGREDIENTS

None of the foregoing would have happened in Memphis without four critical ingredients. First, a sustained grassroots lobbying effort of local government by members of AMI. Second, the realization by the police department that special techniques are needed when working with mentally ill people and could save money, time, effort, lawsuits, and engender highly positive police-community relationships. Third, a group of mental health professionals who became committed to a long-term involvement in training, follow-up, and support of a police program to deal with the mentally ill. And fourth, we had laws on the books allowing officers to transport people who are an imminent danger to themselves or others *and* a place to transport them to safety and medical help.

In Memphis, transporting a person by the police may range from getting them back home, taking them to a local mental health clinic, or bringing them to the crisis-stabilization unit for short-term hospitalization or the psychatric emergency unit of the medical center for observation. While not every community has the hospital resources that Memphis does, each community can reserve an adequate proportion of a hospital or other mental health facility for its mentally ill and designate personnel to transport these patients to such places.

If state laws will not allow police to take the mentally ill into protective custody as opposed to arresting them and throwing them in jail to get them off the streets and out of harm's way, then legislative efforts should immediately be instigated to do so. Each of the foregoing ingredients is necessary, but none alone is sufficient. While all of this may seem a tall order to change, it can be done, and most probably starts with a special-interest group such as a local AMI chapter that is motivated enough to start the ball rolling.

A WORKING EXAMPLE OF CIT OFFICERS IN OPERATION

The following scenario is typical of what happens in Memphis when a family member becomes actively psychotic. The dialogue is representative of the types of responses a CIT officer might make to a relative and to the recipient of services. The narrative interspersing the dialogue discusses the reasons why the officer speaks and behaves as she does. If you have been a recipient of service by your local police department, you may wish to make some comparisons.

> JUANITA (WHO HAS DIALED 911): My name is Juanita Alvarez and I'm calling for the police. I need help with my twenty-one-year-old son Hector. He has schizophrenia. His medication was making him sick and he quit taking it three days ago. Now he's out in the garage wrecking things and yelling and screaming. I live at 2348 Vincino

Street. I'll turn the porch light on and be out on the porch waiting for the police.

If you are calling the police or 911 in regard to a friend or relative who is mentally ill and out-of-control, Juanita's example is a good one. First, be clear in giving your name and address. Things may be pretty wild around you, but remain as calm as you can and give the dispatcher your name and address and very carefully state that you need help with a mentally ill person who is out-of-control. Be concise, clear, and factual. Wait to see if the dispatcher has questions and acknowledges your information. If the person is off his or her medication, or you know what has precipitated the aggressive behavior, briefly say so. Then leave the vicinity of the psychotic person if you are able. Pleading, reasoning, or cajoling with the person to calm down will do little good at this point.

When the police arrive, go up to them in an open stance with your hands visible. (Dispatch messages may get garbled and the police may think you are the deranged person.) As calmly and as factually as you can, tell them what's going on.

> JUANITA: He's my son Hector, and he's just been diagnosed as having schizophrenia. He's been taking Thorazine for just about ten days. He started having some muscle twitches and was feeling dizzy so he quit. About an hour ago he started muttering some real weird stuff and he's been looking for wires or radios or something and then he said he knew they were in the garage where he works on his antique car and went out and started tearing it apart. He's out there now. He's been delusional but never like this. I'm really scared he's going to hurt somebody or himself.

As is typical in so many cases, Hector's medication has caused physical side effects that he doesn't like, and he has quit taking it. Also typical, his previous symptoms have become more pronounced. Conveying this information helps the CIT officer immensely as she attempts to obtain a quick assessment of the situation.

> CIT OFFICER: Hello, my name is Sammie Stokes. I'm on the Crisis Intervention Team and our speciality is dealing with mentally ill

citizens. Has anybody been hurt? Does he have any weapons in there?

JUANITA: No. He hasn't hurt anybody. He just scared me real bad with that crazy talk. Nothing but shop tools, like a hammer and crowbar and stuff like that.

OFFICER: Has he made any threats to you or anybody?

The officer needs to assess Hector's potential lethality both for her own safety and the patient's. She also needs to know if there is anyone else in the garage who might be in danger or is hurt. Being armed with a potential weapon will dictate a very cautious approach. Each MPD CIT officer is additionally armed with a Taser, a weapon that fires dart-tipped wires. Once these darts make contact, they administer a disabling but noninjurious electrical shock. While emphasis is placed on not hurting the mentally ill person, the same holds true for the officer. The Taser is used when the individual cannot be talked down. It should be noted that MPD CIT officers answer thousands of calls and have fired their Tasers less than 100 times.

JUANITA: He said he was gonna get them before they got him, and then he started trashing the place. I don't know who "them" is—I just think they're voices in his head.

OFFICER: Is there anybody with him?

JUANITA: No, he's alone.

The officer continues to query Juanita and gain enough information to make a rapid triage assessment of Hector. She obtains strategic pieces of information about Hector's background, his current and past functioning, level of dangerousness, and enough personal information to establish verbal contact.

As is typical when a police car pulls up, it is not long before a curious crowd gathers. The CIT officer's partner immediately moves the people back and out of the way. The last thing needed is a crowd exhorting the police or the mentally ill person to attack one another. From this point forward, unless the officer asks for assistance, whatever happens will be pretty much her call. If need be, more officers will be called to keep the crowd out of the operation, but only she and perhaps a backup CIT officer will verbally engage Hector.

The officer moves up to the garage door so it is in plain view, but does not enter. She does not wish to intrude into and threaten Hector's space, nor does she want to come face-to-face with the business end of a crowbar. The officer states her name and asks an open-ended, nonthreatening question to establish contact.

OFFICER (IN A WELL-MODULATED, CALM, AND STEADY VOICE): Hector, this is Sammie Stokes, with MPD. What's happening?

HECTOR (HIDDEN FROM VIEW BUT SCREAMING): You goddamn cops never come when somebody needs you, man! First they tried to poison me and now they're trying to kidnap me, find out when I'm in here under the car working and get me. But *I'll* get *them,* so just get out!

Sammie does not respond directly to the paranoid ideation, but acknowledges the feeling behind it and offers to help. The idea is not to affirm the delusions, but to affirm the feelings that go with them and cause the individual to act-out. The offer of help is again solicited.

OFFICER: Hey, man! I hear you're strung out over this, so what can I do to help you?

HECTOR: You can't help me, bitch. You're probably part of them. Yeah, the cops—the FBI—the CIA—they're all part of it. It's the Aryan Nation Brotherhood—they're out to kill me.

OFFICER (THINKING FAST AND CREATIVELY): The Aryan Nation? Hector, I want you to step to the door and just take a look at me and see if you think I'm part of that outfit.

HECTOR (STEPS TO DOOR AND PEERS AROUND IT): So you're black—worse yet! That don't mean nuthin—I'm just another spic to you.

While Hector rejects the officer's attempt to show him that she is not an agent of the Aryan Nation, she does get him to show himself at the door. She now has line-of-sight contact that she can use to further develop trust. She queries Hector on the issue of his medicine.

OFFICER: Hector, I understand you've been taking some medicine that makes you feel bad. Can you tell me about it?

HECTOR (SUSPICIOUSLY): Who told you that?

OFFICER: Your mom did. She's really concerned about you.

Officer Stokes is truthful, as she must be if she is to gain credibility with Hector. She also attempts to use the mother's concern for her son, but this ploy falls on deaf ears and it is soon apparent why.

HECTOR: Hey, man, she's the one that tried to poison me! Right after I ate that funny-smellin' chicken she made yesterday. She's in it with them—wants my antique pickup. But I'll bet you don't believe that.

OFFICER: I don't know if that's right or wrong, but I do understand how you might feel pretty scared, angry, and hurt to think your mom would do something like that.

Again, the officer does not side with the paranoia of the client, but acknowledges the feelings that would go along with such an evil plot. She then attempts to gain compliance by asking him to do something for her.

OFFICER: Right now what I want to do is help you. Would you please put that crowbar down and come on over and sit down with me?

HECTOR: Nobody can help me, man—like I can smell they been here. Can you smell them?

OFFICER: No, but I believe you can. Hector, I need for you to stay right with me. I'm a CIT officer and I can get you to a place to get you some help. But first I need for you to drop that crowbar and come sit down.

Officer Stokes asks Hector to keep his tenuous hold on reality with her. She also uses a broken-record technique to attempt to gain compliance since many people experiencing psychotic episodes need repeated messages of what the officer wants them to do.

HECTOR: Can you make that smell go away? I'm talkin' that stinkin' smell. It makes me sick.

OFFICER: I'm sorry it's making you feel bad. I understand that's really buggin' you. I can't make it go away, but I can promise to get you to some place where they can work on that problem.

The CIT officer makes absolutely no promises that she can't keep. Nothing is more important than maintaining the credibility of the officer. While recipients of service usually are quite psychotic, they tend to have very good memories of who has and who hasn't been truthful with them. Since very few mentally ill people will be one-time recipients of service, it is extremely important for the CIT officers to be known as trustworthy. Finally, the "I understand" statement does not imply agreement with Hector's belief system, but emphatically affirms his feeling state. Such statements go a long way toward making the recipient feel understood and cared for.

HECTOR: Man, I don't know. You'll take me to jail—I don't wanna go to jail.

OFFICER: No, I won't take you to jail. If they were gonna take you to jail, they wouldn't have sent a CIT officer. I've got direct access to the hospital, and I'll take you there right now so you'll be safe and start feeling better. But I really do need for you to put down the crowbar. I'll take you to the Crisis Stabilization Unit. It's a hospital. They can regulate your medicine so that you don't feel so bad.

HECTOR (TAKES A STEP OUT OF THE GARAGE WHILE PENSIVELY HANDLING THE CROWBAR): I dunno, man—I mean, how do I know I can trust you? The cops are bad news around here—I don't know none of that CIT crap or whatever.

OFFICER: CIT means I'm a police officer who's been especially trained to help people. And one of those things is to help people like you who are having trouble with others. Look! I'm standing here talking to you about your problem and listening, right? Nobody's tried to bust your head open, and they won't, 'cause it's my job not to let anyone get you. So put the crowbar down and let's get you to a safe place.

HECTOR (PUTS DOWN THE CROWBAR): OK—but, man, I get so dizzy— and then the smells and my shoulders started jerkin' real bad, and they say I'm crazy. You think I'm crazy?

OFFICER: I think your medicine's caused a bad reaction and I'd like to get that straightened out. How about coming out to the car with me?

The officer states in a matter-of-fact way what she can do for Hector and why she is able to do so. This calming technique relays that the officer does in fact have the power to help the person feel better. She also makes no value judgment as to Hector's state of sanity, but rather responds again with facts. Finally, she now moves to resolve the situation. As officer Stokes works with Hector, she operates slowly and deliberately. She does not want to frighten or surprise him in any way. Instead of trying to gain immediate compliance by getting him into the squad car, she patiently responds to his feelings and concerns.

HECTOR: You're not gonna bust me with that nightstick or Mace me?

OFFICER: No, but I'll have to put handcuffs on you. I'm sorry to do that, but it's standard procedure. You know that, right?

HECTOR: Yeah, I know (compliantly puts his hands behind his back). You'll take me to the hospital and not let them get me. You wouldn't game me, would you, man?

OFFICER: No way! We might run into each other again, and I want you to know you can trust me.

Hector turns around, is handcuffed for his and the officer's safety, and is transported to the hospital.

This brief scenario shows the use of some of the basic responding skills that can be taught to police officers. Since 1992, dozens of officers from across the country have come to Memphis for training. They have returned to their departments, where variations of the Memphis program have been adopted. Can such a program be adopted in your community? The answer is yes, if someone like you is willing to start the ball rolling.

The National Alliance for the Mentally Ill (NAMI) and Public Citizens Health Research Group make the following recommendations to guarantee basic rights and humane treatment for seriously mentally ill individuals in jail:

1. States with laws permitting jails to be used for emergency detention of people with mental illness not charged with any crime should immediately amend such laws to clearly prohibit this practice. States that do not do so by January 1, 1995, should lose eligibility for federal mental health block grants.

2. Jail diversion programs should be set up to minimize the number of individuals with serious mental illness who end up in jail.

3. All inmates with serious mental illness should be evaluated by a mental health professional within twenty-four hours of admission to jail. Ongoing psychiatric services, including medications if necessary, should be available in the jails on a timely basis.

4. Inmates with serious mental illnesses in jail who need medication and have no insight into their illness should be medicated involuntarily if necessary to protect themselves and others.

5. In counties or states where mental health authorities have failed to set up jail diversion programs and where significant numbers of individuals with serious mental illnesses continue to be jailed on misdemeanor charges or without charges, the department of mental health should be required to transfer funds to the department of corrections.

6. When inmates with serious mental illnesses are released from jails, follow-up psychiatric care as needed should be mandated by the courts as a condition of parole or probation.

7. Corrections officers who work in jails and police officers in the community should receive training on serious mental illness.

8. All state or federally supported training programs for mental health professionals should require trainees to spend a minimum of six hours in on-site training in jails.

9. Mental health professionals should be required to provide pro bono services for two hours per week to public mental health facilities, including jails, as a condition of licensure.

10. Increased resources under the Protection and Advocacy Act of 1986 should be devoted to assisting individuals with serious mental illnesses in jails.

11. Relevant federal and state statistical reporting systems should be modified to reflect the existence of seriously mentally ill persons in jails.

12. For each jail in the U.S., there should be a standing mental illness committee, including representatives from the jail, the local department of mental health, the local public psychiatric inpatient unit, and the local chapter of NAMI.

13. Local chapters of NAMI should closely monitor what is happening in local jails and, when reform efforts fail, seek class-action relief through the courts.

6

At Risk:

Suicide and Schizophrenia

DOLORES FORDHAM IS A THICKSET WOMAN who grew up in difficult times on a Nebraska farm. Her deepset eyes are heavily lined with dark-brown circles that accentuate an ingrained weariness. All her gestures are deliberate; she moves slowly, surely, and phlegmatically. She has a low-pitched voice that never thickens with emotion, no matter how painful the subject. Dolores does not weep.

Her youngest son, Stan, is a Vietnam veteran. He enlisted in the army when he was nineteen. Eight years later he returned home. Dolores said, "He was married before he went to 'Nam and the marriage failed. There was a small child."

Within a week of his return, his mother realized there was something "drastically wrong with Stan, drastically wrong," she said to herself. "Of course he said there was nothing wrong with him. It's my opinion usually that people have to live their own lives whichever way they see fit, as long as they aren't interfering with me—but this was something else."

She believed Stan had a drug problem. She thought drugs had been part of his life before the war, but she emphasized that this was strictly speculation, just guesswork.

"It took me two years before I finally convinced him either he had to get some help or he would be out on the street. During those two years he'd worked long enough to draw unemployment and be able to live by himself. But at one point he completely disappeared for six weeks. I had no idea if he was dead or alive. When he did get back home, he told me that he had hitchhiked all the way to New Orleans and back.

"My, my." Dolores looked bemused. "He was a horrible-looking sight, but there he was, intact.

"From then on I really pushed him to get some help. He went to the Veterans Administration Hospital for ten days. They didn't do much testing or evaluation or that kind of stuff, but they did give him some medication.

"Well, he just upped and walked away from there. He went in voluntarily, so he had the right to walk away voluntarily. But the important thing was that he had had just enough medicine to realize the medication was helpful to him. When I hear other folks' stories about their kids, I know what a difference a positive attitude about taking medicine can make. So he picks up the medicine, which they gave him free, but mind you—there wasn't *any* kind of further follow-up.

"Not too much time went by before he began to complain about his eyes. He was having a lot of soreness in his eyes. Due to his confused mind he was taking the medicine backwards! He was taking a small dose of the antipsychotic medicine and a big dose of the medicine that had been prescribed to handle the side effects of the antipsychotic drug. Ultimately we found out that that was the cause of all this pain. Of course I didn't know what was wrong—and neither did anyone else, because he didn't have any doctor or anyone following his case.

"As I said, I had been worried about Stan for quite a while, so even before he started to complain about his eyes I had already been talking to a very sympathetic doctor up at the University Hospital. This doctor told me there was no way of treating him without his being hospitalized.

"Stan was not being violent, he was not abusive, he was quiet—he was not what they call catatonic—he was just withdrawn. I would say that he was withdrawn even though they did not diagnose it that way. The VA people had told me that Stan was 'very satisfied within himself.'

"There was no easy way to get Stan into the hospital. If he didn't go on his own accord, no one was going to come and make him go there. He wasn't a troublemaker. I guess the way they saw it was that he wasn't worth the bother."

Dolores smiled and reminisced fondly about her son. He had always been a quiet and good boy, not like his obstreperous older brother. "Ken, now he was a livewire, always into everything. Stanley, on the other hand, was the kind of kid who would sit quietly and wait peacefully while I mopped the kitchen floor. He seemed happy just to be around while I did my chores. Stan would sit for hours, watching, always placid, never bugging me while I got on with my housework. He didn't talk much. It was hard to know what he was thinking, but he was such a sweet kid that I didn't worry too much about that. I came to accept that he was never big with communication. Huh." Dolores seemed to be reminding herself. "Come to think of it he's the same now—maybe more so.

"All this time, since he'd returned from the service, I was not thinking about mental illness. I just figured he had severe psychological problems or that something was very unbalanced—maybe even a brain tumor.

"So when he kept complaining about his eyes—he was afraid he was going blind—I kept saying there wasn't a thing I could do about it. I told him that he had to go for treatment, that he should go back and see the doctors. And that if his eyes were that bad, the only thing I could think was causing it was that a tumor might be pressing on the optical nerve.

"I didn't know anything about his taking the medicine backwards. I just knew that he had been given some medicine and that he was taking it. I didn't know anything about the medicine at all. With our confidentiality laws—well, that is just like talking to a wall, they didn't tell me a thing. Here I am, the person who cares for him, and those medical people, the doctors and the nurses, they are telling me next to nothing.

"At that time he was living at home. I knew he couldn't handle himself out on the street, so I put up with quite a bit. I have a lot of tolerance and a lot of patience with him. If he complains about something, the way I handle it is to tell him, 'I'm sorry, I don't know what is wrong with you. I can't help you in any way, shape, or form. I am not a medical professional. For proper help,' I say to him, 'you will have to go see a doctor.'

"I still didn't even think about mental illness. To be truthful, I really didn't know what mental illness was. Schizophrenia—well, of course I had the wrong definition of schizophrenia, like everyone else. I was going by the dictionary: I thought it was a dual personality, you know, that you are two or three different people. Like the movie about a crazy woman which Joanne Woodward was in. She had all these different characters who seemed to be inside her and she never knew when one or the other would take over. I knew he didn't have that. And 'manic depressive,' I'd never even heard of that.

"How ignorant can one be? I was so ignorant that, would you believe, I even have a cousin back home—Marion is her name—who is severely mentally ill, and I still didn't know a thing about this disease. Her family kept it so hush-hush. They felt so disgraced, no one talked about it back there in Nebraska. Oh boy, there had to be so much shame.

"It wasn't that I didn't know that Marion had problems. I knew she had been in the state hospital. She was a very, very intelligent girl—I knew her in her younger years. My theory always was that anyone who was so intelligent couldn't possibly be mentally ill. I used to think that someone who was mentally ill was kind of like the village idiot.

"Pretty stupid." Dolores half smiled. "Again, there you have the ignorance of people. It's just very recently that you hear professionals and families talk about how mental illness does nothing much to a person's intelligence. It's their thinking patterns that are supposed to be affected. But if their thinking patterns are affected, I guess even if they are lucky enough to be intelligent, the intelligence won't do them much good.

"Well, even though I didn't know much about any of this at that time, I became convinced that my own son's thinking pattern was completely off base. I remember one afternoon, Stan was in the living room with the TV on, the sound was turned way up. But he wasn't watching. He was sprawled out on the couch, his big feet on the cushions. He seemed to be dozing, when he said very serious-like, 'I can't hardly believe that the whole world has got problems and is doing everything backwards.' Boy, I knew something was loose: it was his manner—he was talking as though this nonsense made sense. He made it quite clear that he was making an important announcement. He sounded almost like a politician.

"And this was one of his better days, because he actually talked about something. Usually he just lay around. He never fussed, he never argued, he never asked for anything. Like I said before, he was just satisfied with himself. He was like this even before he took medicine. Stanley was not a hyper person. He was very calm, very quiet, what I would call very withdrawn.

"Although that first doctor at the VA said he was not withdrawn and he was not depressed. That doctor said that Stan 'was very satisfied, very happy within himself the way he is.' Stanley is a very peculiar case. Later, when I began to talk with other folk, other families who have mentally ill kids, I found out that he was very different from most of the other cases.

"I've heard some terrible stories. Some of these kids are really abusive with their own parents. They yell and use bad words, they're always angry and irritable and even worse. I've heard of cases where the kids have attacked one or other of their parents, even cut them up. I've never had that kind of trouble with Stan. So maybe you could call me lucky.

Dolores cleared her throat. "But peaceful as he is, Stanley, at that time, was very difficult for me. He was difficult from the standpoint that I am the kind of individual who has no time for lazy people. And here is this man, my son, going on for thirty, who has been married and should be supporting a child, but is lounging around on my couch and I can't move him." Dolores closed her eyes. "It was difficult from that standpoint, but not from the standpoint of him being violent or being demanding or being abusive or even being agitated.

"He'd be in bed by four in the afternoon. I'd ask him if he was sick—no, he wasn't sick. So I'd ask him, 'Why are you in bed?' and he'd say, 'I'm tired.' All he'd ever say was, 'I'm tired.'

"When he talked to me about the world being backwards, I said to him, 'The world is not backwards, that's the way you're seeing it. The world is functioning very well.'

"Well, with the combination of the pain in his eyes and his talking about the world being backwards, I had just enough leverage to convince him that there was something wrong with his brain. I told him that it should be taken care of and that the longer he waited the worse it could be.

"I had remained in touch with the doctor at the University Hospital. He arranged for a bed to be available. So it all fell into place as easy as pie. It turned out to be as simple as if we had just snapped our fingers.

"Stan went to the hospital very willingly and he stayed for six weeks. Then he went back every day as an outpatient. They planned to give him six weeks of occupational therapy, but he had a relapse—the medicine wasn't quite right. It was either too strong or the wrong kind. The doctors didn't communicate with me, and all I knew was that it had something to do with the medication.

"Poor Stan got very confused. Later he told me what he thought had happened. He said he was climbing some stairs, which he was sure would take him up from the main floor to the OT room. But he found himself in the wrong place. And for some reason he couldn't get himself to turn around. He could not get himself back down those stairs. Poor Stanley just couldn't figure things out, so this sick guy stayed standing at the top of that flight of stairs for maybe seven or eight hours. I have to believe that it was a stairwell that was used hardly at all, otherwise how could you account for no one's noticing him?

"They did call me, after he had been missing for about five hours, to see if maybe he'd come home. I'm not usually an excitable person, but the next few hours until he was found were as terrible a time as I can ever remember. Ultimately someone came across him.

"So they put him back in the hospital for another week. He's been in the hospital a few times since then. It seems to go in cycles. But he does take his medicine and he functions pretty well. He works and in some ways he does lead what looks like a normal life. He works as a janitor in an industrial building in northeast Portland.

"Even so, he's not what he was. However much he's come back, he's lost a lot. A lot of him isn't there anymore, whether it is in his physical makeup or in his features, quite a bit of him has left—that's how I can best describe it. It's hard for the moms," Dolores said. "You have these kids who remind you of the way they were before they got sick, but at the same time there are so many little pieces that are no longer there. Stanley is the young boy that I knew, and again he isn't.

"Stan's a very kind individual. He's very sympathetic and sensitive, perhaps more so since the illness. Oh, maybe he was like that before, but he didn't show it as much as he does now."

Dolores almost smiled. "Oh, oh, but he is a conniver. He'd connive me out of my last dime if I let him. Stan's big hangup is money." Dolores went on. "His ongoing problem is not managing his money too well. But I don't bail him out, he has to make his money decisions for himself. I've offered to take care of his finances for him, you know, to help him organize how he does things—but he doesn't want that.

"I can't blame him, because that would be taking another little piece away from him. He has this feeling that if he turned over his money management to me, that would be just another way of saying that he was not competent enough, not capable enough—in other words, it would be like saying he's not normal.

"Even so, many is the time I have tried to convince him that there's an awful lot of business people that never see their money. I tell them they have an accountant who takes care of everything and if it wasn't for that they would probably be bankrupt all the time. But he will have none of it; he doesn't want me butting in."

Dolores was silent. Then, speaking slowly, almost as though she were talking to herself, she said, "I've always wondered about a time when Stanley was still a young fellow; he was in junior high school. He woke up at about one in the morning—I was still up—and he said he was having a horrible nightmare. It was a dreadful night as well, it was pouring rain. A typical Oregon winter night of heavy, heavy rain, so I could see that to come out of a deep sleep it might be kind of eerie and frightening. But on the other hand if you've grown up with this weather, it shouldn't be so much of a surprise.

"I remember saying to him, 'It's only a nightmare, Stan, you're aware of that. You just go back to bed and settle down.' But just the way he looked at me, I was uncomfortable with it, so I sat with him and watched him for quite a while. His stepfather and I could tell there was something real wrong with him.

"He seemed to be hysterical. He wanted his stepdad to make it stop raining. He said he couldn't stand the rain, and he couldn't understand why we were unable to get it to stop—that scared us because that didn't seem right coming from a twelve-year-old boy. OK—maybe—from a little kid, but not from a big fellow going into his teens. He kept jumping around in bed and he just couldn't settle down.

"So we packed him up in the car and took him out to Kaiser. They kept him overnight and got him to sleep. The next morning they called us and told us to pick him up. They didn't say much. All they told us was that he was OK, and that we should take him home. We were surprised when we read his record. They had written that he was hallucinating due to intoxication.

"But I knew that he hadn't had anything to drink—it wasn't possible. He'd come directly home from school at his usual time. It was late in the afternoon, after he finished doing his paper route. I'd have picked up on it right away if he'd been drinking. We had a bite to eat together. Then he'd done his homework, watched some TV, and gone to bed. I'd been home all evening. There wasn't anything untoward going on. He shared a room with his brother; it would have been easy to know if something funny was going on.

"After that he was different, he was—you know—more difficult, more rebellious. I feel now that we should have pursued why he had had such a crazy episode. I can't help feeling that maybe I could have done more for him and that might have prevented these worse things that have happened to him. Even with all I know now—that however you brought them up it wouldn't make a difference—I still have these nagging feelings that I could have done more.

"When Stanley came back from 'Nam and I first found out that he had a mental illness, it was shocking to me. I kept thinking for a long while, really, that I was to blame; that it was something that I did; like I said, not checking more thoroughly after he had his horrible nightmare when he was in junior high.

"I felt maybe I had raised him badly, not helping him enough through the hurdles of life. But I did get to be of the opinion that the brain is part of the body. And who says that that can't get us ill the same as kidney stones, gallstones, or any other part of the body that makes you feel sick.

"The family, his brother and stepfather, they still look on it as a disgrace to be mentally ill. I get no support there. But I was never one of these people to try to hide it or kick it under the carpet or anything else. I talk about it continually. It was and is my whole conversation, my only conversation. I don't care whether people like it or not. I want people to know that there is nothing to be ashamed of."

Pulling herself up straight, Dolores said, "The only way to get help is to talk about it. I tell you educating themselves about mental illness is one of the best things people can do, and they should start right at the very beginning. By the beginning, I mean as soon as a family finds out that they've got a mentally ill kid. That would save a lot of heartache—for everyone, both the family and the mentally sick person.

"If I had my druthers, I would just love to make a routine check at all the hospitals, with new families coming in and tell them what things to watch for. I'd tell them to be patient with a mentally ill person who has just come out of a first-time hospital stay. I'd tell them not to be afraid and to remember the sick person is the one who is afraid and confused. I've heard of families and friends who have pulled back and shunned these poor crippled people.

"So many times I've heard that folks disconnect or change their telephone number, all because they couldn't handle their kids calling home over and over again. It's not uncommon for mentally ill people to make many, many repetitive calls when they're very upset. I think they keep calling because they need to be reassured. But maybe it's just because they're confused and forget that they are repeating themselves.

"What the heck, I don't know why they keep telephoning, they just do. But I do know they can't help it. And I know that they don't mean anything evil by it. Poor souls, they're just sick and they need kindness, just like any other human being.

"I will never forget Stanley's second hospitalization after he had mixed up those medicines that he got from the VA. The young doctor at the University Hospital told me that I had a very, very sick boy. Even though

I had been worried about him, so worried that I was the one who had pressed him to go to the hospital, I remember feeling very shocked.

"I was shocked because I was not prepared for his emphasis on 'very sick.' Here is a guy, my son, who walks around, looks OK, will even do things if you push him hard enough, and he's not even really complaining. So I said to the doctor 'In what way do you feel he is very sick?'

"The doctor repeated himself, 'Stan is a very sick fellow. He has a disease called schizophrenia, and he may have to be institutionalized for the rest of his life.' Well, I thought to myself, I'll just have to pull a little harder on my bootstrings. If he has to be institutionalized, that's just the way it will have to be.

"And that's when they told me that he was very suicidal. At that time I was still thinking about what the first doctor told me, that Stan was very satisfied within himself. That struck me as a far cry from someone who might be thinking about suicide."

Dolores paused. "Well, I kind of put the thought of him killing himself out of my mind. Maybe it's just as well that these things sort of leave you from time to time. You find that you've kind of forgotten about the bad things. Nothing happens, so it just slips your mind.

"Well, that young doctor was right after all." Her face darkened and her features looked thicker and heavier. She said, "Stanley did try to commit suicide.

"Stan had been on a double-blind study with a Dr. Crosswell at the VA. This doctor had a theory that everybody should be able to function on a medication called Haldol. Now whether Stan was on it too long or whether it didn't work, I don't know. I guess I'll never know.

"But when he began to have problems, Stanley went to see Dr. Crosswell and told him that he felt that the medicine should be changed. Dr. Crosswell said he'd never heard of such a thing and he told Stan so.

"Well, they did increase the medicine—to the maximum—and it still wasn't doing any good. So Crosswell said, 'It's possible the kid has something.' *Then* they changed the medicine, but it was already too late.

"One of the sure signs that things are going wrong is when Stan gets into financial trouble clear over his head. As I said, Stan can't manage his money. But it's always hard to sort things out. I can be watching him pretty closely, and even though I know him as well as I can know anyone, I'll still be wondering: is he getting better and can handle more, or is the illness working double-time? It's confusing because he gets very active and takes on more and more activities.

"Generally he'll enroll himself in a very expensive course—the last time he did this it was truck driving. He passed it with flying colors. That makes you stop and think when you find out it cost him five thousand dollars. Can you imagine a person like that going down the highway at the wheel of a big rig? Anyone can sign up for those courses, they take the money and ask no questions.

"So he's getting himself into a manic stage and just before the suicide attempt he was roaring around pretty wild. But up until the last day he was still doing his regular janitorial work. Luckily he works with some real regular guys who are pretty supportive, and they watch out for him.

"Now, the VA knew he was having problems. He had been in to see his counselor just the day before he attempted to kill himself. *I* knew he was having difficulty, so I called this counselor. I wanted to know if he thought that Stan should go into the hospital. None of these people ever call me. If I don't call them I'd hear nothing. No, I'd hear nothing at all.

"The counselor, said, 'Stan seems to be OK. I think he'll be able to handle things pretty well.' I took his word for it. I hadn't been seeing too much of Stanley. Usually I see him about two or three times a week, but it's his habit to avoid me when his problems are getting out of hand. That should have tipped me off that things *were* going downhill.

"The suicide attempt was real crazy. Nobody can put the pieces together. I don't even think he can. Yes, he survived it." Dolores sighed. "And I'm not very sympathetic.

"I said to him, 'You know . . .' " She sighed again and shrugged her shoulders. "What do you say to somebody when he tries to commit suicide? What do you say? He's embarrassed, he can't even succeed in dying is the way you have to look at it. That must be a horrible embarrassment for him.

"When I saw him he didn't seem pleased to be alive. I didn't know what to say. If someone was to come to me with the same situation, if someone had a family member who'd attempted suicide, I'd probably have an answer for them. I'd probably be able to tell them what to do and what to say, but I didn't have an answer for myself."

Dolores sat quite still, visualizing her son's blank gaze, remembering how his shock of black hair lay lackluster and limp across his pale forehead, how the bright white bandage around his neck appeared to support his ashen and bruised face.

She spoke slowly and emphatically. " 'Well,' I said to him, 'you know,

I'm real sorry that life is so miserable for you. I wish I could change things for you—but I can't. I can only be supportive of you.'

"And then I took his hand. It was very cold. He felt so cold. I wanted so much to let him know that I cared for him. I remember I said, 'One thing I'll tell you, if you'd have succeeded I would never have held it against you. I would have missed you terribly and I love you dearly.' And I let it go at that.

"He said not a word. He had sliced his throat. He was down near Pioneer Square, in a restaurant. He'd gone into the men's restroom—that's where he did it." She said, "It was fortunate that someone happened to walk in.

"It was around two thirty in the afternoon when he did this thing. I had taken the day off from work and gone down to Salem. I'd been there all day with other families from the Alliance for the Mentally Ill. We were lobbying the legislature, trying, as usual, to get better care for our sick children. It seemed like a kind of coincidence, almost a bad joke. I didn't get home until about five thirty. No sooner had I walked in the house than I got a call from one of the guys at Stanley's work.

"A real nice kid wanted to know if I knew where Stan was. Well, that didn't upset me, it seemed pretty run-of-the-mill. I think I said, 'He's not doing very well, is he?' And this kid said, 'No, he really isn't, that's why I'm calling. Stan never came back from his lunch break. So we figured one of us should call you because he might need some help.'

"I didn't think too much about that. I guessed that he had gotten too stressed-out and had just left the workplace. He was in the habit of doing that when he got too pressured, when he got too stressed-out, it wouldn't matter wherever he was—he would just leave. Yup, he'd just leave, he wouldn't even take his coat or his belongings, he'd just go home.

"I called his apartment but there was no answer there. That worried me a bit, not too much, just a kind of twinge. So I thought it's better to be sure, and I went ahead and checked with the VA. They told me he was there. But they didn't tell me why he was there.

"Well, I thought to myself, I'll be a real good mom and go over to the VA. I'll be there for him when they get through and admit him or whatever they're going to do with him. You know, let him know that I care.

"I try not to let him lean too hard. I want him to stand on his own two feet because I'm not always going to be here. I'm not always going to be around. So I'm very careful not to be overly protective, none of this fussy, cuddly stuff. I try to be very careful and stay away from that.

"Well, there I was, I'd just got home and I was still dressed—in my street clothes. I figured I still had some pep left in me, so I might as well go over there and give him some support. I wanted to let him know that I care. To tell the truth, I was probably a little uneasy about him.

"I go down there. I sit in that waiting room until nine thirty. I'd been there three and a half hours when a couple of the young doctors finally came out. They said that they were trying to find a bed for him. And I still didn't know a thing. Things were real chaotic anyway. They were moving from the old VA hospital to the new VA hospital. So I thought that was why they were having trouble knowing where to put him.

"I suggested that they send him to another local hospital. They said, 'Uh uh, come on.'

" 'Oh my,' I said, 'is he that sick that you want to keep him for a longer stay?'

" 'No, we want to keep him three or four days for observation.'

" 'Well, if that's all,' I asked them, 'what's the fuss? After all, he's got to get back to work.' I'm thinking that if he's on his feet, he's got to support himself and get back to work.

" 'No,' one of the doctors said, 'it's too severe. We have to keep him in the hospital.'

"By now I'm really in a muddle. 'Why is he worse now than any other time?'

"Then they looked at each other—kind of startled—and one of them said, 'Well . . . he had a very severe suicide attempt.'

"Just like that he said it. And that was the first I knew about it. I wasn't shocked so much as I was surprised. 'Oh—you finally tried,' is what I said to myself.

"You know," Dolores said, "the worst thing about all of this is all those mentally ill people out there who are trying to survive on their own. All those sick people are just being ignored and forgotten. If only they could get some kind of follow-up help.

"See, they have a crisis, they go in the hospital, and then their apartment goes. So they've got no place to live when they get back out. And a lot of times they don't even get their belongings back. So many times they're so confused and muddled that they don't even know what stuff they have. They may not even notice that it's lost. They're like babies. They can't care for themselves.

"We need to make it a little easier for them—when they're down and out—to get back up there. I'm not saying that they would have fewer bad times, fewer psychotic episodes, but when they do they wouldn't be so miserably treated.

"For instance, you see this thing that happened to my son—well, I'm there to see that there is some follow-up. I'm there to see that he's not stranded, that he's not kicked out of the place where he lives. And even so, it's difficult for him. He doesn't get a supplementary income because he works, so when he doesn't work nothing is coming in.

"Here he has a disease that is made worse by stress. Stanley gets overexcited when he's stressed. And yet the way things are when he gets sick, he's thrown into more stress.

"They say that mentally ill people do better with a peaceful life." Dolores sighed. "They sure do get the opposite."

Commentary

BY JEFFREY L. GELLER, M.D., M.P.H.

Dr. Geller is Professor of Psychiatry at the University of Massachusetts Medical School and Director of Public Sector Psychiatry at the University of Massachusetts Medical Center. He is a board certified psychiatrist and a Fellow of the American Psychiatric Association. He is well known for his professional writing and for his consultation, nationally and internationally.

For generations people have been intrigued by how their society provides care and treatment to those with the chronic mental illness we now call schizophrenia. America's fascination with this topic is no better portrayed than through its print media, from Nellie Bly's account in the *World* in the 1880s, through *Life* magazine's portrayals of institutional existence in the 1940s and deinstitutionalized existence in the 1980s, to *Time*'s cover story on "Pills for the Mind" in 1992.

Suicide, too, is a subject frequently portrayed in our print media. Accounts of suicide are regular features in any urban newspaper and are often headlines in suburban or rural papers. These suicide victims, how-ever, are usually established members of the community or else individuals whose method of suicide was public or dramatic. Suicide by individuals with schizophrenia appears to be less newsworthy.

While schizophrenia and suicide have each been matters of longstand-ing interest, suicide by individuals with schizophrenia remains enigmatic. In this chapter I will examine the change in patterns of care and treatment for individuals with schizophrenia and then discuss suicide and schizo-phrenia. One of the more interesting questions is whether the current methods of treatment of schizophrenia affect the suicide rate. Are Stan Fordham and his mother, Dolores, better off now than they would have been two or three generations ago in terms of the availability of help for a young man with schizophrenia and suicidal tendencies?

In colonial America, the "insane" were kept at home or in almshouses or jails, for there simply were no psychiatric hospitals. The first institution devoted exclusively to the care and treatment of the mentally ill in British North America opened its doors on October 12, 1773, in Williamsburg, Virginia. Throughout the nineteenth century there was a progressive increase in the number of institutions devoted to the treatment of the mentally ill. Fundamental to the early ascendancy of institutional care for the mentally ill was the belief that "lunatic hospitals" represented both the most humane and most cost-effective manner of dealing with mental illness. This perspective was grounded in the widely held opinion that hospital treatment would cure insanity. After professionals and the public became disillusioned with the curability of insanity, public psychiatric hospitals continued nonetheless to grow in number and in size. Institutions had become places for care, if not for treatment. State hospitals came to serve a protective function, protecting the public from the sights and sounds of insanity and protecting the mentally ill from their own inability to care for themselves.

Throughout the first half of the twentieth century, the psychiatric-hospital population continued to grow, until at midcentury psychiatric patients occupied every other hospital bed in America. But the quality of the care in public psychiatric facilities had descended to almost barbaric neglect—a fact brought to the public's attention by a series of exposés.

In 1955 the census of state and county psychiatric hospitals in the U.S.A. reached its peak, and there has been an annual decline since (see Figure 1). The movement of patients out of public hospitals (deinstitutionalization) was initially fueled by a confluence of factors including revised thinking about patients' rights and capabilities; the introduction of new, more effective medication, starting with chlorpromazine (brand name Thorazine); President John F. Kennedy's message to Congress and the Community Mental Health Act of 1963; new Federal entitlements, such as Medicare and Medicaid that included benefits for persons whose functioning was impaired by mental illness; and court cases and changes in state law reflecting these new attitudes and resources.

More recently there has been a further push to empty public psychiatric hospitals. This effort, like the one that first led to the establishment of these institutions, has been driven by the dual goals of improved quality of care and costs savings for state taxpayers. Unlike the failed attempt in the nineteenth century to get the Federal Government, rather than the states, to assume a significant cost of the care of the chronic mentally ill, this contemporary endeavor is rooted in such cost shifting.

The outcome of moving patients from psychiatric institutions and into

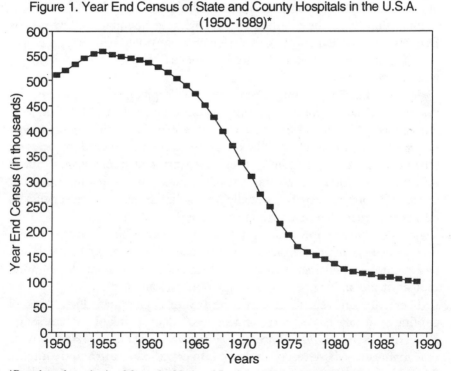

Figure 1. Year End Census of State and County Hospitals in the U.S.A. (1950-1989)*

*Based on data obtained from the National Institute of Mental Health, Division of Biometry and Applied Sciences.

settings in the community has received mixed reviews. Some persons with schizophrenia, who in former eras would have been confined and constrained in state hospitals, now live as productive members of society in as autonomous an existence as possible. For others, life without the asylum functions of state hospitals has meant homelessness and the liberty to be little more than psychotic. For a third group of persons with schizophrenia, deinstitutionalization really has been no more than transinstitutionalization—the movement from the state hospital to another institution or institution-like environment. And for a fourth group the outcome is the least clear. These individuals live constricted lives in semisupervised settings nominally in the community but with interactions limited to caregivers, other ex-patients, and the neighborhood grocer who sells them tobacco and caffeine products.

No matter where an individual with schizophrenia lives in this era of extra-institutional care, there are likely to be times he or she needs acute psychiatric treatment. Obtaining it can be difficult. Some of the problems are illustrated by the plight of Stan and Dolores.

First, Stan is in the community, but without adequate follow-up. As Dolores notes, "He didn't have any doctor, or anyone, following his case." So if Dolores or Stan had questions about his need for acute treatment, whom were they to ask?

Second, if Dolores thought Stan needed hospitalization, but Stan did not agree, Dolores would apparently need to demonstrate that Stan was dangerous to himself or others. As Dolores noted, "There was no easy way to get Stan into the hospital. If he didn't go on his own accord, no one was going to come and make him go there. He wasn't a troublemaker." Stan's difficulty was not his potential dangerousness, but rather his apparent apathy. Dolores lamented, "Usually he just lay around. He never fussed, he never argued, he never asked anything."

And third, if Dolores could get Stan to a facility that might treat him, she could be excluded from the process of evaluation and subsequent treatment, because as she observed, "With our confidentiality laws—well, that's just like talking to a wall—they don't tell me a thing."

There are answers to Dolores' and Stan's dilemmas. First, lack of continuity of care has been recognized as a major failing of contemporary community services. There are service providers, generally referred to as case managers, whose responsibility it is to coordinate care and treatment. Any individual, or someone on the individuals' behalf, can find out about eligibility for such service through the state department of mental health.

Dolores might be able to facilitate Stan's psychiatric admission over his objection even if he does not appear actively dangerous. The procedure for obtaining an involuntary hospitalization varies from state to state. In some states, verbally threatening to commit suicide can be sufficient grounds for a civil commitment, while in other states some act in further-ance of a suicidal threat may be required. It is important that family members like Dolores be familiar with the grounds for civil commitment that apply where they live.

Communication between care providers and persons other than the patient is governed by rules about confidentiality. Information, except in an emergency, cannot be *released* without the patient's permission. What is frequently misunderstood, however, is that information can be *received* by care providers without the patient's permission. If Stan is admitted for treatment, Dolores should not be dissuaded from volunteering whatever information she believes important for those treating Stan.

Even if Stan and Dolores can work together and with care providers to situate Stan in good treatment with adequate supports, how are they to know how great a risk Stan has for suicide? Are there times his risk increases or decreases? When should Stan or Dolores seek more intensive intervention?

The World Health Organization reports that about 1 percent of the general population die by suicide and that about 1,000 people commit suicide each day. In the United States, where suicide is the eighth leading cause of death, there are approximately 35,000 suicides reported annually, with 100,000 being closer to an accurate estimation when one accounts for all suicides reported as accidental deaths. Despite the frequency of suicide, Karl Menninger, the famous American psychiatrist who devoted a consid-erable part of his career to studying suicide, reported, "It's a durn mystery, you know, in spite of all we've written about it."

People commit suicide for many reasons. Edwin Schneidmann, a re-nowned suicidologist, explained, "Suicide is an attempt to solve a prob-lem." And these problems are quite varied. In her well-known suicide, Virginia Woolf filled her pockets with stones and walked into the river. In a note she left for her husband, she told him, "Dearest, I feel certain that I am going mad again. I feel we can't go through another of those terrible times. And I shan't recover this time. I begin to hear voices, and I can't concentrate. So I am doing what seems the best thing to do."

What about suicide in persons with schizophrenia? Eugene Bleuler, the turn-of-the-century psychiatrist who coined the term schizophrenia, noted in an oft-quoted statement: "The most serious of all schizophrenic symptoms is the suicidal drive."

Persons with schizophrenia have a mortality rate that is twice that of the general population. Suicide is the main cause of the increased rate. Patients with schizophrenia account for about 27 to 30 percent of all psychiatric-patient suicides. Twenty percent of all persons with schizophrenia, and about one-third of all individuals with chronic schizophrenia, make suicide attempts. Ten to 12 percent of those with a diagnosis of a schizophrenic disorder die by their own hand.

Stan and Dolores have worked together to obtain treatment for Stan over the course of his illness. He has had many hospital admissions, both at VA hospitals and at university hospitals. Should the fact that Stan has been through the sequence of hospital admission, appropriate treatment, and subsequent discharge lessen Dolores' concern over the possibility of Stan's suicide, even if she is unfamiliar with the suicide potential of individuals with schizophrenia? Unfortunately, no. Various studies have indicated that one-third to one-half of suicides in patients with schizophrenia occur during hospitalization. Of these, about one-quarter occur during the first two weeks of admission and one-third occur by the end of the first month. Even so, 10 percent occur *after* one year of hospitalization. Moreover, one-half of suicides in patients with schizophrenia seem to occur within the first few weeks to a few months after discharge. And, finally, in one study, about half the patients with schizophrenia who committed suicide were seen by their psychiatrists in the week before their deaths.

Dolores is told at the time of Stan's second psychiatric hospitalization that he is a "very sick fellow" and "very suicidal." In fact, some time later Stan does try to commit suicide by slicing his throat. Dolores had previously attempted to deal with the news that Stan was suicidal by putting "the thought of him killing himself out of my mind." What could Dolores have known about the specific suicide risk factors in someone with a diagnosis of schizophrenia? Could such knowledge have better aided Dolores and Stan in recognizing periods of higher risk?

There is a set of risk factors for suicide in persons with schizophrenia that is the same as that for the general population. These are listed in Table 1. Essentially, a white unmarried male; socially isolated, unemployed, with few external supports and a recent loss or rejection; who has deteriorated from a higher level of functioning and now feels a sense of depression and hopelessness is at higher risk for suicide, whether or not he has schizophrenia.

TABLE 1
Risk Factors Shared by the General Population and Persons with Schizophrenia

Depression or depressed mood
Deteriorating health with a high level of functioning before onset of illness
Family history of suicide
Family stress or instability
Limited external support
Loss of parent during childhood
Male
Past history of suicide attempts
Recent loss or rejection
Sense of hopelessness
Socially isolated
Unemployed
Unmarried
White

There is a set of risk factors for suicide specific to persons with schizophrenia. These are not found in the general population. This set of risk factors is listed in Table 2. These risk factors have been determined in studies that compared patients with schizophrenia who committed suicide to persons with schizophrenia who did not and/or to persons who committed suicide but did not have schizophrenia. These data indicate that a young, educated male with schizophrenia, in the early years of his illness, who is realistically aware of his own functioning at below-anticipated levels and fearful of future deterioration to levels even below current functioning, whose pattern of illness is characterized by a chronic course with many exacerbations and remissions and whose functioning after hospital discharges is often not good, who is overly dependent or overly negative about psychiatric treatment is at high risk for suicide. These individuals often demonstrate agitation, irritability, or assaultiveness prior to suicide, do not characteristically give easily recognized warning signs, and use methods that are highly lethal.

Despite what is currently known about risk factors for suicide in people who have schizophrenia, prediction remains problematic at best. There are, however, some factors in the folklore about schizophrenia that are worthy of addressing. These beliefs, or pseudofacts, are often repeated, and even taught, about suicide and schizophrenia, but are either unproven

TABLE 2
Specific Risk Factors for Suicide in Persons with Schizophrenia

Early years of the illness.

Excessive dependence on psychiatric services, or negative attitude toward treatment, or loss of faith in treatment.

Failure to live up to one's own expectations.

Fear of further mental deterioration.

Just prior to suicide, increased agitation, such as irritability or assaultiveness

Last admission was for reasons other than schizophrenic symptoms.

Methods of high lethality.

A high level of education.

Nondelusional assessment of future.

Post–hospital discharge period characterized by high levels of psychiatric symptoms and functional impairment.

Realistic awareness of deteriorating effects of illness.

Severe chronic illness with numerous exacerbations and remissions.

Warning of attempted suicide comparatively rare.

Young (under 45), male.

---

at this time or refuted by data. These myths are listed in Table 3 and discussed on page 221.

In the years after the introduction of antipsychotic medication (mid-1950s) and continuing to the present, there was fear that antipsychotic medication might precipitate suicide by inducing depression or prematurely removing psychotic symptoms in persons with schizophrenia. Studies have not borne this out. There is concern that some of the side effects of the antipsychotic medications, most notably akathisia, a subjective sense of restlessness sometimes accompanied by the inability to be still, might make individuals so uncomfortable that it would increase the likelihood of suicide. There are case reports in the literature that associate suicide attempts with akathisia.

As indicated in Table 2, a realistic assessment by a person with schizophrenia of his or her level of functioning, deterioration from better levels of performance, and a bleak future are high-risk factors. Suicide does not occur as frequently in the most psychotic phases of illness. Further, the oft-cited belief that command hallucinations—auditory hallucinations telling an individual to commit an act—represent high suicide risk is not supported by studies. Suicidal periods are better characterized by periods of hopelessness than by periods of florid or most pronounced psychosis.

TABLE 3
Debunking the Myths About Suicide in Persons with Schizophrenia

Antipsychotic medication does not increase the risk of suicide by inducing depression.

Persons with schizophrenia are not most vulnerable to commit suicide during their most psychotic phase of illness.

Suicide does not commonly occur in persons with schizophrenia in response to command hallucinations.

Persons with paranoid schizophrenia do not have higher rates of suicide than do persons with other subtypes of schizophrenia.

Persons with schizophrenia who commit suicide are not more socially isolated than persons with schizophrenia who do not commit suicide.

There are no data that the shift from institutional-based to community-based care and treatment has increased the risk for suicide in persons with schizophrenia.

Schizophrenia has several subtypes. Those listed in the currently accepted classification of psychiatric disorders (*Diagnostic and Statistical Manual*—DSM-III-R) are: disorganized type, catatonic, paranoid, undifferentiated, and residual type. While folklore has it that persons with the paranoid type are at greater risk than those with other forms of schizophrenia, there are no valid data to support this.

It is often held that persons with schizophrenia who commit suicide are the most isolated. While studies have shown that a lack of family support may be related to an increased suicide risk, the studies do not support a correlation between suicidality and general social isolation. Further, there does not appear to be any clear relationship between suicidality and stressful life events.

Finally, in the early years of deinstitutionalization, and again in these more recent years, popular belief declared that the relocation of patients from institutions to noninstitutional settings or "the community" would increase the risk of suicide in persons who suffer with schizophrenia. While the reasoning behind this has considerable intuitive appeal, there simply is no valid information at this time to either support or refute the proposition.

Having answered many of the questions we posed about Stan and Dolores, we must ask whether they are better off now in terms of Stan's suicidality than they would have been two or three generations ago. There is little to support the idea that they are worse off. External stressors, loss of institutional care or the absence of asylum, antipsychotic medications, more potential isolation—none of these appear to increase the risk of suicide.

On the other hand, there are improved treatments, including new and better medications, improved understanding of the basis for and consequences of cognitive deficits, more sophisticated applications of psychosocial treatments, a vast array of community resources, and a widening effort to decrease stigma, all of which should help Stan and Dolores reduce the risk of suicide. Most important, the current understanding of the suicide-potential and suicide-risk factors in persons with schizophrenia can assist us in the implementation of more informed treatment approaches. Some examples of these approaches are listed in Table 4. Certainly not an all-inclusive list, Table 4 presents ideas for consideration, to be used by patients, family members, and practitioners in our joint efforts.

In the first volume of the *American Journal of Insanity*, in the mid-1840s, the journal's editor, Amariah Brigham, noted that "suicides are alarmingly frequent in this country." Unfortunately, developments over the ensuing one and one-half centuries have made this observation no less true. As this chapter points out, suicide is a particular problem for individuals with schizophrenia.

The victims of a suicide by a person with schizophrenia go beyond the individual himself or herself and include family members and others. This too is an old observation, commented on by Dr. E. K. Hunt in the same volume of the *American Journal of Insanity:* "Too often, notwithstanding the employment of every precaution, the hearts of kindred and friends are made to bleed by the successful tact or ingenuity of the victim to this fearful propensity."

In some ways we have come a long way in approaching the person with schizophrenia and suicidality, and in other ways not.

We are far from the sixteenth-through-eighteenth-century naive notion that suicide can be prevented by admonitions or religious prohibitions. And for some two hundred years we have recognized the need to provide what we would now call "empathy" and "ego supports" aimed at facilitating mastery of life tasks and improving self-esteem. Benjamin Rush, the father of American psychiatry, noted two centuries ago that hospitals needed persons to superintend the "lunatiks . . . to walk with them, converse with them, etc. in order to awaken and regulate their minds."

While scientific medicine struggles to better understand schizophrenia, to improve its treatments and perhaps someday prevent it entirely, persons

TABLE 4
Treatment Considerations in Lessening the Risk of Suicide in Persons with Schizophrenia

Recognize risk factors.

Use care in taking or granting passes or discharge for high-risk individuals and/or during high-risk periods of illness.

Do careful assessments of and use appropriate treatment for secondary depression.

Do careful assessments of self-esteem and address it appropriately.

Do careful differentiation between an inability to function and an unwillingness to function. Set realistic goals.

Ensure there is a supportive, supervised living situation in the community. Avoid isolated residences and high-stress family environments.

Monitor loss and address losses in treatment. There can be losses of family members, friends, treating personnel, and others.

Adjust the environment to need and ability, avoiding too low stimulation (which can lead to withdrawal and apathy) and too high stimulation (which can lead to an increased sense of failure and hopelessness or relapse into active psychosis).

Don't be afraid to discuss suicide. Mentioning or discussing suicide does not generally increase the risk.

Treatment should be experienced by all as supportive and educational.

Work toward making schizophrenia understandable to the population at large as a biologically based disorder that can cause an array of disabilities but does not necessarily make for a disabled person. In other words, decrease stigma.

with schizophrenia and their families can work to improve public understanding of schizophrenia. While suicide by individuals with schizophrenia will surely not be eliminated through increased public awareness and increased public sensitivity, they can only help. As Dolores notes, "They say that mentally ill people do better with a peaceful life. They sure do get the opposite."

7.

Out of Control:

Violence, the Law, and Schizophrenia

"I WILL NEVER FORGET WALKING OUT of University Hall and seeing the headline *Psychiatrist Killed.* 'Oh, my God,' burst from my lips as I saw the photograph of Eric's blood-spattered face. He had shot his psychiatrist, Gordon Campbell, at such close range that the doctor's blood had splashed onto Eric Morgan's face. 'Oh, my God.' I hit that damned newspaper box; I just slammed my fist into that box."

On a wet June day in Portland, Oregon, Eric Morgan killed his psychiatrist. He fired several 12-gauge shotgun blasts, the force of which sprayed blood, bone, and bits of brain from his doctor's exploded head onto his own face.

"I got to know Eric Morgan as a student," Jim Black, a philosophy professor at City University, recollected. "Eric took my 'Theories of Meaning' class, which was a fairly high-level course at that time—he was a philosophy major here. He may have taken other courses with me; certainly he was very involved with the department."

Jim Black is a small, wiry, agile man in his mid-fifties. Chair of the philosophy department at a busy urban university, Jim is peculiarly qualified to deal with the mixed bag of students who make use of a city center school; a keen and knowledgeable motorcycle buff, a scrappy soccer player, an ex-logger, Black's specialty as a Plato scholar is considerably enhanced by his intense and good-humored involvement in his community.

"Eric was a good student, not absolutely outstanding, but he was keen, pretty aggressive, and," Jim's eyes twinkled, "a little inclined to wild philosophical theories. He appeared, however, at that time—and even when I ran into him a little later—clearly sane.

"Sometime after he graduated, maybe after he had just started graduate school, I ran into him. This was at the time when they were drafting people for Vietnam and Eric had just avoided the draft.

"He told me how he accomplished this. Apparently he played the trumpet at the dog races and had learned that blowing hard for a couple of hours elevated blood pressure, so before he went in for his physical he blew like crazy and then rushed over to see the doctor. When they asked him to come back for another test he did it again and was subsequently declared unfit. He wasn't altogether proud of having done this, but like many people at that time he didn't believe in that war and he didn't want to fight.

"A number of years later, I think that he may still have been in graduate school, he came back to visit my class. He walked in one day and announced fairly loudly: 'The great Protagoras has returned.' "

Jim grinned puckishly, "That is a little reminiscent of the setting of the dialogue 'Protagoras,' when Plato's Socrates announces that Protagoras has come to town. I just took it as a joke, but later I began to think he might really have believed it, because he was already a little different. He was harder to deal with. I think his graduate school philosophy department found him very strange—too strange. I don't mean that they thought him insane, rather that he held strong philosophical opinions that were sometimes bizarre and it was hard to understand his reasoning."

What we dismiss as eccentricity can often be an indication of incipient schizophrenia. (Needless to say, eccentricity and mental illness are not necessarily connected.) The early-warning signs can easily go unnoticed or be collusively explained away. But this is no intentional collusion; rather, as we are commonly reactionary in our daily lives—so in the habit of our habits—that we are inclined to stretch what we will accept, being loath to make the effort that any kind of alteration requires.

"It was quite some time after the Protagoras incident that I first learned Eric had schizophrenia." Jim spoke quietly. "It must have been around 1977, and he would have been in his late twenties. Eric called me at my home and asked me to give him a ride home from a mental hospital. I remember telling him I wasn't taking him anywhere as long as he was in the care of a hospital, so he hung up. Ten minutes later I got another call and he said, 'All right, I'm out now, I don't have any money and I don't have a car or anything. I need a ride home.'

"Well," Jim said, "I felt it just wouldn't do to leave him there on the street. Especially if he was as crazy as he sounded, so I went and picked him up. As we were driving to his home he said to me, 'I can't figure it out, are you Jesus Christ or God the Father? I just can't figure that out. Which are you?' " Jim said he remembered laughing somewhat nervously and saying, " 'Well, Eric, I'm sorry but I'm neither of those,' and Eric muttered, 'Lies, all lies.' "

It was quite obvious to Jim that Eric was delusional. Jim was surprised that the hospital had discharged him when he was so clearly psychotic. "Unfortunately, our lives were to intersect far more than I would have wished, and I came to understand only too well how this obviously irrational decision—the hospital having released Eric—had occurred. The hospital, according to the state law, didn't have any choice; they had to let him out because he had been admitted voluntarily—which simply means if he wanted to leave he could. And that is exactly what he did."

Whenever Eric was plainly unable to care for himself, his family—his wife, his parents, and his siblings—had tried to have him committed, to have him hospitalized involuntarily. Repeatedly he had been picked up on the streets by the police, who found him wandering around, screaming obscenities, pissing on the sidewalk, disheveled, filthy—obviously psychotic. They would take him to a hospital, where routinely he would be so heavily medicated that by the time he appeared in court for the commitment hearing, he could manage to behave somewhat appropriately and the judge had no choice but to let him go.

Jim remembered taking Eric home. "He was still living with his wife. I thought it not fair just to drop him there and let him go in, without knowing whether his wife could cope. So I went in to see if she would be all right. She was furious with his being there and actually enraged with me for bringing him." Jim winced at the recollection. "But she determined then to call his psychiatrist, Dr. Campbell, to come over to the house and contend with Eric.

"I never did know how they dealt with him on that occasion. I do remember his wife told him that as a condition for her staying with him he had to give up his Bible reading. It's curious, his delusions were derived from the Bible; the Book of Daniel he regarded as a favorite, there were stories in there that caught his fancy. The other source for his delusions was the *Star Trek* tale about outer-space creatures and other such strange characters."

Eric was especially interested in the *Star Trek* gimmick of beaming up and beaming down. He believed things could be broken down into their atoms and then moved by a beam to another place and reconstituted.

"Later on Eric told me why he picked on me." With an embarrassed shrug and a bemused smile, Jim recalled, "He said he had seen my bookshelf at my office, and it was clear from that that I knew too much to have learned it from so few books. That was what tipped him off. I seemed to know too much, so he concluded I was an alien from outer space.

"What one has to surmise is that, given his interests in philosophy, Eric would have been impressed by the kind of thing that I did in philosophy. All along he had been working on general logical questions, so that would seem to him to be worthwhile work.

"At one point that is why he wanted to kill me. He believed that I had stolen some of his results and was not paying him the royalties that were supposedly due to him. I don't think he ever did any work that one could call sensible. He must have been too ill to actually bring off any results, but he was working at difficult high-level things; he had to have some comprehension of the material even to do what he was doing."

It was quite some time before Jim heard from Eric again. "I don't remember whether he called me on the telephone and then came over to visit me or if he just came by. He did come once or twice when he was really quite delusional. He was always afraid of being shot, as he put it: of being 'plugged.'

"At first when he was talking about his fears of being plugged I wasn't afraid at all. I didn't think him to be dangerous and I still don't think that he was risky to be with at that time. In the beginning Eric never showed signs of bearing any ill-will against me; there was no reason for me to believe that I might have to contend with any future anger or animosity that he might bear toward me."

Jim chuckled. "He treated me as someone who was in this with him. When I didn't converse with him about these crazy 'outer-space' delusions he told me that he understood why I might not be able to talk. 'After all,' he would say, 'you are from outer space and you are in on the secrets that people are controlling my mind by.'

"He believed that some machine from above caused his mental problems. He was adamant that there wasn't anything organic. He was absolutely convinced that there was nothing wrong with him physically. 'I am not sick' was something he was fond of repeating. He insisted that the operation of some device that people 'up there' were messing around with was succeeding in fooling with his brain. Eric was sure that I knew about this and he thought that I could do something about it. As far as I knew, however, he never blamed me for the controlling.

"Eric was quite certain I was an emperor in this galaxy of his. He was sure that I had all these starships overhead and that I commanded them down here on earth. One morning he arrived at my house about seven and he insisted that I instantly beam him up. He told me that I had to get him out of his troubles, that I just had to beam him up in one of my starships. Of course—" Jim laughed—"I couldn't do it. An hour or so later, when I was about to leave for work, he again implored me and I had to tell him: 'Look, Eric—I can't do it.' "

Jim shook his head. "It may sound funny but it wasn't—it was pitiable. Eric had come over to my house by cab. He had left his car at his home because he truly believed that I would agree to beam him up and get him out of his difficulties. When he saw that I wasn't going to do it, he looked pretty sad. 'OK,' he said and called a cab. That afternoon I got a call from him—he was in Reno. He'd taken the taxi to the airport, and since he couldn't get to outer space he'd taken off for Reno.

"Another incident well illustrates Eric's confusion. My parents, who live in Montana, came to visit me. Late one afternoon they were in my house alone and Eric showed up. Of course, they invited him in and offered him some coffee. They presumed—correctly—that he was an old student of mine, so they sat and chatted with him. They found him very strange. I came home after work and there were the three of them talking, so I joined them. We were sitting around the kitchen table. Eric was across from my father. Suddenly Eric leaned over and said, 'I can't figure out who you are.' My dad looked so much like me that it made plausible to Eric my story that my parents lived here on earth. Eric, of course, was sure that I had no ordinary family. According to his perception I had come from outer space and didn't belong here. So he was really puzzled, he couldn't figure out who this guy—my dad—was."

This simple bittersweet story illuminates how this young man, Eric Morgan, was completely trapped by his delusions. His false beliefs created a world which, by its private nature, barred him from straightforward communication with others. An insignificant gathering, elderly parents, their professor son, his past student, drinking coffee, some desultory conversation, an ordinary afternoon—and yet this innocuous and somewhat humorous episode is formed of the same underpinning, the same delusionary material, as a murder.

"Things changed pretty abruptly, and it wasn't very long before his incessant telephone calls started. Eric would inform me that he had a death warrant in my name. He'd say that he was going to have to shoot me. 'I'm coming right over,' he'd tell me and I'd say, 'Well, all right, Eric—you come on over.'

"Eric would drive over to my house and bring his gun—at first he had a fancy automatic pistol—and a box of ammunition. I told him he would have to leave them in the garage if we were to talk. He would take them out and place them on top of an old refrigerator that stood in the garage. Then, after we had chatted for a while, he would pick his gun up and go.

"Other people thought he was very dangerous but I still didn't think so. I was always calm and I felt confident that as long as I could remain peaceful he wouldn't get excited and do anything crazy. Eric had always seemed to me to be a relatively harmless kind of person."

Jim smiled ruefully. "Well, I still don't believe that I was wrong in thinking at that time that he wasn't a real threat, even though he carried a gun and said he was going to shoot me. You see, even though he did eventually kill Campbell, I don't think he would have killed anybody if he had remained in the condition that he was in at that time. What I didn't realize is that this thing is likely to be progressive—that a person who is not dangerous at one stage may, as he gets sicker, as he decompensates, become dangerous.

"From the beginning he did these crazy things only when he was off his medication. When he took his medicine I never saw him. It was quite clear that Eric came to visit me only when he hadn't taken his medicine. Without the control of a regular medication routine he was quite, quite mad.

"As time went on he was more often distraught, desperately unhappy, and fearful for his own well-being. Once, for just what reason I do not know, he wept more violently than I have ever known anyone to weep. You know how children can break your heart with their weeping, this was more piteous than that. What he took to be the control of his mind by these alien forces was not only discomforting but horrific for him. On the other hand, he so hated the side effects of the medicine that he felt himself to be captured and trapped within a terrible double-bind." Jim paused and shook his head. "I cannot think of a more intolerable affliction.

"One evening, early on, Eric came to me in a very bad way. It was obvious that he hadn't taken his medicine for quite a long time. His whole focus was a forcefully expressed distrust of his psychiatrist. From time to time, after that occasion, he would repeat his suspicions about Gordon Campbell. I came to understand that this unfounded paranoia was part of Eric's disease.

"These uncontrollable feelings of persecution were tragically focused on an inappropriate object. Gordon Campbell was an admirable and unusual psychiatrist. He actually made house calls. If his patients were too ill to come to him, he would go to their homes. He treated the sickest people, the worst and most difficult chronic cases of schizophrenia—he took patients other doctors refused to see. He was unflinching in his perform-ance of what he saw as his duty, his obligation to his patients. He knew how dangerous Eric was. In the last few months before his death he told a colleague that he had a patient who really, really could kill.

"At one time, when Eric was threatening to kill me, Campbell called my house to warn me that my life was in danger. I was out and he spoke to Evelyn, my wife. He suggested that she tell me to watch out."

Jim shrugged. "To begin with, I didn't do anything. After all, what do the deer do when people are out hunting? I wasn't going to leave my house. It was a matter of pride that I wasn't going to be run out of my house by a lunatic.

"Gradually Eric became increasingly agitated, less in control. More and more he began talking about killing me rather than about the danger of his being killed. Eventually—I don't remember if it was more than once— he refused to leave his gun in the garage. He kept it with him in the living room. Whether it was the first time this occurred, I couldn't say, but I remember on one occasion he refused to leave his gun and I was pretty sure that he was in a condition in which he could actually shoot me.

"He was very mercurial and I knew that there was considerable danger. I tried to keep near enough to him so that I could interfere if he undertook to load his gun. Unfortunately, the telephone rang. I went to answer it and in the midst of the call I heard him loading the gun. I remember saying, 'Whoops,' and slamming down the phone. I dashed back into the living room, where I successfully restrained him from finishing the job.

"I had developed a strategy. I thought that as long as I was perfectly calm, did nothing to defend myself, nothing to hold him off, nothing to threaten him, he would feel utterly confident, he would be comfortable in coming around with his gun and a box of ammunition—secure that if he needed to he could load his gun. I deliberately did nothing that would make him think he couldn't do that. So I felt assured that when he showed up his gun wasn't loaded. If he had his gun in one hand and his ammunition in the other, I felt certain that all was as it appeared. I had always supposed that a sane person was a little smarter than a crazy person; I was taking advantage of that.

"I had also calculated that Eric saw his role as that of an executioner, not as a hunter. I realized that any killing he would do would be done face-to-face. Furthermore, Eric was quite a lot bigger than I was—that certainly must have made him feel confident. I didn't appear to be any kind of threat. However, I felt secure that in a physical struggle I probably would have gotten the better of him. I had the advantage because he was unaware of that possibility."

Jim Black's professorial mien disguises his athletic prowess. Despite his small, slight stature, he could be a quick and tough physical adversary.

"When I ran to the ringing telephone and heard, almost simultaneously, Eric loading his gun, I knew I had to do something. The time for calm and peaceful theorizing was clearly at an end. I gripped his arm and persuaded him that he simply had to take the gun outside. There was a massive brick fireplace in the living room which would have put me at quite a disadvantage if I had inopportunely hit my head against it. I wanted to be outside if I was going to have to struggle with him.

"Well, I managed to strongarm him out of the house. He was quick to suggest that he place his gun in his car, but I apprised him that that wouldn't do—that I was taking the gun. He certainly balked at that, but by then having maneuvered him out of the house, using a route through the garage, I had succeeded in grabbing a hammer. I put it to him quite simply: 'You take your choice. I'll use this on you and then on your car or you give me the gun.'

"He didn't want to deal with me—and the hammer in my hand—and he didn't want to give way either, so he proposed to sell the gun to me for two dollars. Of course, I agreed.

"I hated to have to resort to this kind of action because it meant that next time he would know that he had to have a loaded gun in order to shoot me. Obviously I couldn't continue with my previous strategy. I had to alter my tactics. Talking calmly is no good when a guy is loading a gun and pulling the trigger. The time for composed conversation had been precluded.

"A few days later his mother came to buy the gun back. Eric had told her about selling it to me, and how much I had paid for it. His family didn't want him having guns, but this was an uneasy and uncomfortable situation for both his mother and me. When I handed the gun over to her, she opened the box and said, 'Wow, that's a really nice one.' I found this to be a rather odd remark, but I'm sure these kind of circumstances get people down. I had the feeling that she found it all very difficult to deal with.

"The family, the psychiatrist, and I were probably by then the only people who were still talking to Eric. The neighbors, I was told, were very afraid of him. He had a malevolent demeanor and they no longer excused him as a harmless lunatic. He walked around the local streets carrying on loud and abusive conversations with the air, and he was quick to accost people, raising his arms in threatening gestures and spitting out foul-mouthed epithets.

"Even I had become afraid. When I heard him loading that gun I was truly scared. I thought I knew him well enough to know when he wasn't likely to shoot and when he was—and I had been right up until then. In the way that a person who gets used to sharks thinks that he knows when one is about to attack, I too felt assured that I knew when he meant to actually fire at me. I cannot dissemble, I was very frightened.

"However, I was determined not to be thrown off course—more than necessary—by this crazy person. I felt a little stubborn about this partly because I knew that there was a lot of danger and I felt a little annoyed that I had to put up with these risks. In knowing my own weakness and fearfulness I was disinclined to give in to him.

"Even so, it was blatantly clear that now I was in some real jeopardy. So after the gun-scuffling business, not wishing to be foolish and impru-dent, I called the police and the District Attorney's office to tell them about Eric's shenanigans. The DA's office was curt and told me that it appeared to be a situation in which they were powerless to intervene.

"The police came around to my house and they were very nice, but they basically gave me the same message: there was nothing they could do unless something occurred. They suggested that I call them when he was actually there. Needless to say, I didn't feel very well protected. It was clear that I was on my own."

Not long after that, Jim Black went on a sabbatical leave to England for eight months. Eric was very concerned about who would be his contact while Jim was gone. Eric consistently held to his delusions that Jim was from outer space and therefore his contact to alien forces. One of Jim's colleagues suggested that Jim give Eric the District Attorney's name as his "contact."

Even though the suggestion was something of a lark, there was a sinister undertone: Professor James Black, a law-abiding man, had found himself in a perilous and untenable situation, without protection from the community of which he was an exemplary citizen. And Eric Morgan, poor Eric, he too was in the position of victim. Not only did he suffer from a chronic disease—paranoid schizophrenia—but he also found himself in a perilous and untenable situation from which his community would not protect him. It was almost as though Eric Morgan were being given a carte blanche to commit murder.

"The first time Eric came to see me after I returned from England, he came to my house without a gun," Jim remembered. "When he left on that occasion, however, I could tell that the next time he would be coming to kill me. It was plain that there wouldn't be any more quiet visits. He had finally made up his mind that he had to eliminate me. There was a distinctly menacing undercurrent in the way he spoke to me and the tone of his voice was greatly altered. He was no longer straightforward about killing me since the time I had taken his gun from him."

When Jim realized that he wasn't going to get any significant support from the police, he began to plan carefully. He started to lock his front door and pull down all the window blinds in case Eric decided to take a shot at him from outside the house.

"I knew I couldn't talk to him anymore, and I was sure that when he next came to my house he would arrive with a loaded gun, fully expecting to kill me. What were my options? Well, I could run out the back door, climb over the fence, and get the hell out of there. However, if I succeeded in escaping, then the next time he came back I'd have to think of something else.

"I was still fairly sure he expected a deliberate response from me. I had never shown any excitement or moved quickly. I'd always faced him, so I was certain that he would count on that kind of behavior. Eric would anticipate that he and I would be standing face-to-face and he would shoot me. I calculated, therefore, that he would not be prepared for me to open the door, burst out of the house, and jump him without even looking to see who was there.

"Late one evening when I heard Eric's heavy walk coming up the path to the house and his subsequent kick on the front door, I had to decide whether I would go through with my plan or chicken out. I felt very pressed and couldn't see any other alternative. I threw the door open, hit the screen with my shoulder, and was on him before he could raise his gun. Eric had his shotgun there, it was loaded and cocked—he was ready to pull the trigger—and he was standing back from the doorway prepared to raise up the gun and shoot.

"I was stupidly overconfident. I had supposed it was a matter of knocking him down, wrestling him for the gun, taking it away, and setting things straight from there. We hit the walk together, both of us skinning our knees. I didn't want to hurt him, I simply wanted to wrest the gun from him. Eric, however, had the stock and I had the barrel and he was succeeding in getting it away from me. I must admit I thought that all was over.

"I distinctly recollect feeling, 'This is it, he's got me.' Amazingly he suddenly stopped, saying, 'All right, I give up. I won't shoot you.' He let me have the gun. He was a little afraid that I might shoot him. I was shaken. I had really thought, for what fortunately turned out to be a brief moment, that I was a dead man."

Both men had propelled themselves into a project. Each had had a discrete plan. But once the action was in motion, it took on its own life and both men were captured by it. Eric was imprisoned by his disease, and Jim was imprisoned by his former student's madness. One man's private insanity had become the other man's deadly dilemma.

Jim kept the gun and called the police. Eric left before they arrived. Jim was in no mood for any further scuffling and had let him go.

The police were pleasant enough. Jim wearily remembered, "Of course they took the gun, but they explained to me that there wasn't anything that they could do. They suggested I call the District Attorney. The District Attorney's office told me they could set up an appointment to talk to me in about ten days. I retorted that in ten days I might be dead. And they replied, 'Well, that's our calendar. You can come and talk to us on that date if you want.' "

Jim did go and talk to an Assistant District Attorney. She told him, "You're on your own. It's none of our business. We couldn't convict this guy even if we took him to court." Jim believes that was irresponsible. Dr.

Campbell had told him that the DA's office *could* have gotten a criminal verdict. This court decision would have required Eric to take medication, and if he refused, they could have had him committed to a mental hospital.

Throwing up his hands, Jim growled, "I learned from that what it must be like to be a hunted animal. The law prohibited me from protecting myself and it refused to restrain the mentally ill man who intended to kill me.

"It's odd how one can remain frightened only for a short time. Initially I used to check out the streets near my house on my way home. Before I approached my house I would look all around my neighborhood very carefully. After a few days I stopped taking all these precautions. I found that I couldn't go around being frightened all the time.

"I did, however, borrow a gun when I became confident that I had no other recourse. It had become apparent to me that I had used up all my other possibilities and that the next time Eric came back there wouldn't be any other way to cope with the situation if I didn't have a gun."

Perhaps two years had passed when very early on a Sunday morning Jim saw Eric marching up to his front door with his hand in his pocket. It was Valentine's Day and Jim had a soccer game planned.

Wryly Jim remembered, "I had borrowed a shotgun from a friend. He had originally bought it in pieces and another acquaintance had put it together. None of us had ever tested it to see if it worked. I had meant to do that.

"I fully intended to take it out somewhere and shoot it just to make sure that the damned thing worked. After all, a nonfunctional gun would certainly not be of much use in the kind of life-and-death circumstance in which I might expect to find myself with Eric Morgan.

"And now here comes Eric up the walk to my house with his hand in his pocket. Needless to say, I didn't open the door. When I refused, he poked his gun through a small grate that serves as a little peephole. Quickly I ducked away and ran and got my borrowed gun of unknown quality. Eric went around to a side door of the house, which has a glass window, and broke it with his gun. He reached in with his arm and easily unlatched the door. We both came into the kitchen, from different directions, at precisely the same time. There we were, the two of us, standing with our guns. I tried to persuade him to drop his. He refused.

"I had intended to shoot him. I had thought it out carefully and had decided that it was the best thing to do. I knew there was no other way to protect myself and equally I had decided it wasn't to his disadvantage to be dead. I knew he was dangerous to other people too, so I thought that I ought to kill him and I actually believed I would.

"Facing his gun, and not knowing if my own gun worked or not, I chickened out. If my gun simply went click then I would have been a dead duck. It would have been all over for me.

"Cautiously, I retreated out of the front door, which I had opened when he went around to the side of the house. Knowing that I could outrun him once I got out the door, I took off. There I was running down the street, carrying a shotgun, with this lunatic, holding a six-shot revolver, chasing me.

"I knew enough about revolvers to know that even a practiced shot couldn't hit anyone at a very great distance, so I didn't feel much in danger as long as I could keep fifty yards between myself and him. Even so, as a precaution I tried to keep a tree or a power pole between us.

"Fortunately there wasn't a soul around, so there wasn't any possibility of someone else being inadvertently hurt. The street was quiet and peaceful, the neighborhood appeared deserted: just the two of us out there, gasping for air, our feet pounding the pavement.

"Eric soon gave up all hope of catching me and quickly grew tired of the chase. He turned and started walking back toward his car and I followed behind with the intent of stopping him from getting away.

"My wife had been at home, and I knew that by now she would have telephoned the police and that, hopefully, they would be on their way. When he reached his car, and I was about thirty yards away from him, I yelled, 'OK, Eric, just wait right there. Drop your gun and stay there.'

"He wasn't about to do that. He just continued getting into his car all the while absolutely ignoring me. So I shot—I couldn't have killed him from that distance—but I shot at the ground between us. The pellets scattered more than I had anticipated. Some of them must have bounced off the pavement because he got some pellets in his leg. This stopped him. He dropped his gun and sat on the curb.

"Then I heard a deep booming voice: 'Drop your gun.' I turned around to find myself facing two guns. The police were hiding behind their car. They had silently pulled up while I was busy concentrating on Eric. Instantly I realized, 'It's me they're after. They have their rifles and shotguns trained on me.'"

Jim's voice dropped to a hoarse whisper. "I really believed I was in at least as much danger from them as I ever was from Eric.

"As soon as I saw the police, I dropped my gun and threw up my hands. They shoved me into their patrol car, clearly unaware that they had the wrong man. Evelyn, my wife, came out and told them that they had got the two of us muddled up, but they only half believed her. They wouldn't let go of me and it took an uncomfortably long time until they had it all sorted out.

"I did feel somewhat wronged. I thought it was unnecessary that they manhandled me. After all, I wasn't behaving in a wild way, so it seemed reasonable that they should find out who was who. They could at least have talked to me. I understand that they might have been confused at the outset. And if I had been unwilling to drop the gun I can see that they might have acted as they did.

"I must say it was altogether unexpected." Jim shook his head and spoke quietly, "It certainly wasn't something that I had anticipated. In the end they were quite civilized and sympathetic once they understood that Eric, intending to kill me, had broken into my house with his six-shot revolver.

"This time Eric was taken to a hospital where the staff showed some intelligence and concern: they didn't give him any medication. They treated his leg wounds but gave him no drugs for his psychosis. They let him go to court in the mental condition that he was in when he had arrived at their facility. Had they not done that, it was unlikely that he would have been committed to the state mental hospital. I have always been very grateful to them.

"Eric's family had urged me to have the police press charges, but when I talked to the police they told me they couldn't. They advised me that it was the responsibility of the District Attorney, but the District Attorney's office refused to press charges.

"They had no reason to feel hesitant about Eric Morgan's being dangerous, but they would not take the step that would have enabled the mental health division people to get a forensic—a criminal—commitment. The District Attorney's office just would not take that step because they felt it wouldn't have garnered them a conviction."

Jim was scathing. "They wouldn't do it because they might not get a score. I consider that Gordon Campbell's blood is on their hands."

There was no criminal hearing. There was a civil-commitment hearing at which Jim testified. The police attended the trial, but the lawyer, the public defender who was representing Eric, successfully petitioned the court to disallow their testimony. The police testimony was ruled as inadmissible evidence. The only testimony that the court could hear was from Jim Black. If Jim had not been at the hearing, nothing would have been done.

During the trial Eric was hearing voices. Unselfconsciously, he carried on long and rambling conversations with unseen creatures. There was no doubt that he was utterly psychotic. Jim remembered, "He told the court that I was the emperor of the evil galactic empire and that he—Eric—had to kill me because I was about to start a thermonuclear war and that the City of Portland would be destroyed if he didn't kill me."

The court ordered Eric committed to the state mental hospital for the maximum six months' civil commitment. After the trial the presiding judge told Jim that Eric Morgan was "the scariest guy" he had seen in a long time. He evinced concern about what could occur when Eric was released and suggested that Jim consider moving to another residence.

Jim said, "I requested that the judge order the hospital administrator to notify me when Eric was going to be released. He said that he would like to, but thought that it was not possible as it might be considered an invasion of Eric Morgan's privacy. Apparently any report concerning a patient's release from a mental hospital is considered to be privileged information because it indicates that that person has been in a mental institution."

Jim Black spoke so quietly that the sibilant sounds seemed magnified. "Even though I had been the principal witness in the courtroom and had testified against Eric Morgan, even though I had been present and heard the judge's decision that considered Eric Morgan to have a mental disorder and appropriately committed to a state mental hospital for the maximum civil commitment, and even though the court demonstrated concern for my well-being, it was still an invasion of Eric Morgan's privacy should I be notified about his release."

One month short of Eric's release a social worker at the state mental hospital sent Jim a note. She wrote that Eric would be released back to the community and that this was against the recommendation of the medical staff. The staff did not believe it was safe to let Eric Morgan out. But because of the current laws they were unable to prolong his civil commitment.

Jim Black never saw Eric Morgan in person again. However, when he saw the newspaper photograph of Eric's blood-splattered face, Jim knew better than most that Eric had been condemned by his community—albeit inadvertently—to commit a murder. The murdered doctor and the schizophrenic murderer were both victims of a clumsy system that had muddled up issues of disease and civil rights.

Commentary

BY JEFFREY L. ROGERS, J.D.

Jeffrey L. Rogers is City Attorney for Portland, Oregon, and Clinical Professor of Psychiatry at the Oregon Health Sciences University. He obtained his bachelor's degree summa cum laude and Phi Beta Kappa from Dartmouth College, attended Harvard Medical School, and received his JD degree from Yale Law School in 1973. Mr. Rogers has published, lectured, and taught extensively in the field of Law and Psychiatry. He participated in the development of Oregon's innovative Psychiatric Security Review Board and was a member and then Chair of that board from 1979 to 1981. Mr. Rogers and his colleagues have conducted intensive research on mentally ill offenders, which has led to recognition of Oregon's approach as one promising model for simultaneously providing patient treatment and community protection.

Most people with schizophrenia are not violent. Studies indicate that, when their psychotic symptoms are treated and not active, they are no more likely to be violent than anyone else. Even when their symptoms are active, almost nine out of ten are nonviolent. Those who abuse alcohol are twice as likely to be violent as persons with schizophrenia, and drug abusers three times as likely.

Nonetheless, the small percentage of people with schizophrenia who are physically dangerous to others have a disproportionately large impact. Because of the media attention to sensational cases like "Eric Morgan" or John Hinckley, many lay people assume that danger is the rule, not the exception. This exacerbates the fear and anxiety that people often feel when encountering those who seem different, even if they pose no actual danger. The misperceptions also cloud our ability to develop constructive approaches to providing adequate treatment resources for nonviolent mentally ill persons.

Of course, statistics are of no comfort when dealing with persons with schizophrenia who are dangerous. The dangerous mentally ill person, and his or her family and friends, may become caught in a confusing web of legal and medical mechanisms that often seem irrelevant, inconsistent, and irrational. Sometimes, as in the case of "Eric Morgan," or that of "Tony Schmidt," in the narrative entitled "Dial 911," the failure of the system to respond adequately to what seems to be an obvious need for intervention produces despair and a warranted sense of helplessness in the face of imminent danger.

There are several reasons the legal and medical systems sometimes fail. Those working in the system are often provided with inadequate funding and resources by legislatures. Also, like anyone, those working in the system sometimes make bad decisions, such as the decision by the Deputy District Attorney not to initiate criminal prosecution of Eric Morgan.

However, in addition to the problems of inadequate resources and human error, there is a more fundamental reason the system produces so much frustration for families of mentally ill persons. The American legal system is intentionally designed to make it difficult to confine a person against his or her will. Just as we have decided to let ten guilty criminals go free to avoid wrongly convicting one innocent person, there are compelling reasons to have a civil-commitment system that strives mightily to protect the civil liberties of mentally ill individuals. But, by zealously protecting precious constitutional rights and erring on the side of liberty, the potential therapeutic value of the commitment process is substantially reduced.

Because families and friends of a dangerously mentally ill person often have no other recourse, civil or criminal commitment may be looked to as a solution of last resort. But, just as the legal system cannot provide a solution to crime, it cannot provide a solution to the suffering wrought by schizophrenia. Even when it functions as it should, the commitment process can only be a temporary palliative, employed when all else has failed. Any legal system has to balance competing values and can never be a panacea for human ills. Eventually, the answer to the scourge of schizophrenia will come from medical research, not from the law.

Meanwhile, however, we must do the best we can with the inadequate tools we have. Civil and criminal commitment and other legal mechanisms are inherently limited in their usefulness. Our communities must do a better job of providing alternatives to coercive legal mechanisms. Preventive treatment, adequate insurance coverage for mental illness, and easily accessible community services are just a few of the tools which are too often unavailable to those who need them.

When alternatives are not available, the law is the last resort. Therefore it is important that families, friends, and others trying to help cope with dangerously schizophrenic individuals have some understanding of legal mechanisms and their limitations. The preceding narrative illustrates how terrifying it can be to seek help from a system which, ironically, may seem as delusionally detached as does the mentally ill person. Although the case of "Eric Morgan" is extreme and unusual, it dramatically illustrates some of the issues that commonly arise when psychiatry and law awkwardly overlap.

THE MENTAL HEALTH PROVIDER'S LEGAL DUTY TO PROTECT

What obligation does a psychiatrist, psychologist, or other provider of mental health services have to protect persons who may be endangered by a patient with paranoid schizophrenia? Can a family member or other person who is in danger of being assaulted expect to receive a warning from the patient's therapist? In the narrative, Dr. Campbell called to warn Jim Black that his life was in danger because the doctor's patient was threatening to kill Jim. Dr. Campbell obviously had concluded that in this case his obligation to try to protect others outweighed his obligation to protect his patient's confidentiality by keeping secret what his patient had told him. Both goals—protection and confidentiality—are legitimate and important. Can a treating psychiatrist be effective if the patient is reluctant to bare his inner thoughts, fearing that the psychiatrist will reveal them? Although there is debate within the profession about whether strict confidentiality really is vital to effective treatment, there is no question that maintaining the privacy of doctor-patient communications is a time-honored principle in the medical profession.

Nonetheless, even before the courts began to intervene in this area of medical practice, many psychiatrists treating patients with paranoid schizophrenia took steps to protect third parties who they believed were endangered by their patients. The psychiatrist might warn others, or initiate civil-commitment proceedings, or try to convince the patient to accept treatment in a secure hospital, or take other actions or combinations of actions. The psychiatrist acted based on his or her best judgment about what was most important in the particular case.

Of course, such judgments are made much more complex by the difficulty of predicting whether a particular patient really is dangerous. In extreme situations, such as when Eric began brandishing loaded guns and making overt threats, the high likelihood of danger is obvious. And after a patient harms someone it may seem easy, in retrospect, to have known that the person was dangerous. But the situations confronted by therapists and by the courts are often complex and subtle. For example, the statement "I'd like to kill the Mayor" can be many things including a joke, a political commentary, an expression of temporary anger or depression, or the genuine threat of a delusional mentally ill person. In retrospect, the meaning may seem obvious; prospectively, it often does not.

We tend to believe, and like to hope, that psychiatrists are experts at predicting dangerous behavior. However, research suggests that they are no better than lay people at predicting most kinds of violence, and that they use the same indicators others use to predict future behavior, primarily past behavior. Nonetheless, our legal system frequently calls on psychiatrists for such predictions regardless of whether or not they have any special ability in this area. As discussed below, the problem of predicting dangerousness is at the heart of the shortcomings of the civil and criminal commitment systems.

A therapist deciding whether to disclose a threat made by a patient has to weigh a certain breach of confidentiality against an uncertain prediction of dangerousness. In recent years, courts have begun to intervene more often in that decision. The best-known case, *Tarasoff*, occurred in California in 1976. A voluntary outpatient at a university hospital told his therapist that he was going to kill a girl, who was readily identifiable as Tatiana Tarasoff. The psychiatrist asked the police to initiate civil commitment, but the police concluded that the patient was rational and released him after he promised to stay away from Tatiana. The psychiatrist took no further action to protect Tatiana and did not warn her or her parents that his patient was dangerous to her. The man later killed her. Her parents sued the university, claiming that the psychiatrist failed in his duty to warn Tatiana or to take other steps to protect her.

The California Supreme Court concluded that psychiatrists in that state have a duty to exercise reasonable care to protect third parties from foreseeable danger presented by patients. This duty can be fulfilled in a number of ways, including warning the potential victim. The court said that a victim, or a victim's relatives, can sue therapists for failing to take adequate steps to warn and protect. Thus, this case created what is sometimes called the "duty to warn" or "duty to protect."

Although the case created a great stir within the psychiatric profession, it was not truly revolutionary. As noted, psychiatrists had customarily been warning others in certain situations. Furthermore, the legal duty created does not have precise boundaries. How clear must the possible danger be before it is reasonable to breach confidentiality? What protective steps are required before a psychiatrist can be certain that a jury will conclude that he or she has exercised "reasonable" care to protect others? These questions are difficult to answer.

The main effect of *Tarasoff* and subsequent similar cases was to subject psychiatrists to possible legal liability for decisions that they have always had to make. A medical decision was converted into a medical and legal decision. Unfortunately for potential victims, the *Tarasoff* doctrine may actually have added little protection. Presumably it has made psychiatrists more inclined to warn, but even that is uncertain.

If a psychiatrist could flawlessly predict whether and in what manner a patient would be dangerous, the decision about warning would be simple. Until that unlikely day, the decision whether to take steps to protect potential victims will be left to the judgment of the individual doctor and second-guessed by everyone including victims, relatives, and courts.

A family member or other concerned person can and should discuss this issue early and openly with the mentally ill person's psychiatrist or other therapist. What general approach does the psychiatrist take to this difficult issue? Would the psychiatrist be willing to breach confidentiality readily, or at least take other steps such as initiating civil commitment, which might not necessarily involve revealing secrets? How would the psychiatrist notify others or take other steps to protect? If others don't hear from the psychiatrist, can they conclude that the psychiatrist believes the patient is not dangerous to them or their relatives? Does the psychiatrist customarily tell the patient at the outset of treatment that if the doctor concludes the patient is suicidal, assaultive, or homicidal that he or she will take steps to protect others, including disclosing confidences? Many psychiatrists who treat people with paranoid schizophrenia or other potentially dangerous mentally ill persons believe that such an understanding does not hinder, and might help, the therapeutic process.

Although the therapist may be unable to give precise answers to these questions, a discussion of them can help alert the therapist to the family's concerns and can help establish good lines of communication. There are no simple rules about whether, when, or how a therapist should act to protect third parties. This makes it all the more important, in each individual situation, to confront and discuss this subject openly and directly before it is too late. If the patient is seen by a series of doctors in several institutions, the same discussion should be repeated with each new therapist.

CIVIL COMMITMENT

Ideally, a person with schizophrenia will recognize the need for treatment and will agree to medication or hospitalization if necessary. But it must be recognized that voluntary treatment is just that. A voluntary adult patient, no matter how ill, has a right to refuse treatment and to leave the hospital—although some states may require a delay or other procedural steps before discharging even a voluntary patient.

Unfortunately, voluntary treatment of a person with paranoid schizophrenia may be inadequate. The disease destroys judgment, and the mentally ill person may be unable to recognize the need for treatment and medication. If the patient refuses hospitalization or insists on leaving prematurely, then involuntary hospitalization is the next recourse. If the unwillingness to take medication is combined with the sort of disruptive and threatening behavior shown by "Eric Morgan" or "Tony Schmidt," relatives and friends also can be terrified. Having run out of alternatives, they turn to the police and the courts for protection and compelled treatment.

In most states the civil-commitment process can be initiated by doctors, police, or a petition filed by one or more persons who know the patient well. If police or physicians do not initiate commitment, family or friends of the ill person may decide to do so themselves. There are several sources of information about initiating civil commitment. The staff of the court that handles civil commitment, often the probate court in the nearest county courthouse, can explain the process and how to initiate it. Similarly, county or city mental health clinics may be able to provide the needed information and forms.

When the civil-commitment process is initiated, a medical problem becomes a medicolegal one. Most nonpsychiatric illnesses are handled purely medically—there is rarely need to turn to the courts for help in treating heart disease, arthritis, diabetes, or most of the vast array of human illnesses. Some forms of mental illness are exceptions. In her introduction to this book, Dr. Andreasen emphasizes that schizophrenia is a physical illness of the brain. She urges that we raise mental illness to equal status with other illnesses. Certainly, once we are able to treat schizophrenia as effectively as we do many other illnesses, it will be easier to respond to mentally ill people the way we do to those with other diseases.

Unfortunately, the symptoms of some forms of schizophrenia may include behavior that poses physical danger to self or others. Although suicidal behavior is not unique to schizophrenia, homicidal behavior is very rarely associated with other "physical," as opposed to "psychiatric," illnesses.

Medication may ease the symptoms and prevent dangerous behavior, but persons with schizophrenia may refuse to take medication voluntarily. Thus, the coercive power of the state may be called on to help compel treatment. Our society is willing to let most sick people decide whether or not to accept treatment. But we cannot afford to let certain mentally ill persons make that decision; they could be incapable of making a wise decision and the risks to others could be unacceptably high. By its very nature, schizophrenia requires us on occasion to respond in different ways than those used with other types of patients. Put most starkly, we don't lock up most sick people in secure hospitals.

As important as it is to provide secure treatment for dangerously mentally ill persons, it is equally important that we ensure that the vast power of the state to confine people against their will is never used to suppress dissent or for other political purposes, as has been done frequently in many countries. In this country we take for granted that our individual liberty is protected. The reason we feel so secure in that freedom is that our courts zealously guard the constitutional limits of government power. When we understandably become frustrated at how difficult it is to civilly commit a person, we are confronting one of the costs of our constitutional rights. We don't encounter that problem with other illnesses because we do not have to turn in desperation to ask the state to confine its victims.

Over the years, the balance between protecting liberty and confining dangerous people has been the subject of innumerable court decisions, with the pendulum swinging back and forth. But even the present conservative Supreme Court has ruled that patients can't be confined against their will merely because they are ill and need treatment. There must be something more: a criminal act committed, or proven danger to self or others. It is this requirement of danger that confounds those who would have the state intervene more readily to require treatment. And it is the difficulty of predicting danger that makes civil commitment even more difficult.

Furthermore, as a society we have been extremely reluctant to confine people for the rest of their life or for any very long period. This is true even regarding those mentally ill persons who have proven their dangerousness by violent acts. We hope that treatment will prevent future violence, and we want to believe in giving second chances. These well-motivated tendencies have combined with the difficulty of predicting dangerousness to produce systems that intentionally make it difficult to commit people or to confine them for long periods.

District attorneys and others involved day-to-day in the legal system know that judges must apply the law and know that the law establishes many obstacles to commitment. Sometimes police and prosecutors are reluctant to proceed with commitment because they know a court cannot order confinement until obviously dangerous acts have occurred. This is one of the most frustrating aspects of the system when dealing with a person who family and friends "know" is dangerous even if it can't be proved under the applicable legal standards.

One way in which families can work to improve the system is to lobby state legislators to change the statutory criteria for commitment. Most states, and many sizable cities, have advocacy groups active in seeking legal reform. Relatives or friends of mentally ill individuals can be compelling and constructive advocates and witnesses before legislative committees. But legal reform is a longer-term proposition of no immediate help to those presently involved in a civil-commitment proceeding.

By contrast, understanding the dynamics of civil commitment can be of some immediate help to those trying to deal with it. The mentally ill person usually has a lawyer appointed by the court and paid by the state. That attorney is duty-bound to advocate what the client wants. If the patient, who is that lawyer's client, wants to avoid commitment, most lawyers believe it is their professional and ethical obligation to seek to prevent commitment, even if the lawyer and others believe release is not in the best interests of the patient's health, or even if it endangers others. This can be enormously puzzling and maddening for family members who have struggled for months or years to get help for their relative and to protect themselves and others. But it is the essence of our advocacy system. To counterbalance the role of the lawyer for the "allegedly mentally ill person," the District Attorney's primary goal is to protect the community and the ill person. Although understandable, little is gained by being angry with the patient's lawyer. Rather, one should recognize the reality of our country's adversarial legal system and consider finding an attorney who will assist in seeking commitment and protection.

Although not routinely done, it could be very helpful for family or friends to find their own lawyer. That lawyer can explain the procedure, list options, advise how best to proceed, and perhaps participate in the commitment hearing. If a private lawyer is too expensive, the local legal aid society or bar association may have a list of lawyers who are willing to provide assistance. Families and friends may not think of having their own lawyer. But it is important to recognize that lawyers are ethically required to represent only one client in any situation.

The decision to commit or not is made in some states by a judge and in others by a jury. The judge or jury hears both sides and then decides if the evidence meets the criteria for civil commitment in their state. Typically those criteria include proving clearly that the person is mentally ill (usually not difficult if the illness is paranoid schizophrenia) and proving clearly that the person will be physically dangerous to self or others. If the evidence doesn't convince the judge or jury that the person meets the legal standard for danger, then the person is discharged no matter how severely ill.

This is seen by many as a huge loophole in the legal system. Shouldn't those who are severely ill and in need of treatment be forced to take treatment? Our legal system, for better or worse, generally answers no. We protect liberty, even if that results in the irony sometimes labeled "suffering with your rights on." Only if the person is clearly dangerous will commitment occur.

Moreover, even if the person is found to be dangerous and is committed, there is little assurance that the problem is solved. This is tragically illustrated by the story of "Eric Morgan." He spent six months in the hospital, the maximum allowed under the laws of his state for civil commitment. Shortly after being released, he murdered his psychiatrist.

CRIMINAL COMMITMENT

If the narrative had followed Eric Morgan to the next step in his tortuous journey through the medicolegal system, we would have read about his prosecution for murder. He could have been criminally prosecuted earlier, after he had assaulted Jim with a gun, and perhaps at several other times.

Unfortunately, prosecution at those stages might have afforded relatively short-lived protection. There can be no justification for the callous attitude of the Assistant District Attorney as reported in the narrative. However, even if the prosecutor had acted professionally, and even if she had filed criminal charges, the actions of Eric, no matter how terrifying to Jim, would probably have resulted only in a misdemeanor conviction, or a finding of not guilty by reason of insanity of a misdemeanor charge. In either case, the state would have had control over Eric for no more than a year. Although this certainly would have been better than nothing, the tragic ending of the story shows that short periods of custody and treatment, followed by complete discharge, do not ensure long-term safety.

If the narrative had followed Eric to the stage of his criminal prosecution for murder, another aspect of the medicolegal system would have become involved. Eric's attorney would have raised the defense of insanity. The insanity defense has been a fixture of Anglo-American law since Daniel M'Naghten was tried in the 1840s for attempting to assassinate the Prime Minister of England. The jury acquitted M'Naghten. Unlike today, there was no mechanism then for confining defendants who were found not guilty by reason of insanity, so M'Naghten was set free.

The uproar that followed prompted the Queen to summon legal experts who developed the rule that formed the basis for insanity defenses in England and the U.S., and is sometimes called the right-wrong test: Was the defendant, at the time of the crime, affected by a disease of the mind that caused such defective reasoning that he did not know the nature and quality of his act or did not know it was wrong? This test was designed to narrow the insanity defense and limit the number of people who met the criteria for acquittal.

Nonetheless, if this test were applied to the case of "Eric Morgan," he likely would be acquitted. He was severely delusional; he did not really know what he was doing or know that it was wrong. Although there is disagreement about whether our law should allow an insanity defense at all, if there is one, a person like Morgan would probably qualify under even the most restrictive tests such as the M'Naghten rule.

Over the years, different states have modified the insanity test. To understand the proceedings, it is important to know the test that applies in the state where a defendant is being tried. Many states have added a second prong to the test: Did the defendant's mental illness cause a lack of substantial capacity to control conduct? In effect, even if the person understands the nature of his or her actions and knows they are wrong, the jury or judge can find the person not guilty by reason of insanity if they conclude the person was so ill as to be unable to avoid committing the criminal act. Thus, for example, if a mentally ill person cannot control his violent impulses, even though he knows that hurting others is wrong, he could be found not guilty by reason of insanity. Applying this part of the test can be confusing since it might not coincide with the medical understanding of mental illness. Thus, this control prong is even more controversial than the first prong of inability to understand the difference between right and wrong.

There is certainly room for disagreement about the insanity defense. Unfortunately, the debate is often based on myths and misperceptions rather than fact. Many people assume that the defense is used frequently and is usually successful when it is used. Research studies, however, show that the defense is typically used successfully in less than one percent of criminal cases. Many people assume that insanity defenses are usually found in controversial, hotly contested jury cases, like the trial of John Hinckley for attempting to kill President Reagan. In fact, most of the relatively small number of insanity cases don't go to trial because the judge and prosecutor agree that the defendant was so severely ill that he or she should be found insane.

Many people cannot understand how a defendant can be found not guilty by reason of insanity when it is obvious that the defendant committed the crime. But the insanity defense is presented only if the evidence proves that the person committed the crime. For example, Hinckley obviously shot the President and intended to kill him. He was guilty in that sense, but the defense attorney argued successfully that he should not be found criminally responsible because he was severely mentally ill in a way that met the test for insanity. To try to ease the confusion, some states have changed the name of the verdict; for example, Oregon now says that the defendant was found "guilty except for insanity."

But the name is less important than the consequences of the defense. Many people assume that a person who successfully asserts the insanity defense "gets away with murder" and is quickly released. Although this used to happen, during the past several decades most states have developed mechanisms to confine those found legally insane for as long or longer than they would have been imprisoned if found guilty. Oregon has led the way in ensuring that the insanity defense provides protection for the community as well as treatment for the defendant. The young man with schizophrenia in the "Dial 911" narrative was eventually placed in this system, and his family felt hopeful for the first time in years. It is worth discussing Oregon's system because it is now being copied in part or whole elsewhere and it illustrates how the insanity defense can become a positive force in the medicolegal system.

After a defendant in Oregon is found "guilty except for insanity," the judge decides whether he or she is still mentally ill (which almost always is true) and whether the defendant is dangerous to others (which the judge usually finds, partly because the defendant's crime usually demonstrates dangerousness). If mentally ill and dangerous, the defendant is committed to the locked wards of the state hospital and placed under the supervision of a group called the Oregon Psychiatric Security Review Board, the PSRB. This board consists by law of a psychiatrist, a psychologist, a lawyer, a parole and probation expert, and a lay citizen.

The board monitors the defendant's progress in the hospital and decides if and when it is appropriate to allow him or her to leave the hospital and reenter the community, but under close supervision continuously monitored by the PSRB. As long as the person remains mentally ill, even if in remission, and as long as the person remains dangerous or *potentially* dangerous, the board keeps him under its jurisdiction and supervision, although this cannot be for a total period longer than the *maximum* sentence the defendant could have received if he had been found guilty. These criteria mean that defendants found insane are often confined and supervised for longer than they would have been if convicted and imprisoned, since those found guilty are often given less than the maximum possible sentence and paroled before the end of their sentence.

Even more important, when an Oregon insanity acquittee is released (this release being technically comparable to criminal parole), the PSRB places the person in an intensive community treatment and support program, with very close monitoring. Typically, the patient must attend day treatment five to seven days per week. The patient is subject to many conditions including random urinalysis. If the person stops taking medication or fails to follow all the terms of conditional release, the PSRB can promptly return him or her to the secure hospital. This stands in sharp contrast to criminal parole, which often can provide only monthly check-ups of the parolee's progress. Studies have shown that patients are better able to stay out of trouble when they are supervised under intensive community treatment programs like the PSRB conditional release system. Thus, the system provides significant protection for others.

In addition to providing good security, Oregon's PSRB system provides intensive psychiatric treatment and social support in the community. Help is provided with employment if possible, with housing, and with handling money and other personal affairs. By providing intensive treatment and support, the PSRB system also makes it less likely that mentally ill persons will commit another crime and perhaps be placed next time in prison, where there are many mentally ill inmates receiving little or no treatment for their diseases.

The Oregon system is strongly supported by a surprisingly wide range of groups: family advocacy groups, prosecutors, judges, mental health professionals, and even civil liberty groups and defense attorneys. These groups support the PSRB combination of tight security with intensive treatment and extensive community support. In a sense, the Oregon PSRB mechanism provides what the deinstitutionalization movement envisioned, but never achieved, because the resources were not made available to provide adequate community treatment and supervision.

What is the drawback to the Oregon system? It is expensive. However, it seems worthwhile to allocate public money to obtain a system that provides effective handling of those suffering from an illness that can cause enormous suffering, fear, and danger.

This is another area in which lobbying for legislation can be important in dealing better with dangerously mentally ill individuals. The staff of the Oregon Psychiatric Security Review Board can provide information to anyone interested in trying to establish a similar system in other states. Their offices are in Portland, Oregon, and they are listed under "Oregon State Government" in the Portland Telephone Book.

ASSISTING THOSE WHO HAVE BEEN COMMITTED

Relatives can help those committed by trying to put aside frustrations with the system and learning as much as possible about the legal and medical realities. Most employees working in the system act in good faith, trying conscientiously to do what is best. However, like the relatives of persons suffering from schizophrenia, those working in the system experience repeated frustrations. Medicine doesn't yet know how to cure this terrible illness, and has a difficult time containing it. The law doesn't know how to ensure protection or prevent crime. Legislatures provide inadequate resources.

Those in the system confront intense and conflicting pressures from all sides: treatment versus protection versus civil liberties versus lack of money versus prejudice against mentally ill people. Just as these mentally ill people and their relatives often feel misunderstood and rejected, so do those working in the medicolegal system.

Thus, families and friends can help patients by approaching those working in the system as allies. Try to put aside anger and frustration. Try to understand why things are they way they are. Then work on what can be realistically accomplished within the existing limitations of knowledge and resources.

Above all, stay actively involved with your relative or friend. This can be exceedingly difficult after years of struggle, but it can be pivotal. Those deciding about treatment, release, and support systems will be better able to help if there are concerned and involved family members and/or friends.

In the broader perspective, family members can be invaluable in proposing and advocating new legislation and increased funding of services for the mentally ill, and, most important in the long run, more money for medical research. As previously stated, legal systems are not, and cannot be, a solution for the personal and community problems caused by schizophrenia. The law is inherently an inadequate last resort. Let us work toward the day when we don't need to turn to it at all in responding to this disease of the brain.

References and Notes

References for the Preface

Camus, Albert (1955). *The Myth of Sisyphus: And Other Essays*. New York: Alfred A. Knopf.

Hatfield, Agnes (1991). *The Iris Times*. January newsletter of the Mid-Valley Alliance for the Mentally Ill, Corvallis, Oregon.

Lefley, Harriet (1987). "The Family's Response to Mental Illness in a Relative," in *Families of the Mentally Ill: Meeting the Challenges*. San Francisco: Jossey-Bass.

MacDonald, Michael (1981). *Mystical Bedlam: Madness, Anxiety, and Healing in Seventeenth Century England*. Cambridge: Cambridge University Press.

Scull, Andrew (1989). *Social Order/Mental Disorder: Anglo-American Psychiatry in Historical Perspective*. Berkeley: University of California Press.

Sontag, Susan (1977). *Illness as Metaphor* (New York: Farrar, Straus, and Giroux).

Wilson, Colin (1972). *New Pathways in Psychology: Maslow & the Post-Freudian Revolution*. Haverhill, Suffolk: St. Edmundsbury Press.

References for Chapter 2, Commentary by Harriet P. Lefley, Ph.D.

Anderson, C. M., Reiss, D. J., and Hogarty, G. E. (1986). *Schizophrenia and the Family: A Practitioner's Guide to Psychoeducation and Management*. New York: Guilford.

Bernheim, K. F., and Lehman, A. F. (1985). *Working with Families of the Mentally Ill*. New York: Norton.

Carpentier, N., Lesage, A., Goulet, J., Lalonde, P., and Renaud, M. (1992). "Burden of Care for Families Not Living with Young Schizophrenic Relatives. *Hospital & Community Psychiatry*, 43, 38–43.

Dearth, N., Labenski, B. J., Mott, M. E., and Pellegrini, L. M. (1986). *Families Helping Families: Living with Schizophrenia*. New York: Norton.

Falloon, I. R. H., Boyd, J. L., and McGill, C. W. (1984). *Family Care of Schizophrenia*. New York: Guilford.

Group for the Advancement of Psychiatry (1986). *A Family Affair: Helping Families Cope with Mental Illness*. New York: Brunner/Mazel.

Hanson, S. M. H., and Sporakowski, M. J. (1986). "Single Parent Families." *Human Relations,* 35, 3-8.

Harding, C. M., Brooks, G., Ashikaga, T., Strauss, J. S., and Breier, A. (1987). "The Vermont Longitudinal Study of Persons with Severe Mental Illness, II: Long-term Outcome of Subjects Who Retrospectively Met DSM-III Criteria for Schizophrenia. *American Journal of Psychiatry,* 144, 727-735.

Hatfield, A. B. (1990). *Family Education in Mental Illness.* New York: Guilford.

Johnson, J. T. (1988). *Hidden Victims: An Eight-Stage Healing Process for Families and Friends of the Mentally Ill.* New York: Doubleday.

Lefley, H. P. (1987). "Aging Parents as Caregivers of Mentally Ill Adult Children: An Emerging Social Problem." *Hospital & Community Psychiatry,* 38, 1063-1070.

Lefley, H. P. (1992). "Expressed Emotion: Conceptual, Clinical, and Social Policy Issues." *Hospital & Community Psychiatry,* 43, 591-598.

Lefley, H. P. (1989). "Family Burden and Family Stigma in Major Mental Illness." *American Psychologist,* 44, 556-560.

Marsh, D. T. (1992). *Families and Mental Illness: New Directions in Professional Practice.* New York: Praeger.

McFarlane, W. R., Lukens, E., Link, B., Dushay, R., Deakins, S., Dunne, E., Horen, B., Newmark, M., and Toran, J. (1991). "Multifamily Groups and Psychoeducational Treatment of Schizophrenia: A Research Demonstration Project." In National Association of State Mental Health Program Directors, *The MASMHPD Research Institute, Inc. Second Annual Conference on State Mental Health Agency Services Research, October 2-4, 1991,* 211-235. Arlington VA: Author.

Noh, S., and Turner, R. J. (1987). "Living with Psychiatric Patients: Implications for the Mental Health of Family Members. *Social Science & Medicine,* 25, 262-272.

Selvini, M. (1992). "Schizophrenia as a Family Game: Posing a Challenge to Biological Psychiatry." *Family Therapy Networker,* 16(3), 81-86.

Terkelsen, K. G. (1982). "The Straight Approach to a Knotty Problem: Managing Parental Guilt About Psychosis." In A. S. Gurman, ed., *Questions and Answers on the Practice of Family Therapy,* vol. 2, 179-183. New York: Brunner/Mazel.

References for Chapter 3, Commentary by Marsha Martin, D.S.W.

Bachrach, L. L., and Nadelson, C. C. (1988). *Treating Chronically Mentally Ill Women.* Washington, D.C.: American Psychiatric Association.

Blau, J. (1992). *The Visible Poor.* New York: Oxford University Press.

Burt, M. R. (1992). *Over the Edge.* Washington, D.C.: Urban Institute Press.

Chacko, R. C. (1985). *The Chronic Mental Patient in a Community Context.* Washington, D.C.: American Psychiatric Association.

Helping Mentally Ill Homeless People. Washington, D.C.: American Public Health Association (1989).

Hopper, K., and Baxter, E. (1981). *Private Lives, Public Spaces.* New York: Community Service Society.

Lamb, H. R. (1984). *The Homeless Mentally Ill.* Washington, D.C.: American Psychiatric Association.

Martin, M. A. (fall, 1990). "Creating Community and the Development of Networks of Support with the Homeless Mentally Ill," with Nayowith, S., in *Social Work with Groups,* special edition edited by Lee, J.

Martin, M. A. (1988). "Homelessness Among Chronically Mentally Ill Women, in *Treating Chronically Mentally Ill Women,* edited by Bachrach, L. L., and Nadelson, C. C., Washington, D.C.: American Psychiatric Association Press.

Martin, M. A. (October 1989). "The Homeless and Community-based Care: Changing the Mind Set," in *Community Mental Health Journal,* special edition edited by Goldfinger, S.

Martin, M. A. (1990). "The Homeless Elderly: No Room at the End," in *The Vulnerable Aged,* edited by Harel, Z., Ehrlich, P., and Hubbard, R., New York: Springer Publishing Company.

Martin, M. A. (1987). *Implications of NIMH Supported Research for Homeless Ethnic and Racial Minorities.* Rockville, MD: National Institute of Mental Health.

Martin, M. A. (1982). Strategies of Adaptation. Unpublished dissertation, Columbia University.

Memminger, W. W., and Hannah, G. (1987). *The Chronic Mental Patient/II.* Washington, D.C.: American Psychiatric Association.

Outcasts on Main Street, Washington, D.C., National Institute of Mental Health, 1992.

Reaching Out. Washington, D.C.: Interagency Council on the Homeless (1991).

Tessler, R. C., and Dennis, D. C. (1989). *A Synthesis of NIMH-Funded Research Concerning Persons Who Are Homeless and Mentally Ill.* Rockville, MD: National Institute of Mental Health.

Torrey, E. F. (1988). *Nowhere to Go.* New York: Harper and Row.

What You Can Do to Help the Homeless. Washington, D.C.: National Alliance to End Homelessness (1991).

Working to End Homelessness. Washington, D.C.: Interagency Council on the Homeless (1991).

References for Chapter 4, Commentary by Judith B. Krauss, R.N., M.S.N., and Diane M. Gourley, R.N., B.A.

Anthony, W. A. (1991). "Recovery From Mental Illness: The New Vision of Services Researchers." *Innovations and Research,* 1(1), 13–14.

Henderson, V. (1966). *The Nature of Nursing*. New York: Macmillan.

Keil, J. (1992). "The Mountain of My Mental Illness." *The Journal*, 3(2), 5–6.

Kessler, N. (1992). "From Sister to Social Worker." *The Journal*, 3(1), 9–10.

Marsh, D. (1992). "Siblings: Forgotten Family Members." *The Journal*, 3(1), 3–4.

Shore, M. F., and Cohen, M. D. (1990). "The Robert Wood Johnson Foundation Program on Chronic Mental Illness: An Overview." *Hospital and Community Psychiatry*, 14(11), 1212–1216.

Sontag, S. (1977). *Illness as Metaphor*. NY: Anchor Books, Doubleday.

Weisburd, D. (1992). Publisher's note, siblings. *The Journal*, 3(1), 1–2.

Notes for Chapter 5, Commentary by Richard James, Ph.D.

The writer wishes to thank Commander Walter Crews and police training officer Deborah Davis, both of the Memphis Police Department, for their critical review and helpful comments in the construction of this critique. Commander Crews helped initiate the CIT program, and officer Davis is a graduate from the first CIT class.

References for Chapter 6, Commentary by Jeffrey L. Geller, M.D., M.P.H.

Table 1. (1990) From Caldwell and Gottesman.

Allebeck, P. (1989). "A Life-Shortening Disease." *Schizophrenia Bulletin*, 15, 81–89.

Barner-Rasmussen, P. (1986). "Suicide in Psychiatric Patients in Denmark, 1971–1981." *Acta Psychiatrica Scandinavia*, 73, 449–455.

Bly, N. (1887) "Ten Days in a Mad-house." *World*, October 9.

Brier, A., and Astrachan, B. M. (1984). "Characterization of Schizophrenic Patients Who Commit Suicide." *American Journal of Psychiatry*, 141, 206–209.

Bromberg, W. (1954). *Man Above Humanity*. Philadelphia: J. B. Lippincott.

Caldwell, C. B., and Gottesman, I. I. (1990). "Schizophrenics Kill Themselves Too: A Review of Risk Factors for Suicide." *Schizophrenia Bulletin*, 16, 571–589.

Cheng, K. K., Leung, C. M., Lo, W. H., and Lam, T. H. (1990). "Risk Factors of Suicide Among Schizophrenics." *Acta Psychiatrica Scandinavia*, 81, 220–224.

Colt, G. H. (1991). *The Enigma of Suicide*. New York: Summit.

Cotton, P., Drake, R., and Gates, C. (1985). "Critical Treatment Issues in Suicide Among Schizophrenics." *Hospital and Community Psychiatry*, 36, 534–536.

Dolce, L. (1992). *Suicide*. New York: Chelsea House.

Drake, R. E., Gates, C., Cotton, P. G., and Whitaker, A. (1984). "Suicide Among Schizophrenics. Who Is at Risk?" *Journal of Nervous and Mental Disease*, 172, 613–617.

Drake, R., Gates, C., Whitaker, A., and Cotton, P. G. (1985). "Suicide Among Schizophrenics: A Review." *Comprehensive Psychiatry*, 26, 90–100.

Friend, D. M. (1981). "Emptying the Madhouse." *Life,* May, 56–70.

Hunt, E. K. (1845). "Statistics of Suicide in the United States." *American Journal of Insanity,* 1, 225–234.

Maisel, A. Q. (1946). "Bedlam 1946." *Life Magazine,* May 6, 102–116.

Roy, A. (1986). "Depression, Attempted Suicide, and Suicide in Patients with Chronic Schizophrenia." *Psychiatric Clinics of North America,* 9, 193–206.

Roy, A. (1985). "Suicide and Psychiatric Patients." *Psychiatric Clinics of North America,* 8, 227–241.

Wallis, C., and Willwerth, J. (1992). "Awakenings." *Time,* July 6, 52–57.

References for Chapter 7, Commentary by Jeffrey L. Rogers, J.D.

Monahan, John (1992). "Mental Disorder and Violent Behavior." *American Psychologist,* 47 (4), 511–552.

Tarasoff vs. Board of Regents of the University of California. 551 P2d 334, 17 Cal. 3d 425, 1976.

Suggested Reading

Anderson, C. M., Reiss, D. J., and Hogarty, G. E. *Schizophrenia and the Family: A Practitioner's Guide to Psychoeducation and Management.* New York: Guilford, 1986.

Andreasen, Nancy C. *The Broken Brain: The Biological Revolution in Psychiatry.* New York: Harper & Row, 1984.

Andreasen, Nancy C., and Black, Donald W. *Introductory Textbook of Psychiatry.* Washington, D.C.: American Psychiatric Press, 1991.

Bernheim, K., and Lehman, A. *Working with Families of the Mentally Ill.* New York: Norton Press, 1985.

Bernheim, K., Lewine, R., and Beale, C. T. *The Caring Family.* New York: Random House, 1982.

Bouricius, Jean K. *Psychoactive Drugs and Their Effects on Mentally Ill Persons, NAMI Book No. 3.* Arlington VA: NAMI, 1989.

Gorman, Jack M. *The Essential Guide to Psychiatric Drugs.* New York: St. Martin's Press, 1990.

Dearth, Nona, Labenski, B. J., Mott, M. E., and Pellegrini, L. M. *Families Helping Families: Living with Schizophrenia.* New York: Norton Press, 1986.

Falloon, Ian, Boyd, J. L., and McGill, C. W. *Family Care of Schizophrenia.* New York: Guilford, 1984.

Hatfield, Agnes B. *Coping with Mental Illness in the Family: A Family Guide, NAMI Book No. 6.* Arlington VA: NAMI, 1991.

Hatfield, Agnes B. *Family Education in Mental Illness.* Washington, D.C.: American Psychiatric Press, 1990.

Hatfield, Agnes B., ed. *Families of the Mentally Ill: Meeting the Challenges.* In *New Directions for Mental Health Services,* no. 34. Edited by Richard H. Lamb. San Francisco: Jossey-Bass, 1987.

Hatfield, Agnes B., and Lefley, Harriet P. *Families of the Mentally Ill: Coping and Adaptation.* New York: Guilford, 1987.

Isaac, Rael Jean, and Armat, Virginia C. *Madness in the Streets.* New York: The Free Press, 1990.

Johnson, Julie. *Hidden Victims.* New York: Doubleday, 1988.

Lefley, Harriet, and Johnson, D. L., eds. *Families as Allies in Treatment of the Mentally*

Ill: New Directions for Mental Health Professionals. Washington, D.C.: American Psychiatric Press, 1990.

Liberman, Robert P., ed. *Psychiatric Rehabilitation of Chronic Mental Patients.* Washington, D.C.: American Psychiatric Press, 1991.

Marsh, D. T. *Families and Mental Illness: New Directions in Professional Practice.* New York: Praeger, 1992.

Porter, Roy. *A Social History of Madness: The World Through the Eyes of the Insane.* New York: E. P. Dutton, 1989.

Rothman, David J. *Conscience and Convenience: The Asylum and Its Alternatives in Progressive America.* Boston: Little, Brown, 1980.

Rothman, David J. *The Discovery of the Asylum: Social Order and Disorder in the New Republic.* Boston: Little, Brown, 1980.

Russell, L. Mark. *Future Care Planning Guide.* Evanston IL: First Publications, 1989.

Scull, Andrew. *Social Order/Mental Disorder: Anglo-American Psychiatry in Historical Perspective.* Berkeley: University of California Press, 1989.

Sedgwick, Peter. *Psycho Politics.* New York: Harper & Row, 1982.

Selzer, M. A., Sullivan, T. B., Carsky, M., and Terkelsen, K. G. *Working with the Person with Schizophrenia.* New York: NYU Press, 1989.

Snyder, Solomon. *Drugs and the Brain.* New York: W. H. Freeman, 1986.

Sontag, Susan. *Illness as Metaphor.* New York: Farrar, Straus and Giroux, 1977.

Steadman, Henry J., et al. *The Mentally Ill in Jail: Planning for Essential Services.* New York: Guilford, 1989.

Torrey, E. Fuller. *Freudian Fraud: The Malignant Effect of Freud's Theory on American Thought and Culture.* HarperCollins, 1992.

Torrey, E. Fuller. *Nowhere to Go: The Tragic Odyssey of the Homeless Mentally Ill.* New York: Harper & Row, 1988.

Torrey, E. Fuller. *Surviving Schizophrenia: A Family Manual,* 2nd. edition. New York: Harper & Row, 1988.

Torrey, E. Fuller, et al. *Care of the Seriously Mentally Ill: A Rating of State Programs,* 3rd edition. A Joint Publication of Public Citizen Health Research Group and National Alliance for the Mentally Ill, 1990.

Turnbull, J. Rutherford. *Disability and the Family: A Guide to Decisions for Adulthood.* Baltimore: Paul H. Brookes Publishing Co., 1989.

Walsh, M. *Schizophrenia: Straight Talk for Family and Friends.* New York: Warner, 1985.

Wechsler, J. A. *In a Darkness.* New York: Irvington, 1983.

Wrobleski, Adina. *Suicide: Why?* Minneapolis: Afterwords, 1989.

Resources

Helpline 1-800-950-NAMI

The National Alliance for the Mentally Ill (NAMI) Helpline is a toll-free telephone outreach service to the public. Volunteers staffing the Helpline offer comfort, information, and resources to callers. Most important, the volunteers provide callers with the names and telephone numbers of our local affiliates and state organization in the caller's location.

NAMI members are reminded that the Helpline is not a business line. Calls cannot be transferred between the Helpline lines and the business lines. Nami cannot ask the very dedicated and hardworking volunteers to take and deliver messages for the staff. Business calls should be placed to 1-703-524-7600, Monday–Friday from 8:30 A.M. to 5:30 P.M., holidays excepted.

The Helpline is open twenty-four hours a day, seven days a week, 365 days a year. Volunteers staff the lines between ten and five, Monday through Friday. At other times an answering machine will take messages.

Alliance for the Mentally Ill (AMI) State Organizations

Alabama AMI
3322 Memorial Parkway S.
Suite 66
Huntsville, AL 35801
800/626-4199 (in Alabama only)
or 205/880-3918

Alaska AMI
4050 Lake Otis Pkwy.
Suite 103
Anchorage, AK 99508
800/478-4462 (in Alaska only)
or 907/561-3127

Arizona AMI
2441 E. Fillmore St
Phoenix, AZ 85008
602/244-8166

Arkansas AMI
4313 W. Markam
Hendrix Hall, Room 233
Little Rock, AR 72205
501/661-1548

California AMI
1111 Howe Ave., Suite 475
Sacramento, CA 95825
916/567-0163

Colorado AMI
1100 Fillmore St.
Denver, CO 80206-3334
303/321-3104

Connecticut AMI
62 Alexander St.
Manchester, CT 06040
203/643-6697

AMI DC-Thresholds
422 8th St., SE
Washington, DC 20003
202/546-0646 or 202/397-1395

AMI of Delaware
4 Street Plaza, Suite 12
2500 W. 4th Street
Wilmington, DE 19805
302/427-0787

Florida AMI
400 S. Dixie Hwy #17
Lake Worth, FL 33460
407/586-4500

Georgia AMI
1256 Briarcliff Rd. NE, Rm. 412-S
Atlanta, GA 30306
404/894-8860

Hawaii AMI
1126 12th Ave., Suite 205
Honolulu, HI 96816
808/737-2778

Idaho AMI
331 N. Allumbaugh
Boise, ID 83704
208/376-4304

AMI Illinois State Coalition
110 W. Lawrence, Suite B
Springfield, IL 62704
217/522-1403

Indiana AMI
P.O. Box 22697
Indianapolis, IN 46222-0697
317/236-0056

AMI of Iowa
5911 Meredith Dr., Suite C-1
Des Moines, IA 50322
515/254-0417

Kansas AMI
P.O. Box 675
Topeka, KS 66601
513/233-0755

Kentucky AMI
333 Guthrie Green, Suite 310
Louisville, KY 40202
502/584-2009

Louisiana AMI
2431 S. Acadian, Ste. 420
Baton Rouge, LA 70808
504/928-6928

AMI of Maine
Box 222
Augusta, ME 04332
207/622-5767 or 207/464-5767

AMI of Maryland
2114 N. Charles St.
Baltimore, MD 21218
410/837-0880

AMI of Massachusetts
27–43 Wormwood St.
Boston, MA 02210
617/439-3933

AMI of Michigan
24133 Northwestern Hwy, #103
Southfield, MI 48075
313/355-0010

AMI of Minnesota
1595 Selby Ave., Ste. 103
Minneapolis, MN 55104
612/645-2948

Mississippi AMI
3500 Hwy 90 East
Ocean Springs, MS 39564
601/875-1771

Missouri Coalition of AMI
208-B East High St.
Jefferson City, MO 65101
314/634-7727

Montana AMI
P.O. Box 1021
Helena, MT 59624
406/443-1570

Nebraska AMI
215 Centennial Mall South
Rm 22, Lincoln Center Building
Lincoln, NE 68508
800/245-6081 (in Nebraska only) or
  308/345-3013

AMI of Nevada
1027 S. Rainbow Blvd., #172
Las Vegas, NV 89128
702/254-2666

AMI of New Hampshire
10 Ferry St., Unit 314
Concord, NH 03301
603/225-5359 or 800/242-NAMI

New Jersey AMI
114 W. State St., 2nd Flr
Trenton, NJ 08608-1102
609/695-4554

AMI-New Mexico
P.O. Box 9049
Santa Fe, NM 87504
505/983-6745

AMI of New York State
260 Washington Ave.
Albany, NY 12210
800/950-3228 (in New York only)
or 518/462-2000

North Carolina
3716 National Dr., #213
Raleigh, NC 27612
800/451-9682 (in No. Carolina only)
or 919/783-1807

North Dakota AMI
401 S. Main
Minot, ND 58701
701/852-5324

AMI of Ohio
979 S. High St.
Columbus, OH 43206
614/444-2646 or 800/686-2646

Oklahoma AMI
1140 N. Hudson
Oklahoma City, OK 73103
405/239-6264

Oregon AMI
161 High St., SE
Suite 212
Salem, OR 97301
503/370-7774

AMI of Pennsylvania
2149 N. 2nd Street
Harrisburg, PA 17110-1005
717/238-1514

AMI of Rhode Island
P.O. Box 28411
Providence, RI 02908
401/464-3060

South Carolina AMI
P.O. Box 2538
Columbia, SC 29202
803/779-7849 or 800/788-5131

South Dakota AMI
Box 221
Brookings, SD 57006
605/692-5673

Tennessee AMI
1900 N. Winston Rd., #511
Knoxville, TN 37919
615/531-8264

Texas AMI (TEXAMI)
1000 E. 7th St., Ste 208
Austin, TX 78702
512/474-2225

Utah AMI
P.O. Box 58047
Salt Lake City, UT 84158-0057
801/584-2500

AMI of Vermont
230 Main Street, Suite 203
Municipal Center
Brattleboro, VT 05301
802/257-5546

Virginia AMI
P.O. Box 1903
Richmond, VA 23215
804/225-8264

AMI of Washington State
4305 Lacey Blvd., Ste 11
Lacey, WA 98503
206/438-0211 or 800/877-2649

West Virginia AMI
1418 MacCorkle Ave., SW
Charleston, WV 25303
304/744-5562

AMI of Wisconsin
1245 E. Washington Ave.
Suite 290
Madison, WI 53703
608/257-5888

Wyoming AMI
1949 E. A St.
Casper, WY 82601
307/234-0440

Colleague Organizations

American Academy of Child & Adolescent Psychiatry
3615 Wisconsin Avenue, NW
Washington, DC 20016
202/966-7300

American Association for Partial Hospitalization, Inc.
901 N. Washington, #600
Alexandria, VA 22314
703/836-2274

American Association of Retired Persons
601 E. St. NW
Washington, DC 20049
202/434-2277

American College of Neuropsychopharmacology
P.O. Box 1823-Station B
Vanderbilt University
Nashville, TN 37335
615/327-7200

American Federation of State, County & Municipal Employees (AFSCME)
International Headquarters
1625 L St., NW
Washington, DC 20036
202/452-4800

American Hospital Association
840 Lake Shore Drive
Chicago, IL 60611
312/280-6000

American Psychiatric Association
1400 K Street, NW
Washington, DC 20005
202/682-6000

American Psychological Association
750 First Street, NE
Washington, DC 20002
202/336-5500

Anxiety Disorders Association of America
6000 Executive Blvd., Ste 513
Rockville, MD 20850
301/231-9350

The ARC *(formerly Assoc. for Retarded Citizens)*
500 E. Border St.
Arlington, TX 76010
817/261-6003
and
The ARC
Office of Govt. Relations
1522 K St. NW #516
Washington, DC 20005
202/785-3388

Boston University Center for Psychiatric Rehabilitation
730 Commonwealth Ave.
Boston, MA 02215
617/353-3549

Brain Tissue Resource Center
McLean Hospital
Harvard Medical School
115 Mill Street
Belmont, MA 02178-9106
617/855-2400

The Center for Community Change
Trinity College of Vermont
Colchester Avenue
Burlington, VT 05401
802/656-0000

Center on Organization and Financing of Care for the Severely Mentally Ill
The Johns Hopkins University
School of Hygiene and Public Health
624 N. Broadway
Baltimore, MD 21205
401/955-6562

Child & Adolescent Psychopharmacology Information Center
Univ. of Wisconsin
Dept. of Psychiatry, B6-227 CSC
600 Highland Avenue
Madison, WI 53792-2475
608/263-6171

Compeer
259 Monroe Avenue, Suite B-1
Rochester, NY 14607
716/546-8280

Depression & Related Affective Disorders Association (DRADA)
Meyer 3-181
600 N. Wolfe St.
Baltimore, MD 21205
301/955-4647

Epilepsy Foundation of America
4351 Garden City Dr.
Landover, MD 20785
301/459-3700

Foundation for Biomedical Research
818 Connecticut Ave., NW
Suite 303
Washington, DC 20006
202/457-0654

Fountain House
425 W. 47th Street
New York, NY 10036
212/582-0340

Information Exchange on Young Adult and Aging Research
20 Squadron Blvd., Suite 400
New City, NY 10956
914/634-0050

Institute for Health, Health Care Policy and Aging Research
Rutgers University
30 College Avenue
New Brunswick, NJ 08903
908/932-8415

International Association of Psychosocial Rehab. Services
10025 Governor Warfield Pkwy.
Suite 301
Columbia, MD 21044

Joint Commission on Accreditation of Health Care Organizations
1 Renaissance Blvd.
Oak Brook Terrace, IL 60801
708/916-5600

Lithium Information Center
c/o The Dean Foundation
8000 Excelsior Dr., Suite 203
Madison, WI 53717
608/836-8070

Mental Health Law Project
1101 15th St., NW, Suite 1212
Washington, DC 20005
202/467-5730

Mental Health Policy Resource Center
1730 Rhode Island Ave. NW, #308
Washington, DC 20036
202/775-8826

National Alliance for Research on Schizophrenia & Depression (NARSAD)
60 Cutter Mill Road, Suite 200
Great Neck, NY 11021
516/829-0091

National Association of Developmental Disability Councils
1234 Massachusetts Ave., NW
Suite 103
Washington, DC 20005
202/347-1234

National Association of Private Psychiatric Health Systems
1319 F Street, NW, Suite 1000
Washington, DC 20004
202/393-6700

National Association of Protection and Advocacy Systems
900 2nd Street, NE, Suite 211
Washington, DC 20002
202/408-9514

National Association of Social Workers
750 1st St. NE
Washington, DC 20002
202/408-8600

National Association of State Mental Health Program Directors (NASMHPD)
66 Canal Center Plaza, Suite 302
Alexandria, VA 22314
703/739-9333
and
NASMHPD
444 No. Capitol St., NW, Suite 417
Washington, DC 20001
202/624-5837

National Council of Community Mental Health Centers
12300 Twinbrook Pkwy.
Suite 320
Rockville, MD 20852
301/984-6200

National Depressive & Manic Depressive Association
730 N. Franklin, #501
Chicago, IL 60610
312/642-0049

National Information Center for Children & Youth with Handicaps
7926 Jones Branch Dr., #1100
McLean, VA 22102
703/898-6061

National Foundation for Depressive Illness
P.O. Box 2257
New York, NY 10116
212/268-4260

National Mental Health Association
1021 Prince Street
Alexandria, VA 22314
703/684-7722

National Rehabilitation Association
1910 Assoc. Dr. #205
Reston, VA 22091-1502
703/715-9090

Obsessive Compulsive Foundation
P.O. Box 9573
New Haven, CT 06535
203/772-0565

President's Committee on Employment of People with Disabilities
1331 F St., NW
Washington, DC 20004-1107
202/376-6200

Public Citizens Health Research Group
2200 P Street, NW, #700
Washington, DC 20036
202/833-3000

Research & Training Center for Children's Mental Health
Dept. of Child & Family Studies
Florida Mental Health Institute
University of South Florida
13301 Bruce B. Dones Blvd.
Tampa, FL 33612-3899
813/974-4657

Research and Training Center on Family Support & Children's Mental Health
Portland State University
Regional Research Institute
P.O. Box 751
Portland, OR 97207
503/725-4040

The National Coalition for the Mentally Ill in the Criminal Justice System
600 Stewart Street, Suite 520, Seattle, WA 98101-1217
Telephone: 206/628-7021

The National Coalition includes as members many of the national organizations listed below. These organizations have information, resources, programs, or activities about in-jail or jail diversion programs for people with mental illness.

American Correctional Association
8025 Laurel Lakes Court
Laurel, MD 20707
301/206-5098

American Jail Association
1000 Day Road, Suite 100
Hagerstown, MD 21740
301/790-3930

American Psychiatric Association
1400 K Street, N.W.
Washington, DC 20005
202/682-6000

Community Action for the Mentally Ill Offender
Human Services Strategic Planning Office
Alaska Building, Suite 1350
618 2nd Avenue
Seattle, WA 98104
206/628-7021

International Association of Chiefs of Police
1110 North Glebe Road, Suite 200
Arlington, VA 22201
703/243-6500

John Howard Association
67 East Madison, Suite 1416
Chicago, IL 60603

Mental Health Law Project
2021 L Street, N.W., Suite 800
Washington, DC 20036
202/467-5730

National Alliance for the Mentally Ill
2101 Wilson Boulevard, #302
Arlington, VA 22201
703/534-7600

National Association of State Mental Health Program Directors
1101 King Street, Suite 160
Alexandria, VA 22314
703/739-9333

National Center for State Courts
300 Newport Avenue
Williamsburg, VA 23187-8798
804/253-2000

National Council of Community Mental Health Centers
12300 Twinbrook Parkway, Suite 320
Rockville, MD 20852
301/984-6200

National Mental Health Association
1021 Prince Street
Alexandria, VA 22314-2971
703/684-7772

National Sheriffs Association
1450 Duke Street
Alexandria, VA 22314
703/836-7827

Western Interstate Commission for Higher Education
P.O. Box Drawer P
Boulder, CO 80301
303/541-0200

List of Major Organizations That Help the Homeless (reprinted by permission of the National Alliance to End Homelessness, Washington, D.C.)

The American Institute of Architects
1735 New York Avenue, NW
Washington, DC 20006
202/626-7300

American Red Cross
National Headquarters
17th and D Streets, NW
Washington, DC 20006
202/639-3610

Better Homes Foundation
189 Wells Avenue
Newton Center, MA 02159

Catholic Charities, USA
1319 F Street, NW
Washington, DC 20004
202/639-8400

Center on Budget and Policy Priorities
236 Massachusetts Ave., NE
Suite 305
Washington, DC 20002
202/544-0591

Council of Jewish Federations
227 Massachusetts Ave., NW
Washington, DC 20002
202/547-0020

Emergency Food and Shelter National Board Program
601 N. Fairfax Street, Suite 225
Alexandria, VA 22314-2088
703/683-1166

Enterprise Foundation
505 American City Building
Columbia, MD 21044
301/964-1230

Habitat for Humanity
Habitat and Church Streets
Americus, GA 31709
912/924-6935

HandsNet, Inc.
303 Potrero Street
Suite 54
Santa Cruz, CA 95060
408/427-0527

Homelessness Information Exchange
1830 Connecticut Ave., NW
Washington, DC 20009
202/462-7551

Housing Assistance Council
1025 Vermont Avenue, NW
Suite 606
Washington, DC 20005
202/842-8600

Interagency Council on the Homeless
451 7th Street, SW
Washington, DC 20410
202/708-1480

Local Initiatives Support Corporation
666 Third Avenue
New York, NY 10017
212/949-8560

Mental Health Law Project
2021 L Street, NW Suite 800
Washington, DC 20036-4909
202/467-5730

National Alliance to End Homelessness
1518 K Street, NW Suite 206
Washington, DC 20005
202/638-1526

National Association of Community Health Centers
1330 New Hampshire Avenue, NW Suite 122
Washington, DC 20036
202/659-8008

National Association of Social Workers
7981 Eastern Avenue
Silver Spring, MD 20910
301/565-0333

National Coalition for the Homeless
1439 Rhode Island Ave., NW
Washington, DC 20005
202/460-8110

National Council of Churches of Christ in the USA
110 Maryland Avenue, NE
Washington, DC 20002
202/544-2350

National Governers' Association
Hall of the States
444 North Capitol Street, Suite 250
Washington, DC 20001
202/624-7819

National Institute of Mental Health
Office of Programs for the Homeless Mentally Ill
5600 Fishers Lane, Room 7C-06
Rockville, MD 20857
301/443-3706

National Resource Center on Homelessness and Mental Illness
Policy Research Associates, Inc.
262 Delaware Avenue
Delmar, NY 12054
800/444-7415

Neighborhood Reinvestment Corporation
1325 G Street, NW Suite 800
Washington, DC 20005
202/376-2400

Salvation Army
799 Bloomfield Avenue
Verona, NJ 07044
201/239-0606

Second Harvest Eastern Region Office
343 South Dearborn, Suite 408
Chicago, Ill 60604
312/341-0581

Second Harvest Eastern Region Office
4 East Biddle Street
Baltimore, MD 21202
301/539-4944

Second Harvest Western Regional Office
5121 Port Chicago Highway
Concord, CA 94520
415/682-4555

Travelers Aid International
1001 Connecticut Ave., NW Suite 504
Washington, DC 20036
202/659-9468

U.S. Conference of Mayors
1620 Eye Street, NW
Washington, DC 20006
202/293-7330

United Way of America
701 North Fairfax Street
Alexandria, VA 22314-2045
703/836-7100

World Share
5255 Lovelock Street
San Diego, CA 92110
619/294-2981

Federal Programs

Research and Services

Medicare: Health Care Financing Administration
Medical Bureau Public Affairs Office
202/690-6113

Medicaid: Health Care Financing Administration
Medical Information
410/966-5659

SSI, SSDI: Social Security Administration
Public Information
1/800/772-1213

Research: NIMH Public Inquiries Branch
5600 Fishers Lane, Room 15-C05
Rockville, MD 20857
301/443-4513
and NIMH Office of Scientific Information (Statistics)
5600 Fishers Lane, Room 15-105
Rockville, MD 20857
301/443-3600

Services: Substance Abuse and Mental Health Services Administration
(SAMSA)
Public Information & Questions
301/443-4513

and Center for Mental Health Services
Office of Consumer, Family and Public Information
301/443-0747

Housing

Fair Housing: Department of Housing and Urban Development (HUD),
Office of Fair Housing & Equal Opportunity
202/708-4252

Shelter and
Care, Safe
Havens
Program: HUD Office of Special Housing
202/708-2730

Public and
Indian
Housing: HUD Div. of Public and Indian Housing
202/708-0950

Education and Employment Training

State Voc
Rehab: U.S. Department of Education Rehabilitation Services Administration
202/205-8303

State and
Local
Special Ed: Department of Education Office of Special Education Programs
202/205-5507

Research
on Rehab: National Institute of Disability and Rehabilitative Research
202/205-5867

Americans with Disabilities Act (ADA)

Publications
About and
Information
Referral: Equal Employment Opportunity Commission
1801 L Street NW
Washington, DC 20507
ADA Hotline 1-800-669-EEOC

Questions
    on the
        Act: U.S. Department of Justice
            Civil Rights Division,
            Office on the ADA
            PO Box 66118
            Washington, DC 20035-6118
            ADA Hotline 202/514-0301

Index

Advocacy
  information, 141–43
  role of, 40, 82
Akathisia, 69, 80, 220
Alabama, AMI in, 261
Alaska, AMI in, 261
Alcohol abuse, effects on schizophrenia,
  66–67, 239
Alliance for the Mentally Ill (AMI). *See*
  National Alliance for the Mentally
  Ill (NAMI); *under specific state*
Almshouses, 214
Alzheimer's disease, 33, 35, 36
American Academy of Child &
  Adolescent Psychiatry, 265
American Association for Partial
  Hospitalization, Inc., 265
American Association of Retired Persons,
  265
American Civil Liberties Union, 119
American College of Neuropsycho-
  pharmacology, 265
American Correctional Association, 269
American Federation of State, County &
  Municipal Employees (AFSCME),
  265
American Hospital Association, 265
American Institute of Architects, 270
American Jail Association, 269
American Journal of Insanity, 222
American Psychiatric Association, 266,
  269
American Psychological Association, 266
American Red Cross, 270

Americans with Disabilities Act (ADA),
  79, 82, 273–74
Amphetamines, 66
Andreasen, Nancy, 21–22, 245
Anger, felt by family members, 55–56, 83
Anthony, W. A., 162
Antipsychotic medication
  list of, 67
  suicide and, 220
Anxiety Disorders Association of America,
  265
ARC (formerly Association for Retarded
  Citizens), 265
Arizona, AMI in, 261
Arkansas, AMI in, 261
Arthur, Kate, 86–87
Auditory hallucinations, 38
  medications for, 67

Baxter, Ellen, 138
Benztropine, 69
Better Homes Foundation, 270
Bipolar disorder. *See* Manic depressive
  disorder
Black, Jim, 224–38
Bleuler, Eugene, 35, 217–18
Blood cell counts/chemistries, 66, 71
  reduced white, 70
Blood pressure, low, 69, 70
Boston University, Center for Psychiatric
  Rehabilitation, 265
Brain
  relationship to mental illness, 34
  relationship to schizophrenia, 36–37, 67

scans, 66
tumors, 66
Brain Tissue Resource Center, 265
Brigham, Amariah, 222

California, AMI in, 261
Campbell, Gordon, 224, 230, 241
Camus, Albert, 14
Care, lack of continuity in, 216–17
Carpentier, N., 95
Case management, 72
  adaptation to residential living and role
    of, 139
  nursing and, 164–65
Case managers
  educational background of, 57, 58
  role of, 57, 74, 75, 216
Catatonic schizophrenia, 221
Catholic Charities, USA, 270
Cavett, Dick, 40
Center on Budget and Policy Priorities,
  270
Center for Community Change, 265
Center for Ethics in Health Care (Oregon
  Health Sciences University), 20
Center for Mental Health Services, 140
Center on Organization and Financing of
  Care for the Severely Mentally Ill,
  266
Chlorpromazine, 67, 69, 70, 215
Civil commitment, 65, 217
  See also Danger/harm to self or others
  difficulty in getting, 245–47
  limitations of, 240–41
  who can initiate, 244
  who makes final decision, 247
Civil rights/liberties, 32
  involuntary treatment and, 64–65
Child & Adolescent Psychopharmacology
  Information Center, 267
Clozapine, 70–71, 182
Cocaine, 66
Cogentin, 69
Cohen, M. D., 160
Colorado, AMI in, 262
Command hallucinations, 220

Community Action for the Mentally Ill
  Offender, 269
Community Mental Health Act (1963),
  215
Community mental health programs,
  services provided by, 60–61, 74
Compeer, 266
Computerized tomography (CT), 36, 37
Confidentiality laws, 147, 154, 161, 203,
  217
  right to privacy versus duty to protect
    endangered persons, 238, 241–44
Conflict
  between community and family
    members, 19
  between legal issues and mental health
    professionals, 19–20
Confusion (initial), among family
  members, 17–18
Connecticut, AMI in, 262
Constipation, 69
Consumers (clients), 79, 108
Control of one's life, importance to
  caregiver, 107
Council of Jewish Federations, 270
Counselors
  educational background of, 57, 58
  role of, 57
Crime
  See also Violence
  committed by people with
    schizophrenia, 80
  instrumental versus expressive, 183–84
  people with schizophrenia as victims of,
    80
Criminal commitment
  conditional release system, 250–51
  insanity defense, 248–50
  limitations of, 240–41, 248

Danger/harm to self or others, 61, 129
  hospitalization and constraints of, 19,
    63
  involuntary treatment and, 64–65, 91
  Lindsey case story, 92–94, 104–5
  Morgan case story, 224–39

right to privacy versus duty to protect
endangered persons, 238, 241–44
Decompensation, 91, 98, 99, 100, 229
Deinstitutionalization, 32–33, 39, 214–16
Delaware, AMI in, 262
Delusions, 38
medications for, 67
Dementia praecox, 35
Depression & Related Affective Disorders
Association (DRADA), 266
Diagnosis of schizophrenia, 66–67
Diagnostic and Statistical Manual
(DSM-III-R), 221
Diarrhea, 71
Disclosure of illness, 157
Disorganized type of schizophrenia, 221
District Attorney's office, lack of action
by, 232, 233, 234–35, 237, 248
District of Columbia, AMI in, 262
Dopamine, 67
Drop-in center services, 137–38
Drug abuse, effects on schizophrenia, 49,
66–67, 239
Drugs. *See* Medications
Dry mouth, 69
Duke, Patty, 40

Eccentricity, 225
Economic issues. *See* Financing mental
health care
Education
federal programs, 273
role of, 40–41, 100–101, 155–57
Emergencies, involuntary treatment and,
64–65, 93
Emergency Food and Shelter National
Board Program, 270
Employment
federal programs, 273
importance of, 73
versus unemployment, effects of, 32
Enterprise Foundation, 270
Environmental causes, 37
Epilepsy, 66
Epilepsy Foundation of America, 266
Expressed emotion, 102

Families of mentally ill people
anger felt by, 55–56, 83
coping reactions by, 103
effects of illness on, 52–53, 54–55,
88–90, 94, 101–4, 114, 173–74
feelings of, 15–19
feelings of loss felt by, 18, 45–46, 54
how they can be helped, 105–8
problems confronting single caregivers,
83–94
roles of, 16, 40
Federal entitlements, 215
Federal programs, 272–74
Finances, personal, 73–76
Financing mental health care
community programs and, 60–61
cost of hospitalization, 78
deinstitutionalization and, 32–33
health insurance and, 78–79
Medicaid and, 76–77, 78
Medicare and, 77
reluctant providers and, 59–60
Flaubert, Gustave, 12
Florida, AMI in, 262
Fluphenazine, 69
Food, delusions about, 75–76
Food stamps, community mental health
programs and access to, 60, 74
Fordham, Dolores and Stan (case story),
201–13
Foundation for Biomedical Research,
266
Fountain House, 266

Geller, Jeffrey, 24–25
General Assistance, 74, 77
Genetic risks, 159
Georgia, AMI in, 262
Golden, Martha, 149, 150, 162
Gourley, Diane, 23–24
Group advocacy, 40
Group housing, 49, 79–80, 87–88
Guilt, parental, 97–98, 112

Habitat for Humanity, 270
Haldol, 67, 69, 209

Hallucinations, auditory, 38
    medications for, 67
Hallucinations, command, 220
Haloperidol, 67, 69
HandsNet, Inc., 270
Hatfield, Agnes B., 16, 95
Hawaii, AMI in, 262
Health insurance, 33, 63, 78–79, 172
Henderson, V., 162
Hinckley, John, 80, 239, 249
Homeless/homelessness
    adapting to, 132–34
    characteristics of, 127–28
    drop-in center services, 137–38
    emergency and transitional housing
        services, 138–39
    how people become, 130–31
    finding missing people, 140–44
    Mathews case story, 145–65
    outreach services, 136–37
    role of families, 143–44
    social service system for, 134–36
    sources of information on, 270–72
    statistics on, 127
Homelessness Information Exchange, 270
Hopper, Kim, 138
Hospitalization
    commitment laws and voluntary, 48
    cost of, 78
    involuntary treatment and, 64–65, 91
    problems confronting families, 51
    reasons for, 46–47, 61, 63
Hospitals
    danger/harm to self or others and
        access to, 19, 61, 63, 64–65
    general, 63
    lengths of stay in, 63
    lunatic, 214
    private psychiatric, 63
    psychiatric services at, 61–62
    restrictions on personal liberties at,
        62
    Schmidt family relationships with,
        175–76, 177–78
    state mental, 50, 62–63
    types of, 62

Housing
    community mental health programs
        and access to low-income, 60
    emergency and transitional housing
        services for homeless, 138–39
    federal programs, 273
    HUD, 80
    need for improved and alternative,
        160–61
    nursing homes, 79
    problems with finding, 39, 49, 87–88
    Section Eight, 80
    sheltered care/group, 79–80
    single-room occupancy (SRO) hotels,
        79
Housing Assistance Council, 270
Hunt, E. K., 222

Idaho, AMI in, 262
Illinois, AMI in, 262
Illness as Metaphor (Sontag), 153
Inderal, 69
Indiana, AMI in, 262
Information Exchange on Young Adult
    and Aging Research, 267
Insanity
    See also Mental illness
    defense, 248–50
Institute for Health, Health Care Policy
    and Aging Research, 267
Interagency Council on the Homeless,
    271
International Association of Chiefs of
    Police, 269
International Association of Psychosocial
    Rehab. Services, 266
Involuntary treatment
    hospitalization and, 64–65, 91
    Morgan case story, 224–39
Iowa, AMI in, 262

James, Richard, 21, 24
John Howard Association, 269
Johnson, Julie, 101
Joint Commission on Accreditation of
    Health Care Organizations, 266

Kansas, AMI in, 262
Keil, Jeanette, 153, 154
Kennedy, John F., 215
Kentucky, AMI in, 262
Kraepelin, Emil, 35
Krauss, Judith, 23–24, 160

Lefley, Harriet, 20, 22–23
Legal issues
  See also Danger/harm to self or others
  civil commitment, 65, 217, 240–41,
    244–47
  conflict between legal mental health
    professionals and, 19–20
  confronting police, 184–85
  criminal commitment, 240–41, 248–51
  mental health provider's duty to
    protect, 241–44
  Tarasoff ruling, 64, 242–44
Liberties
  See also Right(s)
  need for restrictions on personal, 62
Life, 213
Lindsey, Joni and Stuart (case story),
    83–94
Lithium, 71
Lithium Information Center, 266
Local Initiatives Support Corp., 271
Loss felt by families, feelings of, 18,
    45–46, 54, 98–99
Louisiana, AMI in, 262

MacDonald, Michael, 11
McFarland, Bentson, 22
McFarlane, W. R., 105–6
Stewart B. McKinney Homeless
    Assistance Act (PL 100–77), 135
M'Naghten, Daniel, 248
Magnetic resonance imaging (MRI), 37
Maine, AMI in, 262
Manic depressive disorder, 33, 40, 67, 71
Marsh, Diane, 158–59
Martin, Marsha, 23
Maryland, AMI in, 262
Maslow, Abraham, 15
Massachusetts, AMI in, 263

Mathews, Shirley, Neal, and Anne (case
    story), 109–26, 145–52
Medicaid, 76–77, 78, 215
Medical history, importance of, 66–67
Medicare, 77, 215
Medications
  See also specific names
  failure to take, 71–72, 98, 229–30
  high-potency, 69
  list of, 68
  low-potency, 69
  monitoring of, by community mental
    health programs, 60
  negative symptoms and, 38, 68, 71
  positive symptoms and, 38, 67–68
  right to refuse, 65
  role of, 59
  side effects, 69–70, 71, 220–21
  suicide and, 220
Mellaril, 69, 85
Memphis Police Department Crisis
    Intervention Team (CIT)
  coordination between police and
    mental health workers, 190–91
  example of a typical scenario, 192–200
  history of formation, 185–87, 191–92
  results of, 189–90
  training of officers, 187–89
Menninger, Karl, 217
Mental Health Law Project, 266, 269,
    271
Mental Health Policy Resource Center,
    266
Mental health professionals/providers
  See also specific types
  conflict between legal issues and, 19–20
  duty to protect, 241–44
  failure by, to communicate and
    educate, 99–101
  Mathews family relationships with,
    113–14, 115–16, 119, 121
  reluctant, 59–60
  role of, 57, 58
  Schmidt family relationships with,
    169–70, 172, 175
  types of, 57, 58

Mental health system
  Memphis response to, 185–87
  need for reform, 160–61
  reasons for failure of, 240
Mental illness
  historical attitudes toward, 28–29, 214
  origins of attitudes toward, 29–35
  relationship of the brain to, 34
  sources of information on, 261–74
Michigan, AMI in, 263
Mind/body dichotomy, implications of, 29–31
Minnesota, AMI in, 263
Missing relatives, finding. *See*
  Homeless/homelessness
Mississippi, AMI in, 263
Missouri, AMI in, 263
Montana, AMI in, 263
Morgan, Eric (case story), 224–39
Mortality rates, 218
Motivation, lack of, 38–39
Motor restlessness, 69, 220
Mourning (perpetual), among family
  members, 18

National Alliance to End Homelessness, 141, 271
National Alliance for the Mentally Ill
  (NAMI), 16, 40, 100, 269
  Helpline telephone numbers by state, 261–64
  Homeless and Missing Mentally Ill
    Network, 141–42
  recommendations regarding basic rights
    and humane treatment, 198–200
  Sibling and Adult Children Network, 101
National Alliance for Research on
  Schizophrenia & Depression
  (NARSAD), 268
National Association of Community
  Health Centers, 271
National Association of Developmental
  Disability Councils, 268
National Association of Private
  Psychiatric Health Systems, 268

National Association of Protection and
  Advocacy Systems, 267
National Association of Social Workers, 267, 271
National Association of State Mental
  Health Program Directors
  (NASMHPD), 267, 269
National Center for State Courts, 269
National Center on Homelessness and the
  Law, 141
National Coalition for the Homeless, 141, 271
National Coalition for the Mentally Ill in
  the Criminal Justice System, 268–70
National Council of Churches of Christ
  in the USA, 271
National Council of Community Mental
  Health Centers, 267, 269
National Crime Information Center
  (NCIC), 148
National Depressive and Manic
  Depressive Association (NDMDA), 40, 268
National Foundation for Depressive
  Illness, 268
National Governers' Association, 271
National Health Care for the Homeless
  Council, 140
National Information Center for Children
  & Youth with Handicaps, 268
National Institute of Mental Health
  (NIMH), 135, 271
National Mental Health Association, 267, 269
National Rehabilitation Association, 267
National Resource Center on
  Homelessness and Mental Illness, 140, 271
National Sheriffs Association, 270
Navane, 69
Nebraska, AMI in, 263
Neighborhood Reinvestment Corp., 271
Neuroimaging, 37, 41
Neuroscience, 34, 41
Nevada, AMI in, 263

New Hampshire, AMI in, 263
New Jersey, AMI in, 263
New Mexico, AMI in, 263
New York, AMI in, 263
Noh, S., 108
North Carolina, AMI in, 263
North Dakota, AMI in, 263
Nurse practitioners
  educational background of, 57, 58
  role of, 57
  role of psychiatric, 161–65
Nursing homes, 79

Obsessive Compulsive Foundation, 267
Ohio, AMI in, 263
Oklahoma, AMI in, 264
Oregon, AMI in, 264
Outreach services, 136–37

Paranoia, 14–15
Paranoid schizophrenia, 221
Peers, relationships with, 99
Pennsylvania, AMI in, 264
PL 100-77. *See* Stewart B. McKinney
    Homeless Assistance Act
Police
  legal issues confronting, 184–85
  Mathews family case story and, 124–26,
    148–50
  Memphis, Tennessee example, 185–200
  Morgan-Black case story and, 232,
    234–35, 236–37
  reactions by, 183–84
  Schmidt family case story and, 175, 176,
    183
President's Committee on Employment of
    People with Disabilities, 267
Prisons, recommendations regarding basic
    rights and humane treatment in,
    198–200
Privacy, duty to protect endangered
    persons versus right to, 238,
    241–44
Prolixin, 69, 169
Propranolol, 69
Protect, duty to, 238, 241–44

Providers. *See* Mental health
    professionals/providers
Psychiatric nurses. *See* Nurse practitioners
Psychiatric Security Review Board
    (PSRB)(Oregon), 181, 250–51
Psychiatrists
  educational background of, 57, 58
  role of, 57
Psychiatrists, relationships with family
    members
  Lindsey family, 85, 96–97, 99, 99–100
  Schmidt family, 169, 170
  Talbott family, 46–47, 48, 50–51,
    53
Psychologists, clinical
  educational background of, 57, 58
  relationship with Mathew family,
    113–14
  role of, 57
Psychopharmacologists, 57
Psychosocial treatment, 72–73
Psychotic symptoms, 38
Public Citizens Health Research Group,
    198, 268

Rain Man, 41
Rationing benefits concept, 33
Rehabilitation
  psychosocial, 57, 72–73
  vocational, 44–45, 73
Research
  federal programs, 272–73
  role of, 41
Research & Training Center for
    Children's Mental Health, 268
Research & Training Center on Family
    Support & Children's Mental
    Health, 268
Residual type schizophrenia, 221
Respite, importance of, 106–7, 159–60
Rhode Island, AMI in, 264
Right(s)
  involuntary treatment and, 64–65
  to privacy versus duty to protect
    endangered persons, 238,
    241–44

recommendations regarding basic rights
and humane treatment in prisons,
198–200
to refuse treatment/medication, 19, 64,
65, 129
of self-determination, 19
Right–wrong test, 248
Robert Wood Johnson Foundation,
(RWJF), 160–61
Rogers, Jeffrey, 25
Rush, Benjamin, 222

Salvation Army, 148, 271
Schizophrenia
age of onset, 59
defining, 35–37
diagnosis of, 66–67, 155–57
environmental causes of, 37
impact of, 153–54
improving conditions for people with,
39–41, 80–82
long-term outcome of, 39
myths regarding, 15
negative symptoms of, 38–39
positive/psychotic symptoms of, 37–38
relationship of the brain to, 36–37, 67
subtypes of, 221
Schizophrenogenic, 15
Schmidt, Lucille, Jack, and Tony (case
story), 166–82
Schneidmann, Edwin, 217
Second Harvest, 272
Section Eight, 80
Seizures, 70
Selvini, Matteo, 100
Shame, feelings of, 15–16, 53, 83, 112
Sheltered care housing, 79–80
Shore, M. F., 160
Siblings
effects on, 101–2, 114, 158–59
support from, 171
Single caregivers
case story of, 83–94
problems confronting, 101–4
Single-room occupancy (SRO) hotels, 79

Social Security Administration, 74
letter-forward services of, 141
Social Security Disability Income (SSDI),
74, 75, 77
Social workers, clinical
educational background of, 57, 58
role of, 57
Sontag, Susan, 13, 153–54
South Carolina, AMI in, 264
South Dakota, AMI in, 264
Styron, William, 40
Suicide
case example, 209–13
civil commitment and, 217
during hospitalizations, 218
media reaction to, 213–14
mortality rates, 218
myths regarding, 220–21
reasons for, 217
risk factors for, 218–20
statistics on, 36, 217
treatment of, 221–23
Supplemental Security Income (SSI), 74,
75, 76
Support
from family, 16, 171
from friends, 53
importance of group, 105–8, 171
Symptom management, 156

Talbott, Joe and Mark (case story), 43–56
Tarasoff ruling, 64, 242–44
Tardive dyskinesia, 70
Tennessee, AMI in, 264
Terkelsen, Kenneth, 98
Texas, AMI in, 264
Thioridazine, 69
Thiothixene, 69
Thorazine, 67, 69, 215
Thyroid gland, 66, 71
Time, 213
Transinstitutionalization, 216
Travelers Aid International, 272
Treatment
See also Medications

hospitalization and involuntary, 64–65, 91

importance of inclusive plan for, 157–58

methods of, 65–66

psychosocial, 72–73

right to refuse, 19, 64, 65, 129

suicide and, 221–23

Tremors, 71

Tumult (inescapable), among family members, 18–19

Turner, R. J., 108

Two-doctor hold, 177

Undifferentiated schizophrenia, 221

U.S. Conference of Mayors, 272

U.S. Department of Housing and Urban Development (HUD), 80, 161

United Way of America, 272

Urination, excess, 71

Urine tests, 66, 250

Utah, AMI in, 264

Vermont, AMI in, 264

Veterans hospitals, 62, 202

Violence

acts committed by people with schizophrenia, 46–47, 80, 93, 105, 173, 174, 179

Morgan case story, 224–39

Virginia, AMI in, 264

Vocational rehabilitation, 44–45, 73

Voices, hearing. *See* Auditory hallucinations

Washington, AMI in, 264

Weekend syndrome, 51

Weight gain, 70, 71

Welfare, community mental health programs and access to, 60, 74

Western Interstate Commission for Higher Education, 270

West Virginia, AMI in, 264

Wilson, Colin, 15

Wisconsin, AMI in, 264

Woolf, Virginia, 217

World, 213

World Health Organization, 217

World Share, 272

Wyoming, AMI in, 264

X rays, 66

A health care ethicist, Patricia Backlar serves on the bioethics committees at two state mental hospitals. Educated at Vassar College and Yale University, she is a Senior Scholar at the Center for Ethics in Health Care, Oregon Health Sciences University, and an adjunct faculty member at Portland State University.